GIMME SHELTER

Mary Elizabeth Williams

SIMON & SCHUSTER
New York   London   Toronto   Sydney

Simon & Schuster
1230 Avenue of the Americas
New York, NY 10020

First Simon & Schuster hardcover edition March 2009

SIMON & SCHUSTER and colophon are registered trademarks
of Simon & Schuster, Inc.

For information about special discounts for bulk purchases,
please contact Simon & Schuster Special Sales at
1-800-456-6798 or business@simonandschuster.com

Designed by Suet Y. Chong

Manufactured in the United States of America

1   3   5   7   9   10   8   6   4   2

Library of Congress Cataloging-in-Publication Data

Williams, Mary Elizabeth, date.
Gimme shelter / Mary Elizabeth Williams.
p.   cm.
Includes bibliographical references.
1. Real property—New York (State)—New York. I. Title.
HD268.N5W55 2009
333.33 ' 8097471—dc22   2008014169
ISBN-13: 978-1-4165-5708-1
ISBN-10:   1-4165-5708-3

In memory of
Elizabeth Rosalie Mansfield

CONTENTS

AUTHOR'S NOTE

This is a true story, albeit viewed through the lens of one person's experience. Whenever possible, I have relied on notes, journals, emails, and interviews to recount events and dialogue, and am deeply indebted to everyone who assisted. I have at times changed names and identifying details to preserve the privacy of certain friends, some unwitting participants, and numerous homeowners whose bad taste was generously displayed through the open house process.

However, there really are condos by the live poultry market. They're not cheap either.

No money is better spent than what is laid
out for domestic satisfaction.

—*Samuel Johnson*

GIMME SHELTER

HOME-SHOPPING

Of course I want a home. I'm American; it's encoded into my cultural DNA.

My country was founded by stragglers looking for a place to put down roots. Its wilderness was built by people lured by the promise of a plot of land. Its sales pitch to the world, even now, is that this is where everybody else comes to forge a life. Home is what we fantasize about and sacrifice for; it's what we go into debt over and fight wars over. It's what *The Wizard of Oz* and *Gone With the Wind* and *Battlestar Galactica* are all about—that wrenching, primal need to have a place in the world that belongs to us and to belong to it.

I walk by the house, even though it's out of my way, and sneak a fleeting peek through the windows. Sometimes, I cross the street, the better to play the part of someone who's not interested, and cast a coy glance right as I go past. I pray no one I know sees me here on Sackett Street in the middle of the morning, off my usual route and with no good excuse. There's nobody in there that I'm interested in; the place is empty anyway. No, I'm fixated on the house itself. I'm stalking an inanimate object.

I saw it a few weeks ago, and now it haunts me, a crush I can't get out of my head. I shut my eyes and try to remember the precise leafy design of the ceiling medallion, the color of the bricks in the back yard. I've got it bad. So I walk past, hoping not to see signs of people moving around, people moving in. Someday soon I will, and I'll have to stop coming around like this.

Most of our friends have already made the leap. Mortgages happen. They happen to the buttoned-up friends who work for the government, and they happen to the burnouts who never miss a Burning Man. They happen to the single and the married, the gay and the straight. But not us, not yet.

We live in the most expensive shantytown on earth. It's the place we can get bok choy at 3 A.M. but the supermarket runs out of toilet paper. Where we can share a pediatrician with one of the Beastie Boys and get felt up by junkies on the bus. How many other places boast luxury lofts above skeevy bars? And where else, outside the refugee community, is obsessing over shelter the chief local pastime? Where else but New York City—Brooklyn, to be exact? The grandly named County of Kings used to be an afterthought, a bridge-and-tunnel punch line. Now it's rapidly becoming a *Zagat* guide destination of its own, with rock star residents and CEO-priced real estate.

I had never been to an open house before I saw the place on

Sackett. I hadn't any need. I've recently decided, however, that this is the year our family buys a place of our own, the year *Rent* will become just a musical instead of a way of life to us. The average American moves 11.7 times in a lifetime. By my count, I'm already on my fifteenth residence. I've clocked in six of those with Jeff, in four cities and a dozen years. The world is full of nomads, to be sure, but I have done enough wandering. Even here in dense, cramped Brooklyn, I believe there's a space to truly call our own. I just have to find it before we're priced out.

Enter my new Sunday pastime—snooping in other people's closets, flushing strangers' toilets. It's easier and more constructive than brooding, which is how I've spent the previous few weeks.

It is the winter of 2003. Since Lucy turned three in January, Jeff and I have been on the fence about whether to have another child. At thirty-seven I'm not exactly decrepit—yet—but my breeding years are finite. Whatever we choose, I'd rather it be an active choice rather than something we forgot to discuss until it's too late. The way things have been between us lately, though, we may not ever have sex again, let alone babies.

We have a spectacular spat on Court Street, on the way to a kiddie birthday party. I badger Jeff about when we're going to have the conversation, and he mopes that I'm pressuring him. We fight again on the F train. "You promised we'd talk in February!" I snap, providing the morning's drama for the occupants of our car. "February's not over!" he lobs back, narrowing his brown eyes at me.

"You'd better get it together," I hiss before storming out at Jay Street, "because it's a short month."

When we finally have the discussion, one exhausted night

when work and parenting and the seventh straight day with no sunlight have put us in the optimum frame of mind to make a life-changing decision, neither of us is surprised what my vote is.

I'm not one of those women who gets off on her fecundity. I didn't enter marriage, or even parenthood, raring to produce multiple offspring. Having a child didn't do much to quell my ambivalence about kids as a species either. When friends started having their perfectly timed second children two years after their firstborns, I felt no urgency to join them. I shudder when anyone I didn't give birth to calls me a mommy.

Yet I deeply relish the sweet, silly intimacy of motherhood, and I love my kid with more ferocious tenderness than I ever thought possible. Expanding on the adventure of family, this time with Lucy in the role of big sister, is exactly what I'm up for. Despite all the financial and career and time and sheer stamina concerns that another child would kick up, I'd like to try. There's more to it than that, though.

"I look at our table," I tell Jeff, shifting my gaze all of two feet from the couch to the spot where we eat our dinner, "and I see someone else at it."

It's not that I want some imaginary Gerber-jar baby. It's that I'm ready for the child I'm convinced we're meant to have. You can overanalyze, you can list your reasons why you want the things you do, but in the end the big stuff defies explanation. Sometimes, you feel life pulling you, and so you go.

A year ago, at Andrew and Ruth's wedding in New Orleans, I splurged at Marie Laveau's for a tarot reading. "I see you with two daughters," the fortune-teller informed me.

"That's pretty good," I said, "I have one daughter."

She smiled indulgently at me, the way you do when a child puts her shoes on the wrong feet, and repeated herself. "I see you with two daughters."

"So do I," I said.

My husband isn't so sure. We're an ordinary middle-class family. By that I mean a true working middle-class family, not the people you see on the cover of *New York* magazine wringing their hands because a half-million-dollar salary doesn't go as far as it used to.

When we moved back to New York in 1999 after several peripatetic years of freelancing and grad school, Jeff had to reinvent himself at a lower-level office job. Even now after a few raises and promotions, he's still in a not terribly lucrative position in the not terribly lucrative world of publishing.

I work from home at a half-time job for a Web site, and do freelance writing as well. When the Internet boom went bust, my company gutted much of its staff. I was one of the lucky ones who got to stay. Salaries were cut and I haven't had a raise since. I don't make six figures a year. My husband and I put together don't make six figures a year. We've never owned a car. We rarely go out. Our main expenses are rent and parenting.

"I worry about money," Jeff tells me, and I do too. "I'm scared I'll be trapped in my job forever," he says. I suspected this response was coming. That whole cringing whenever I'd broach the subject thing was a tip-off. "I can't fathom how much harder all of it would be with a baby. I'm so tired all the time now."

He's a good man, and he wants to do the right thing. "I keep looking for a sign," he says. He's searching my face for the answer. "Maybe you being so sure is the sign. If this is what you want, then we'll do it."

And then I say something that stuns me.

No.

This isn't how I pictured it at all. I wanted to have a baby the way we had Lucy, to be utterly, romantically on board for the experience. It isn't like having the chicken or the fish for dinner; it isn't a "whatever you want, honey" decision. I can't go through trying to conceive and pregnancy and swollen ankles and pushing a human being out a reluctant orifice and raising a child with someone who's so-so on the idea.

Jeff and I are both only children ourselves. We know you don't need siblings to have a family. I'll resign myself to accepting what we have as more than enough. I'll give away the maternity clothes and little baby things I'd packed up. I'll get over it. I'll flail around for a while, missing like mad this child I didn't even have, but I'll live.

"If it's not right for both of us, it's not right, period," I tell him. "That's our deal, right?"

He puts an arm around me. "Then I guess it's settled," he says, and it feels like something inside of me just broke.

I had so blithely assumed this spring would be all about conception and pregnancy, based on little more than my own wishing. Now that the plan is off the table, I badly need a distraction from the grief. I need to channel that nesting instinct into something. If we're not expanding the family, then that's one less big expense in our lives, and a space requirement that's more or less settled. The idea seizes me almost immediately. If I can't have a baby, I'll get a home.

The Sunday after the big talk our family is crammed around a tiny table at Bagel World, loading up on carbs. As I flick through the paper, I make my intentions known. "Maybe we should start looking to buy a place," I say, "because the housing market is heating up."

Jeff is somewhat less hesitant about homeownership than he is about having two children. "I guess we can see what's out there," he answers noncommittally.

Before we can see what's out there, though, we need to know what we can spend. We start by reducing our contributions to our 401k's so our take-home pay is higher and we have more savings at the ready. We have some money put aside already, but not a lot. I twiddle with a mortgage calculator and, based on our rent, get a rough idea of what we could pay each month. We're looking at, absolute maximum, a $400,000 investment. The sum is staggering, but it's a blip in the New York housing market. Houses that went for $600,000 two years ago can fetch close to a million dollars now.

Jeff and I have a talent for finding neighborhoods just as they're becoming impossible to afford, arriving, on average, a year before the middlebrow chain stores and coffee bars. We are drawn to places when they're on the cusp, still alive with that electrifying mix of old ladies in house dresses, goateed artists, and sleepy new parents.

The problem is that nothing ever stays the same, and change is happening at such a breathtaking pace that yesterday's vibrant melting pot is today's homogenized playground.

My fantasy is that we'd find someone to go in on a two-family house with us. That's the formula my nonhomeowning friends and I keep talking about, although none of us are actually doing it.

While I generally bristle at anything with such hippieish associations as co-ownership, sharing is appealing. I'm not greedy. I could share a yard; I could even share a washer-dryer. Maybe someone else out there has the same idea.

The house on Sackett is offered at $775,000. It's a two-family, brick but not brownstone, and close to the dead zone of warehouses and the Gowanus Canal. It's no great shakes. But *madre de dios*, the potential.

I crowd in to the open house on a sunny Sunday, and the joint is jumping. It's a mostly straight-up white crowd, with a smattering of preppy guys and their Asian wives. Everybody looks younger and more prosperous than the scruffy lady all by herself that the realtor is studiously ignoring.

It's seriously tiny. The downstairs is occupied by two bedrooms and a bathroom, where a miniaturized washer-dryer lurks across from the toilet. The garden level consists of a sitting room and an eat-in kitchen. Upstairs, there's a very humble one-bedroom apartment.

This is not a home to go halfsies on.

There also appears to be one working outlet in the whole house. Every appliance, every fixture, is connected via an elaborate system of extension cords and adaptors. Paint is falling off in imposing chunks.

It's too late, though. I don't care about anything anymore, because I'm besotted. The house has all the details that always divert me from glaring problems. For starters, there's a tin ceiling. When I look up and see a tin ceiling, I see heaven itself. The kitchen has vintage glass cabinets and a built-in armoire. There is subway tile in the bathroom. Outside, there's a small, sunny yard where Tibetan flags flap in the breeze. It's all that I desire, a patch of earth in the city, a place to have friends over to cook out, to drink my coffee on a summer morning, to plant flowers with my daughter.

When I return from the Sackett Street open house and rapturously describe the place to Jeff, he nods blankly. He not only doesn't share my ardor, he doesn't understand it.

"It's too expensive, right?" he says. "So why bother thinking about it?" As far as he's concerned, we should stick to pursuing things in our price range. He is so on my shit list.

We're not usually this discordant. Jeff and I met in New York, when he lived in the East Village and I had a place in Hoboken. I was leaving the early showing of *Roger & Me* with a girlfriend; he was going in to the late show with his friends. My friend knew him from work. She introduced us, and right there in the lobby of the Eighth Street Movieland, we fell for each other.

After we married, we spent years bouncing around San Francisco and Boston, until the pull of Gotham became too great to ignore. When we were ready to return, we wanted a new neighborhood for a new chapter of our lives.

Brooklyn was terra incognita, a place we'd visited only once or twice. A few friends tried to steer us to the Williamsburg section of town, which was fast becoming the new East Village—Trendy! Edgy! See also: Desolate! Now it teems with expensive bars and strollers, and we couldn't afford it if we tried.

Most people we knew figured we'd wind up in Park Slope. Park Slope is what Berkeley is to San Francisco and Cambridge is to Boston—the crunchy, liberal, and pleased-with-itself sibling to the posh big city across the river. It's the neighborhood that has a food co-op and a wildly expensive private school. It's also the place bookish, academic people go when they're ready to settle down and make babies, which, our friends and family rightly assumed, was what we were settling in New York to do.

We tried to warm up to Park Slope when we invaded for a whirlwind weekend of apartment-searching, right before Christmas. We ate burgers on Seventh Avenue and checked out Prospect Park and looked at an insane number of places, in elegant old brownstones and delicately beautiful limestones. Everywhere we went, Jeff was thinking what I was thinking: Pffffffft. Nothing. Nada. Zip.

Jeff and I know one way to love—at first sight. No second-guessing, and no doubt. It's why I couldn't have a baby knowing he was unsure. It's why we couldn't bring ourselves to live in Park Slope either. We didn't get it.

At the time, Jeff's oldest and best friend was living on Smith Street in Cobble Hill, in a railroad apartment above Johnnie's Bootery. I didn't know what a bootery was, but I liked that there were places in the world that still needed them. After another fruitless afternoon in the Slope, we went to visit Peter and to check out his neighborhood. I was a goner before we even got to his door.

We had stepped off the train at Jay Street, in the center of Brooklyn's downtown. It was as urban and uninspiring as anything we'd ever seen in lower Manhattan. Then, when I wasn't expecting it, something clicked into place. We crossed Atlantic on Court Street and entered Cobble Hill.

It had the feel of a true neighborhood, where produce stands and burrito joints mixed with more upscale-aspiring storefronts. There were trees and side streets full of brownstones and brick and oil lamps. And people. People everywhere, speaking in Spanish and Japanese and French and Italian. Little kids and old guys with cigars. A palpable pulse.

By the time we got to the movie theater, with its Art Deco marquee and crudely rendered murals of Scarlett O'Hara and Laurel and Hardy, I was sure this was exactly where we were destined to live. We ate lunch at a Middle Eastern restaurant called Zaytoons and stuffed ourselves with soft, fragrant flatbread. "I can't believe this great neighborhood was sitting next to Manhattan all this time," I said, humbled by my ignorance, "and we never knew it."

"This is the one," Jeff replied.

We met with a real estate agent who apprised us nervously. He rose from his chair and came up three inches from my face and half a head shorter than it. "I'm using my twenty years in this business to read you now," he said to my chin. "I *think* you're people I can trust." He grabbed his coat and walked us several blocks farther from downtown into the neighborhood of Carroll Gardens.

Carroll Gardens's main claim to fame is that it is the setting of the movie *Moonstruck*. It's where Al Capone got married. It's home to several funeral parlors, pizzerias, bakeries, and plaster Virgin Marys. You could say it has something of an Italian vibe.

The Carroll in its name comes from Charles Carroll, one of the original signers of the Declaration of Independence and the sole Catholic in the group. The second part of the moniker has to do with the jewels of the neighborhood—the Place blocks. On First, Second, Third, and Fourth Place, the houses are mostly brownstones, nineteenth-century head-turners straight out of an

Edith Wharton novel or *Sesame Street*. In an urban planning quirk, they're set back from the sidewalk, giving the streets an unparalleled feeling of light and spaciousness, and leaving room in the front for squares of green. The Gardens.

That December weekend we came down from Boston to look in Brooklyn, there were only two apartments on the rental market in Carroll Gardens, both on Fourth Place. The street was decked out for the holidays, not in the tasteful white lights and pine wreaths of our Brahmin neighborhood, but in good old-fashioned plastic and a Vegas-worthy array of twinkling lights. We stopped to gawk at a life-size nativity featuring Mary, Joseph, and an empty manger where Baby Jesus would arrive on his birthday. Instead of Wise Men, Santa and a giant snowman stood guard over the tender scene. *We have arrived,* I thought. This is where we belong.

The first landlady we met, whose departing tenant had left behind an apartment full of paper and debris, didn't agree. Maybe it was because we're not Italian, or because we were from out of town. Whatever the reason, she turned us away. Another landlord, in a three-family a few doors up, seemed suspicious too, but offered us a lease on a minuscule upstairs apartment. We leapt at it.

A year later, I had a newborn in my arms, a lease that had expired, and a landlord who'd decided to convert our building into a one-family and kick us out. Sleep-deprived, hormonal, and historically overemotional on the subject of geography anyway, I spent days heaving and snuffling to Jeff, envisioning worst-case scenarios that would fling us to unchartered boroughs. "Wah-wah-wah we-re g-g-g-gonna have to move to Queeeeeeeeens!" I'd hyperventilate at him while Lucy screeched along sympathetically.

Instead, fate smiled on us. One morning on the way to the

subway, Jeff passed by a nondescript storefront, a law office that shared space with a real estate agent. A handwritten sign in the window advertised a one-bedroom "plus den" at the high end of our price range. The "den" is Brooklynese for the cell-like side room that every apartment seems equipped with. It's where you stick the crib after you've gone from couplehood to familyhood and before you get fed up and move to Jersey. The apartment we were living in was also a one plus den. It probably measured 750 square feet in its dreams.

That evening, while Jeff made spaghetti in our kitchen built for one, I dutifully strapped Lucy in the BabyBjörn and went over to the office. The broker, Vivian, grew up in Carroll Gardens. "I've lived down the street my whole life," she told me. She was open and friendly. "I think you'll like this apartment."

"I'm a little worried about size," I said. "We've got two adults and a person whose main job these days is growth."

"It's big," she promised, but I've lived enough places and looked at enough apartments to assume that God created realtors to make lawyers and publicists look honest.

We walked through the darkness to a block where the houses are the widest and grandest in the neighborhood. Vivian steered me to a stately brownstone with a requisite statue of Saint Anthony in the front yard.

A petite blonde was standing outside in the cold, smoking a Parliament. "Hey, Viv," rasped the landlady, "how's the family?" She held out a hand. "I'm Gina. I live downstairs, with my daughter and my granddaughter. What a beautiful baby. God bless her."

"Be careful with the banister, it's broken," Gina warned as Vivian, Lucy, and I lurched up a dusty flight of stairs. She unlocked the door and said, "Let me open the light."

She flipped a switch, and I gasped. "Excuse me," I said, "I need to make a call."

The apartment was almost twice the size of our other place, and, at $1,800 a month, only $200 more. The kitchen and bath were bigger, though still psychotically claustrophobic, but the bedroom was almost preposterously large. The "plus den" room could fit the crib and contained a closet, and there was a whole extra middle room, ideal for our office.

Jeff showed up in a heartbeat. "Do you think it's too big?" he mused.

"That's not a question people who live in a city should ever ask," I replied. A few weeks later we had moved in. We've been there ever since.

There's a lot to appreciate about our apartment—the high ceilings, the hardwood floors. There are plenty of drawbacks too: the water leaks that have sent brown rivers cascading down into our kitchen cupboards, the broken banister that forces us to go up and down the stairs clinging to the wall, the temperamental toilet that regularly goes on strike and refuses to flush, the stink of smoke from our nicotine-addicted neighbors that creeps into our air space, the ceiling collapses that have unleashed plagues of shiny flying roaches. There are days it feels like the last freaking book of the Bible in there.

It has not for one moment ever felt too big either. Not any of the times we've cringed when a well-meaning relation has gifted us with a supersized toy, not every morning when I roll out of bed to navigate the scant floor space between the garment rack and the bed, not when I'm so frazzled over where to put our shoes or our papers or our laundry detergent that I have to go to the Container Store to calm down and cheer up.

But the thing I like least about our apartment is that it will never be ours. The tenants upstairs, Sheila and her grown daughter Marilyn, have lived in the building for thirty years. They're great people. My biggest dread in life is turning into them.

I've lived in other people's houses my whole life. The first was my grandmother's, right on the other side of the Hudson River in Jersey City. I don't want my child to grow up in somebody else's home too.

"We should get our credit reports," I tell Jeff one lazy evening as we park, semidazed, in front of a movie. "Sure," he says, and soon after, we've ordered them.

More than your blood type, more than your astrological sign, more, even, than your SATs, your credit score is your identity. It determines what kind of a dream you can buy.

There are three major credit-scoring bureaus in America: Equifax, TransUnion, and Experian. These businesses collect information on how you spend your money and how on the ball you are about paying your bills. Late with a student loan? Delinquent with a car payment? Running up a lot of debt and paying only the minimum balance? They're the ones keeping tabs.

Your score is a calculation on a scale of 300 to 850 of how likely you are to default on your debts. The lower the number, the riskier a prospect you are. Jeff and I are in good shape in this regard. In the Venn diagram of our relationship, we overlap on an appreciation of bacon, Philly soul music, and having as little plastic as possible and carrying as little revolving balance on it as possible.

Jeff's scores are 738, 790, and 785. Mine are 810, 808, and 805. All we do is not use our cards too much and pay our bills on time, and our credit is considered "excellent." It's still a long road though, from getting a good score to scoring a house.

I arrange a playdate for Lucy with her friend Harry. It's really an excuse to get together with his mother, Jennifer. Jennifer and I are in a codependent real estate relationship. We can spend entire afternoons discussing the minutiae of the *New York Times* real estate section, from the Thursday "Recent Sales" column to the merits of the current week's "If You're Thinking of Living In" neighborhood report to the price tags on any building or condo or co-op in a five-mile radius. We can talk for hours about boilers and wiring, coaxing out intimate details of other people's countertops and closet space, and it doesn't get old for either of us.

Jennifer is from a midsized Ohio town that the housing bubble has conspicuously passed by, where one could easily purchase ten homes for the cost of one Brooklyn brownstone. When I met her, she and her husband were living in a microsized rental on President Street. It predated the relationship, belonging first to Vincent and a revolving series of roommates, but eventually straining, like a size-twelve ass in a size-six pair of jeans, to accommodate a wife and child. The rent was cheap and they scrimped and saved. Then a death in the family brought them some extra money. In 2001 they bought a fixer-upper three-family brownstone around the block from us for $780,000. It was a good price then. It's an impossible one now.

Meticulous, diligent Jennifer throws herself wholeheartedly into whatever she does. She was a self-educated home buyer, who as an owner learned on the fly the ins and outs of renovation. Becoming a homeowner didn't dampen Jennifer's taste for the hunt either. She still checks out open houses and reads the Web sites of every broker in town. She's also got a real knack for it, an instinct for what's a good investment and what's a clunker, a sense for how much work a house will need and how much it'll cost. Her continuing research also reassures her she got an excellent house at a wise price. As she says, "If I can go out for a few minutes on a Sunday and look at a place and that makes me feel good, why not?"

Now that I'm dipping my toes into the market, Jennifer has become an enthusiastic supporter of the quest. She gets to house-hunt vicariously through me. I get to home-own vicariously through her. She's the one, even in this cutthroat market, who keeps saying to not be afraid to bid and to bid low. "All they can do is say no," she says with the confidence of someone who negotiated the kind of deal on her house that any realtor would have said couldn't be done.

When I tell her about the house on Sackett Street, I can hear neurons firing up in her head. "There's another open house this weekend," I say, enticing her with those original fixtures.

"Call me Sunday, when you're heading out," she says. "Maybe I'll check it out with you." This is Jennifer code for "on it like white on rice."

Jennifer at the open house projects a vicious beauty. She's a quiet woman who wears ponytails and glasses. Get her around anyone unloading property, though, and she is a shark. As we stroll through the rooms, she grills the broker about the concrete on the sidewalk. About the roof. About why the water pressure is so low, relentlessly knocking thousands off the asking price. I'm so dopey-eyed over the plank floors, I can't even form a question, but Jennifer makes it all look as straightforward as a mob hit.

I follow Jennifer with a notebook like a cub reporter, scribbling furiously. I know I will never live in this house, even as I stand here contemplating how loud the foot traffic is at night and whether the closets are big enough. Since when has not being able to have something stopped anyone from aching for it? At least I'll sound a whole lot sharper the next time I go out on the prowl.

I need any bit of savvy I can get. Something has to compensate for what we don't have much of—money.

We have friends in other parts of the country who bought their homes with practically nothing in their pockets, with not much more than their smarts and local incentives. I keep hoping that we can use our pluck and wits to find a relative bargain and finance it through some magical loan.

I look into Housing and Urban Development programs for first-time homebuyers, but our family isn't financially or vocationally qualified for any. I spot a boarded-up brownstone on a less desirable block and make numerous calls to the city. Eventually, I track down some info on the owner, who, it turns out, is still paying taxes and is not violating enough quality-of-life laws for the house to be officially designated abandoned.

There are homes in Brooklyn available at auction, thanks to a foreclosure rate that's creeping steadily upward all over the country. But most of them require massive rehabs and are located in the absolute shittiest parts of town. I'm not afraid of elbow grease or investing our family in a growing neighborhood. This is more than that. It's crap schools, high crime, and more money than we could spend for renovation.

I'd never before given much thought to whether or not Jeff and I would own a home. We married young; we conceived as soon as we started trying. I'd assumed if I wanted another baby, I'd have one. I'd equally assumed that home ownership would be waiting for us when we were ready for it. I had the cockiness of one for whom other milestones have come easily. Only a few weeks into the house hunt, and already the reality of what we're facing here and the subtext that we have failed economically, are only making the disappointment of not having another baby even worse.

After school one cold March afternoon, Lucy and I go to see Margot and her new daughter. Margot grew up in Brooklyn Heights, not far from right where she's living now. She has the in-born confidence of a native New Yorker, with a low threshold for the indirect, the unsure, and the passive. She moves quickly and she expects you to keep up.

She and her husband Simon bought their two-family in Cobble Hill in 1999. The house was a disaster and they paid $250,000 for it. They lived there through a nerve-scraping year of renovation, surviving microwaved meals and workers tramping in and out. They endured it all through a pregnancy and the birth of a first baby, because that was the only way they could afford to do it.

Margot's daughter Bette has been Lucy's best friend since before the girls could even crawl. Now, and for the rest of her life, Bette is also someone's sister. Margot knows that's not in the cards for us. When, in her ninth month, she cheerfully queried, "So when are you going to have your next one?" I responded with the glum assertion, "I'm not."

Harper is snoozing in the bouncy seat when we arrive bearing a tray of spinach lasagna. I peer at the baby under her blanket, her long eyelashes casting shadows on her cheek. She's so stunning it's an icepick to my psyche.

By the time I come home, I can barely speak. It's hit me why I'm so pissed off at Jeff. It's not that he doesn't share my certainty about a baby. It's that he's reneging on our deal.

We have a pact that's sustained us through our entire relationship: to make our decisions based on our desires, not our fears. It stems from our earliest days after meeting each other. He said it's what made him call me for the first time. It's why I got off the corporate track years ago. It's how we chose to live in California and Boston for a few years. We'd never lived there and we wanted to do the things we hadn't tried. Now, when I think back to our baby conversation, I remember all I heard from Jeff was a litany of worries.

We're washing the dishes after Lucy is asleep. "I have to say something," I tell him, "and then I'll let it go. If you're completely satisfied with everything we have now, if you don't want to have another baby, then fine. Just do me a favor and ask yourself if that's it, or if you're not saying yes to something that could be fantastic because you're scared. You don't even have to tell me what the answer is," I say, and I mean it, "but promise you'll think about it. We always said we wouldn't chicken out."

"Okay," he replies softly, and sticks a plate back in a crowded cabinet.

I don't expect him to change how he feels, I don't expect anything to change at all, but I needed to ask. I needed to be sure.

A short time later I pass a sign in another real estate office, a listing for someone with "patience, vision, and stamina." There's a picture of a brick house, not the familiar brownstone of my street or the stately red of Cobble Hill, but a yellowish beige-ish baby-poop hue. The price is $625,000, "firm," the ad notes, and there's an address.

It's located at the farthest end of a dead-end street, a few yards before the Gowanus Canal. An enormous tree in front of it has burst through the sidewalk, ripping up pavement and blocking out the view of its upper levels. From where I stand, I can ascertain a few things. The area past the rust-crumbling gate is similarly cracked, the windows are far too filthy to see in, and what is at best ivy and at worst a virulent strain of Venus flytrap is crawling up the façade and tearing up the bricks. To call it a blight would be an insult to blight.

I stand in front of the house wondering if I could wheedle a better price than "firm" from the seller and pondering whether the inside is full of fabulous, untouched details like stained glass and sliding doors. An older man materializes from the house next door with a broom and begins sweeping his stoop.

"There are mushrooms growing in there," he says. Come again? "Mushrooms" he repeats. "Nobody's lived in there for twenty-five years. Owner lives on Staten Island. The whole block has been trying to get him to sell it for years. He'd rather not sell it than not get his price."

Part of me is intrigued. I picture a primeval interior overrun with fungus, moss, and elves. The more sensible parts of me, my feet, turn and walk away.

On Saturday, it feels like spring outside. We still need sweaters and jackets, but the air is soft and there isn't a cloud for six counties. We decide to treat ourselves to breakfast out and head for the greasy spoon at the end of Court Street, directly under the overpass. The diner lacks ambiance and drinkable coffee, but it's cheap and close and the waitresses fuss like mad over my daughter.

I'm cutting up her pancakes when Lucy blurts, "Mommy's going to have a baby."

I can feel my heart cracking. Jeff's a great father. I get swoony and sentimental when I see him with Lucy, their close relationship teaching me of how much fathers and daughters can mean to each other.

"No," I tell Lucy, trying not to glare accusingly at Jeff, "I'm not."

"Yes you are!" she insists. She rubs my stomach. "There's a baby in there and she's going to come out." I'm sure this is just some weird reaction to Bette's new sister, but she's playing it to the hilt. She leans down to kiss my belly. "Hi, baby," she coos. "Daddy, touch Mama's belly."

Then she looks up at me. "Why are you crying?"

"I'm not," I say, as the waterworks flow so copiously that I can't even fool a three-year-old. We can't have a baby, we can't find a home, how much less together could our act be? While Jeff pays the tab, I escape to the bathroom to pull myself together, splashing my face and staring at the Bob Marley poster in the ladies' room until I'm composed enough to come out. Everything's gonna be all right. Everything's gonna be all right.

We step out in the morning light, and Lucy busies herself singing the score of *Annie*. "I don't need anything but you!" she belts.

That's when Jeff whispers: "I've been thinking about what you said. You're right. I was scared. I want to have a baby. I want Lucy to have a sibling; I want two kids running around the dunes on Cape Cod in the summer, playing together. I knew it for sure when I saw Lucy kissing your belly. I've been looking for the sign. That was the sign."

This is exactly what I've been wishing to hear for weeks. There's only one thing to say.

"What the hell are you doing to me?" I roar. "Are you crazy? I thought we made a decision." I'm so angry and sad and confused over this whole stupid pancake breakfast fiasco I could run away. "I can't be on the roller coaster anymore. It's too late. Forget it."

Three and a half weeks later, I drop Lucy off at nursery school and then I duck into the drugstore on the way home. When I get there, I shut myself up in the bathroom for a few minutes, and when I emerge, I dial Jeff's work number. I'm pregnant.

Co-ops are buildings that are owned and run—surprise—cooperatively by their shareholders, who usually, but not always, live in them. If you buy into a cooperative, you don't exactly own your apartment; you own a percentage of a whole building. In addition to whatever you've paid for your shares, you pay into a monthly maintenance fund to upkeep the common areas and provide whatever predetermined services the shareholders designate.

Like other businesses, a co-op will have an elected board of officers. Sales of units within the building usually have to be approved by the board, which assesses a buyer's finances and character and can veto a potential resident without any explanation. Even if a seller says yes to a buyer, even if the bank approves, the board can still say no. Some of the most prominent people on the planet have been rejected by New York City co-ops. Money alone can't buy your way into an exclusive address. You have to distinguish yourself as the right kind of person for the building, as co-op rejectees like Mike Wallace, Barbra Streisand, Ronald Perelman, and Madonna can attest.

Increasingly, however, real estate is becoming less a test of character and more a transaction like any other. Why would anyone with the right financials put up with the debasement of having to prove personal merit? Co-ops are markedly more difficult to get into than condos, and subsequently, harder to sell.

Since the 1980s, condominiums have become the preferred choice for new multiunit residences. When you buy a condo, you own your niche in your building outright. A seller and buyer can negotiate a property transaction independent of any intermediary body, free of the possible mortification of a board rejection. Now construction is booming in the city, with condos sprouting up wherever there remains a sliver of untapped land.

The four-unit co-op near the Brooklyn-Queens Expressway we're walking toward tonight isn't going to hold us to the same ultraschmancy standards that a Park Avenue address would, but that extra hurdle-jumping we'd have to do to get in is an unpleasant consideration. The imminent addition to our brood, has made us step up the search and consider more options.

"I guess we can't live at Gina's forever," Jeff had said recently as he panned our bedroom for a corner in which to stick the crib. "Can we?"

"No," I'd replied. "We can't."

We've been discerning in our choices of apartments, but always with the understanding that the sum of our risk was a security deposit and a broker's fee. Tonight is the first time Jeff and I have ever looked at a place together as potential owners. It feels different with our life savings and credit ratings on the line.

The owners of the co-op have two tween sons and have recently bought a brownstone on Third Place. Their apartment is bright and in great condition. It even has a small, stackable washer and dryer. It's also the same size as our last apartment, the one that was too small when there were only two of us. Oversized, baroque furniture fills almost every inch of the space—all 750 square feet of it.

It's the boys' room that does Jeff in. The small chamber looks even more constricted because of the massive dresser and bureau, both of which seem to be vying to engulf the huge bunk bed. This is where these ten- and twelve-year-old boys sleep, in a veal pen where they have to sidle in to climb up and crash on their mattresses.

Jeff wears the same appalled expression on his face as when we toured Alcatraz a few years ago. His upbringing was modest. Still, he had his own room, had the luxury of suburban breathing space.

A single, middle-aged gay man is viewing the apartment with us. He takes a perfunctory stroll through the rooms and says, "I'd like to make an offer."

As we dejectedly trudge home to munch our cold hamburgers, Jeff asks, "Why should we settle for less? We don't act out of fear, right? We hold out for what we want. We'll know it when we see it." I'm convinced he's right, and I'm wracked with concern he isn't.

I can chalk up my belief that there is a home out there for us to inherent boundless optimism. Too bad I also got my mother's talent for angst. My life is a happy path of hope, paved with determined fretting.

The following Tuesday night, I walk around the corner to watch *Buffy the Vampire Slayer* with Sharon, as I do every week. Sharon is Lucy's godmother, and my best friend.

We met in San Francisco in the mid-nineties, when she was an ambitious young compensation analyst working for a boutique firm. I was her temp. Our pale Irish features are similar enough that people in the office assumed we were related. Maybe that's why we clung to each other like family so fast. Sharon's parents are both dead; she's taken care of herself since she was a teenager. In her twenties she was creating stunning organizational charts and elaborate payout plans for CEOs. I was stuffing envelopes and answering phones. We bonded the day she overheard me chatting amiably to one of the company's big clients in my smoothest receptionist voice.

"You're good with people," she'd observed.

"That's funny," I'd unprofessionally confessed, draining a Coke and studying my nails, "because I don't like most of them."

She'd arched a quizzical eyebrow over her horn-rimmed glasses. Then she'd leaned in and said conspiratorially, "Me neither."

We've been inseparable ever since. We misanthropes have to stick together.

The difference between us is that Sharon is a more reluctant urbanite. She's a woman who finds her true solace in tranquil spaces, nature, and the company of animals. I, meanwhile, am drawn to denser environments. I figure among 8 million people there have to be a few I can love. Cities give better odds.

A few years ago Sharon decided to, in her words, give New York a shot, and moved here. It was around the time Vincent and Jennifer were buying their house. She needed an apartment. They needed a tenant. I happily played matchmaker. It's an idyllic arrangement—with Sharon above and Vincent, Jennifer, and Harry below, this one building provides our family a regular concentrated dose of camaraderie.

As *Buffy*'s familiar theme music swells, Sharon goes to the fridge and pulls out two Sam Adams. "No thanks," I say.

She does not miss a beat. "You're pregnant, aren't you? You never turn down a beer."

"That's not true," I retort. "Sometimes I'm already drinking one."

There is a gleam of triumph in her eye. "Maybe this time it'll be a son," she says, flipping the cap off her beer. "See if you can grow me a boyfriend, would you?"

"That's what friends are for," I reply.

A few days later, I am once again uncharacteristically turning down a beer. Jeff and I are at a potluck dinner at the home of some friends from Lucy's school. As our collective offspring dart around, the adults drink and talk of real estate. Most of the people in the room own their homes, and they banter about their mortgages and their contractors while I sullenly sip my Canada Dry.

"What's up with you two?" asks Ron brusquely. Ron, tall and thin as the omnipresent toothpick dangling from his lips, is hovering near his perpetually silent wife Naomi. He has a small but lucrative consultancy business. Perhaps that's why he's so generous with his opinions. "Still in that apartment?"

"For now," I say, "but we're looking to buy."

Like Vincent and Jennifer, Ron and Naomi bought a two-family in the neighborhood a few years ago, and pay their mortgage with the income their tenant provides. "Why can't you do that?" he interrogates. "Interest rates are so goddamn low right now, anyone who doesn't buy is nuts. And anyone who gets a one-family," he throws in for good measure, "is an idiot. Why do anything that doesn't make money?"

We know that interest rates are at record lows right now. They've been dropping weekly, setting homeowner friends scrambling to refinance. Thirty-year fixed rates that were flying above the 8 percent zone a few years ago are now down around 5 percent. Adjustable rate loans can be had for even less, often considerably so. It's an economic moment that comes along once in a lifetime.

What good does that do, though, when housing prices are rising faster than interest rates are falling?

"We don't have enough for the down payment for a multifamily," Jeff says, his face burning.

Ron looks at him witheringly. "You can't come up with a down payment? You can't dip into your retirement money?" It seems to genuinely perplex him that we're not more prosperous, that we don't have some secret reserves to tap.

Our accountant often expresses similar incredulity, much to the deflation of our egos. We're not paycheck-abusing yuppies who could have a fantastic investment portfolio if we cut out the luxuries. Lord, I wish. I've crunched the numbers, and if I eliminate my once-a-week mocha, it'll take four thousand years of savings to get a home.

We don't have well-to-do relations itching to bankroll us either. My father has never given me anything. My mother has almost no money of her own; everything she has belongs to my stepfather. She's not even speaking to me again this month, for reasons I can't recall, so a wad of cash is probably out.

I used to figure that if we ever got jaded or fed up or anxious enough, we could sell out to the Man. I could hustle for corporate work, or get a full-time office job instead of spending afternoons in the park with my daughter. Eventually, I realized the Man wasn't that eager for my services.

Jeff and I are not at this accountant-offending economic level because we're trying to make a statement here. We're at this level because this is what we get paid to do the things we do. Which, in a city full of millionaires, is something of a handicap. Can't summon up the gross national product of a small nation to dump into a house? There are a couple of thousand guys behind you who can.

"If you're putting ten percent down on a house here, that's around seventy or eighty thousand dollars," Jeff says. "That's not even including closing costs. That's a lot of money."

Then Ron delivers the *coup de grâce*. He looks at us with naked disgust and says, "Man, I'm just glad we bought when we did."

That night, as we sort through a stack of bills, Jeff correctly observes, "Ron is an asshole. The way he kept asking in front of everybody why we're losers."

"What we need is a time machine," I tell him. "Then we could take the savings we have today to buy a house in 1979. That could be Ron's next helpful idea."

Still, I can't ignore the fact that other, nonasshole friends have tenants, and they get to live in nice houses with yards. I rethink my original mortgage calculation of $400,000 as just a suggestion, and decide that securing a loan that's double our budget would probably be a minor obstacle. Why say we can't do it before we even try? It feels like anybody and everybody can obtain a mortgage now. Besides, I want to be able to go upstairs. Ditto downstairs. To have rosebushes and still live in the city. I want a house.

On a bracing spring morning soon after, I am looking at a brick two-family on Nelson Street offered for a comparatively paltry $575,000. It's well beyond our budget, but the fact that it's a house with income potential and only $275,000 more than that miniscule co-op we looked at makes it seem somehow worth investigating. What's $275,000? That's just six short years of my annual salary!

Nelson Street is farther away from the heart of Carroll Gardens and closer to the expressway. I have to beg for days to get

Edward, the broker, to take me, because he's positive it's not right for us. "It needs work," he says, "and a buyer who can handle it." I think that because I can distress a dresser and put drawer pulls on it, I'm Ty Fucking Pennington.

This house needs work like Ground Zero needs work. The upstairs is inhabited by an elderly tenant and, by the sounds of things, an exceptionally large dog that is having a psychotic episode. I can't be sure, because the old woman refuses to let us in.

"Helloooo? Antoinette?" Edward shouts as he raps on the door. *"Okay then,"* he says uncomfortably, above the barking, *"some other time."* All I glean from the visit is that her bathroom is outside the apartment in the stairwell.

He next leads me to the top level of the downstairs owner's unit. The bedrooms are so profoundly water-stained that the walls have developed the wrinkly texture of a pile of wet laundry. Below, in the generously named garden level, there's a front room, an eat-in kitchen with a low ceiling and ripped-up floors, and a bathroom big enough to accommodate a filthy shower with no hot water. The garden itself is so overgrown I'm afraid to enter it, especially when I see something large and furry darting through the grass. The basement is a festival of more water damage, odors I've never encountered before, and no boiler. None.

Edward takes me back upstairs, and we stand in the front bedroom. There's a small cot still there, and an ancient space heater with a wide grate and cinnamon-bun coils.

"What's the story with this place?" I ask him. "Who's the seller?"

"It's the owner's son," he explains. "She just passed away. He wants to unload the place as fast as possible, and it's a good price.

Don't worry about the lady upstairs, she's been evicted. She has to be out by June first."

My eyes survey the surroundings, and I try to go into mental decorating mode. I try to push a kitchen and sitting room up here, and turn the downstairs into bedrooms. I try to enlarge the bathroom and clean out the yard. I try, but all I see instead is an old woman shivering in her bed in this cold, fetid house with no boiler. All I keep thinking is, you would have to shake hands with someone who let his mother live like this, who asks for over half a million dollars to throw out his elderly tenant.

We don't have the money for this house. We certainly don't have the few hundred thousand dollars more it would take to renovate it. But more than anything else, I don't have the stomach for it. I couldn't live with myself if I lived here.

Because we don't earn a lot and because we don't have much saved, Jeff and I know we may not be the best candidates for a mortgage anyway. All we have in our favor, really, is our sterling credit. Not that bad credit is stopping anyone from getting a home these days.

If you want to know what pumped up the housing bubble, look no further than the hot air blowing around the subprime mortgage industry. Subprimes are a means of giving mortgages to homebuyers—and often second mortgages to existing home-owners—who might otherwise never obtain them. They're the choice of borrowers whose credit is less than stellar, and those with even bigger black marks in their histories—like foreclosure or bankruptcy.

They operate on a simple conceit. The borrower gets mortgage approval, but for higher interest than the market—or prime—

rate. Sometimes the rate is set enticingly low to start, and then rises later. The prime interest rate might for example be 6 percent, while a subprime loan can be 8 percent. For a $400,000 loan, those extra points add up to an extra $536 and change every month.

A generation ago, interest rates were a less pliable affair. Most states had set legal limits on them to prevent usury lending practices. Then in 1978, in the *Marquette v. First of Omaha Service Corporation* decision, the Supreme Court ruled that national banks could charge customers the highest interest rate allowed in the bank's home state, not the borrower's. Banks, smelling profits, flocked to states with loftier interest limits, leading other states to rush to raise their maximums.

The old usury laws both protected consumers from high interest rates and made it more difficult to obtain loans. Once interest could be put on a more tiered system, rates could fluctuate based on elements like the borrower's risk potential. The *Marquette* decision revolutionized the industry, creating a new population of borrowers. And lots and lots of personal debt.

The mortgage industry took note and now operates on similar principles. It wasn't always this aggressive, though. But in the early nineties, as homeownership rates began to level off, lenders had to come up with novel ways of stimulating more loans. Lenders began reaching out to less attractive prospects. All those who've ever watched their own standards decline in proportion to the toxic cocktail of poor judgment and slim pickings can probably relate. It's just that our individual faulty decision-making isn't on the macroeconomic level.

Now more people can obtain loans, with more kinds of loan

options, and more varieties of interest rates. Behold the dawn of the subprime.

I can get behind the logic that people with a dubious track record should pay a higher premium than a compulsive accounts settler like me. I can even understand why the risk doesn't seem so risky—there are properties in our neighborhood currently going for tens of thousands of dollars more than they were earlier this year. We've had friends sell their places for nearly double what they paid two years ago. In the right hands at the right time, getting your hands on a mortgage—even one with a higher interest rate—sounds like money in the bank.

Lenders, meanwhile, have relied on the safety net of mortgage-backed securities, bundling mortgages together and thereby coating potentially dodgy-looking loans into shiny, unthreatening-looking new packaging.

The blue-sky assumption that lenders and borrowers have been operating on is that housing prices are going to keep inflating. Buoyed by the robustness of the housing market of the past few years, lenders have gone from merely courting subprime borrowers to doggedly pursuing them. People with spotty histories, who thought they'd never own homes, have eagerly latched on.

The other explanation for the rise in subprimes is that some lenders are plain predatory, peddling sometimes staggeringly high interest rates to borrowers who don't know the questions to ask, who don't read the fine print, who have trouble seeing beyond the next paycheck. Who's more vulnerable to taking on an unreasonable debt than someone who already has a history of doing so?

For those people, subprimes can be the crystal meth of

mortgages—cheap, seductive, poisonous to the user, hell on the community. It's the downright nonsensical logic behind ads that read, "Why let past credit problem or uncontrolled debt prevent you from getting the home loan you really want?" It's the get-rich-quick pitch so many would-be real estate flippers have fallen for.

It's not just about greed, though, or foolishly living beyond your means. For a lot of people—ones who will eventually fall behind on their payments and go into foreclosure—it's about the dream. It's about wanting the security of a home so badly you'll go about it in the most potentially devastating way.

If the value of your home has been overestimated (a likely scenario when the housing market is euphoric), if you're trying to sell and the market softens, if you lose your job and you can't keep up with those high interest payments, if any number of things that often happen in the real world occur, you're screwed. If borrowers can't pay their mortgages, they'll start defaulting en masse on their loans and going into foreclosure. And if that happens, lenders may at best have to stop processing subprime loans and, at worst, go under entirely. Which in turn ripples out to the stock market and screws the economy.

This is what happens when ebullience runs amok. I'm not an economics person. I can barely, reluctantly balance my checkbook. I may not have a great sense for leverage or speculation, but I do have a shiftless enough coterie of relatives to know this: if you lend money to people who aren't adept at paying off their debts, you might not get your money back. Or, as the saying goes, if I owe the bank a hundred dollars, I've got a problem. If I owe the bank a million dollars, the bank has a problem. More than what you might someday be able to refinance or sell your home for, at the end of the month, the only thing that really matters is, can you pay your mortgage?

With our respectable credit scores, Jeff and I don't need to cast our economic fate into the murky, higher-interest subprime waters. It's a good thing, because they scare the daylights out of us. And I have enough distraction going on already. Like the fact there's a human being growing inside me.

I've gotten off easy in my pregnancies. I don't get nauseated or woozy. I surge on with only a raging appetite and an ever-widening ass to proclaim my fertility. I am nevertheless deeply aware that another person is coming. I go for a doctor's appointment and watch an infinitesimally small heart beating underneath my own. Another chair at the table, another bed with someone in it. I'm consumed with figuring out where this child is going to grow up.

Yet for all my preoccupation, I've been keeping a low profile. Hardly anyone knows about the pregnancy, and I've been actively putting off telling my mother.

My mother is a world-class worrier. Her anxiety is as much a part of her identity as her cornflower blue eyes and talent for pancake flipping. She worries about everything—whether it'll rain, if the neighbors are gossiping about her, where a serial killer in Mexico is hiding out. When I was a child, I could feel her tense up each time we crossed the street together, holding her breath until we got to the curb. She still does.

Usually, when she asks me how I am, I say that I'm great, and she tells me I sound sick, or sad. I'm estimating she'll stress out twice as much when she learns there are two of us now, housed in one body. Especially because I am, as my mother anxiously points out, so very old.

"When your age," she likes to say, "I was raising a teenager." If fate had dealt her a different hand, she says, she'd have had a houseful of kids.

At twenty-one my mother was still living with her parents and Auntie, her mother's unmarried sister. Her five siblings were all either married or off fighting in Vietnam by then. She was working at Sears and dating a handsome coworker. Her life was pretty quiet and orderly. Then the doctor told her she was having a baby. She's said that when she found out, she wished she had cancer instead.

My father reluctantly married her, and they set up house in my grandparents' finished basement. Then one August morning when Mom was six months pregnant, he took off for work and said, "I won't be coming back." He never did. He disappeared without so much as a forwarding address, robbing her of the family she believed she was meant to have.

"I'm expecting again," I mention casually one morning when she calls to check in.

"Well," she says, a slight tremor in her tone.

Years ago, my mother confided how, when she learned of her condition, she'd tried to miscarry. One day when she was alone in the house, she climbed over the railing on the second-floor landing and hung there by her wrists. She said she thought she could somehow dislodge me from her womb. I don't know how long she stayed, hoping for an end to her morning sickness and shame. I often ask myself if there's an unspoken part of the story where she contemplated letting go, or if she did. I only know I didn't budge.

"That's wonderful," she says tonelessly. "We could use some

good news around here for a change." There's a beat and then, "Are you feeling okay? You sound so tired."

Jeff's parents will be easier to tell. They worry less. I think it's because of God. We are spending the weekend at their home in White Plains, a prim suburb outside of the city. They wound up there the way they arrived everywhere in their lives—because that's where the church sent them. Jeff's father is a retired Baptist minister, as is his mother. They met, providentially to say the least, in seminary. They too had wanted more children, but, as they say, God had a different plan.

For most of Jeff's life, his parents lived in the homes the church provided, homes they occupied but didn't own. They bought their first house shortly before they retired a decade ago. It is beautiful—a 1920s Tudor full of charm and character, rising from a swell in the land toward the treetops. On their first excursion as prospective buyers, they took a drive through an attractive neighborhood and saw two FOR SALE signs. They bought the house that stood behind the second one.

While Lucy is playing with her Fisher-Price people in the other room and I'm hoovering up my second bowl of cereal of the morning, Jeff tells them, "You're going to have another grandchild." They hug us and offer congratulations.

After the requisite queries into how I'm feeling and when the baby is arriving, my mother-in-law floats the other inevitable question. "Do you think you'll stay in that apartment?"

"We're looking," Jeff says, "but it's hard. Not much out there in our price range."

If we want to "get in the game," to use the parlance of everyone who advises us to just buy something already, we need to get a mortgage broker. A mortgage broker acts as a conduit between the lender and the buyer, shopping for the best type of mortgage and best interest rate for her clients. Her presence greases the wheels of the loan approval process, which lets sellers know that a prospective buyer isn't some Sunday afternoon tire-kicker. Being able to walk into an open house and say we're preapproved to spend a certain amount of dollars might give us a slight edge over the competition.

I ask Margot for a reference one afternoon as we're schlepping the kids from preschool. Harper is strapped to Margot's chest, her arms and legs dangling like a Whoozit.

"Talk to our broker. She's the *best*; she got us a really good rate," she says briskly. "You should have no trouble getting a place. You don't need much space anyway; it's not like you're having any more kids."

I am awkwardly silent.

"You're not, are you?" she asks. Then we both break into sly grins. The girls are walking ahead of us, oblivious to our boring adult talk. Margot stops, and with her baby between us, envelopes me in a teary hug.

Later in the week Jeff's mother calls him. "We have a few stocks," she says, "that we inherited from your grandmother. We've been hanging on to them for something special. If you need help with a down payment, we can probably throw in a few thousand dollars."

It's an unexpected blessing, one that tips the scales for us from impossible to maybe.

I mention this later when I speak to Roz, Margot's mortgage broker. I tell her our household income, how pitifully little we have saved, and that I'm aware of exactly how profoundly this limits our searching. "We want a home," I say, "and the market's so crazy. I think we're running out of time."

"You're not going to get much," she replies. She is even more no-nonsense than Margot, direct but not discouraging. We're simpatico about trying to get our paperwork in order before there isn't a square inch of affordable real estate left in the boroughs or New Jersey. "You're ahead of a lot of people already. You wouldn't believe how many come to me with less than you've got and want to buy a brownstone. You should look for a condo," she explains, "because they'll usually accept a smaller down payment, or a co-op sponsor sale, because the requirements aren't as tight." Sponsor sales are typically units held over from before the building converted and still owned by the original developer. They usually don't require board approval.

"Can I get you to draw up a preapproval letter, then?" I ask.

"No," she replies. "There's no point. What you're going to do instead is use my name if you make an offer on a place. Then I can tailor a letter to the bid. You don't want the realtors to know you're approved for more than you're offering," she explains. "If they think you're at your maximum, they won't try to get you to bid more."

This makes perfect sense and I never would have thought of it.

"So what do you think our maximum is?" I ask.

I hear her pounding on the keys of her calculator. "If you're paying $1,800 a month rent now, and you'd have maintenance charges and interest and homeowners' insurance"—*tap tap tap*—

"you're looking at a max of $400,000. More like $350,000, $300,000 if you can find it."

"This is all so helpful," I tell her. It's what I'd calculated too. Almost anywhere else, we'd be able to get a great house for that money. We are not rich, but to be able to swing that much makes us tremendously fortunate.

What I think is, *Oh cripes, we're never going to find anything at that price.* Our neighborhood is comprised almost entirely of multifamily houses, where the landlords live in and rent out the other units. There are almost no condos or co-ops, and what there are tend to be developments on the other side of the Brooklyn-Queens Expressway.

I lie here in my bed now, agonizing that we've missed the real estate boat, while Lucy is dreaming in the little room off ours. The white-noise function on our clock radio is cranked up.

That staticky drone is there to drown out the street noise, and to drown out the noise of the apartment itself. The only doors here are for the bathroom and the closets. If Jeff wants to stay up late to watch a movie in the living room, or I want to have a phone conversation, or we have dinner guests, we don't want to risk disturbing the slumbering child in the back. Hence the sound machine.

The white noise is also there for sex. Sex in our apartment means waiting until Lucy is deep asleep and the lights are out. No squeaky bedsprings, no porno-movie-style cries of ecstasy. I'm so pleased we conceived a second child. I'm impressed when we exercise our connubial rights at all.

So we're ready for a home. One with a door or two and a small measure of privacy. And though it's a bitch to admit, if we're ever going to make it happen, Jeff and Lucy and I are going to have to look outside our neighborhood.

I'm trying to approach the exploration of other neighborhoods with the same openness I've been applying to having another baby. It'll be an adventure; it'll be fun. It'll be a means of depleting all our physical and emotional resources.

"It's a big borough," I whisper to Jeff in bed, and I can feel his skepticism in the darkness.

"I like it here," he says. "But I guess it wouldn't kill us to look around."

On a sunny Sunday morning, our blossoming family has decided to make an excursion to the Brooklyn Botanic Garden. It's cherry-blossom time, so we're off to watch our daughter dance on a carpet of fragrant pink petals. And what could be more efficient for a pregnant woman, a preschooler, and an ambivalent spouse than working in an open house or two on the way?

The listing that has made me do a double take today is for a house in Prospect Heights, right off Franklin Street. It's described as a "turn-of-the-century brick one-family," and the asking price is $295,000. It has to be a typo—even a bombed-out shell should be going for nearly double that.

I look at the map. This is the far-from-gentrified side of Prospect Heights. In fact, it's Bedford-Stuyvesant.

A neighborhood's reputation is like your own elementary school one—it takes about twenty years to live down. My impression of Bed-Stuy still stems largely from its Reagan-era infamy for crime and crack, and one warehouse party I wound up at in the nineties.

Now people are starting to reconsider the area. I've read the newspaper and magazine stories about it and other "up and coming" neighborhoods. The articles usually follow the same formula—long ago, it was a bustling immigrant area, then the gangs and the drugs moved in, but lately it has been attracting artists and creative types priced out of nearby neighborhoods. The subtext is: Be not afraid, vanguard bourgeois bohemians! Get in now while housing is cheap, and panini and American Apparel will follow! Even areas like the South Bronx—now straight-facedly rebranded as "SoBro"—are being touted as the next big boom areas. High-end developers have been swooping in to zones where cabdrivers still won't venture after dark.

Maybe that's urban improvement. Maybe it's colonization. Maybe it's both.

The subway station is dismal and the street is run down, with crumbling stoops and broken windows. Some of the buildings seem deserted. The one we're looking at however, a narrow white two-story, is in immaculate condition.

A cursory visual sweep of the photos on the walls tells us the occupants are an attractive African-American couple. There are elegant wooden mantels in the living room and main bedroom, and beautifully stained plank floors. The kitchen is small but recently renovated. The outdoor space is stamp-sized but its very existence is a boon. Prospect Park is a short walk away. Most of all, if we lived here, we could have a whole house, a beautiful brick house, in Brooklyn.

This beautiful brick house is also a few feet from the main drag of Franklin, and the pulse of radios and cars horns and kids yelling back and forth at each other vibrates in through the closed windows. We're here on a sleepy springtime Sunday afternoon—what is it like on a Saturday night in July?

"Is this my room?" Lucy asks cheerfully as she skips into a sunny upstairs chamber.

"Maybe," Jeff and I say together.

We take the information sheet from the realtor, then we go home and do our own research. While the neighborhood is getting safer, the 79th Precinct still has one of the highest violent crime rates in the city. I look at the reports for the public school we'd be zoned for—the test scores are distressingly low and the vaguely defined "incident rate" is high. Could I trust that my children would get a decent education there? Or would we be the people who send their kids to outside schools, buying in one neighborhood but really living in another?

Wherever we go, we're not just buying a home; we're getting an educational system and a peer group in the deal as well. The thought is even more intimidating than a mortgage. You grow where you're planted. Where do we plant our kids?

"It's too soon," Jeff says. "We need to look around more."

It sure was a pretty house though.

If you live in a city, you spend your days moving through different worlds, often in the span of a few blocks. Race and class and money are in your face and in your mind all the time. Whatever language you speak, whatever color your skin, whatever God you worship or don't believe in, however much you earned or didn't last year, whatever genitalia you possess or gender you prefer, there are places where the neighbors don't want your kind because of exactly who you are. You'll bring down the property values or you're a carpetbagging poseur. Your music is too loud, or you're a classist snob if you think someone else's music is too loud. You're a townie if you've been in the neighborhood too long, a yuppie if you've arrived too late.

As we begin to consider other neighborhoods, we're not yet able to distinguish the places where we could weave ourselves into the community from the ones where we'd always be outsiders. What we do know for sure is that there is nothing like a house-hunting walk through Bed-Stuy to bring on a whole boatload of soul-searching.

The person who buys this house will be getting a bargain, and making an investment in a neighborhood that's only getting better. In just a few years, in fact, that low-rated school will become one of the best in the district. If the us of a decade ago were in sync with the neighborhood of five years from now and the house and its price today, it would be perfect. It's not though. It's not our home. We have to keep hoping ours is out there, just waiting for the current occupant to decide to move. Because time is a luxury we don't have.

A TOMB
WITH A VIEW

The ad says the house is in "Greenwood Heights," and the map shows a street adjacent to a large patch of emerald. Two subway transfers, several stairwells, interminable waiting, and a lengthy walk down the industrial eyesore that is Fourth Avenue later, we're at the address. It's two blocks from the Gowanus Expressway, Interstate 278, and half a block from Brooklyn's tremendous Green-Wood Cemetery.

"At least the neighbors are quiet," Jeff notes. And classy—the house is on the edge of Leonard Bernstein's final resting place.

We might be able to process the comedown of the location were the house itself not such a $400,000 nightmare. The color scheme is brown, light brown, and paneling. A large deck has metastasized over the small yard. There are three inconsequential bedrooms, two of which are, surprisingly, triangular.

The broker stands in the center of all this wreckage, his face a rictus of chipper denial. "You ready to make an offer?" he inquires of Jeff.

"I think we need to talk it over," he understatedly replies.

As we leave, Lucy trips down the front step. Her forehead opens up in a scarlet gash. Jeff scoops her wailing little form up, and carries her through the blocks and blocks of Fourth Avenue, to the three trains that will, eventually, get us back home.

It's another weekend, another round of house-hunting.

The next day, undaunted, I take my bandaged child out for a sweep of Windsor Terrace. Windsor Terrace is the next neighborhood past the more upscale Park Slope, so it's not as pricey. Jeff stays home to work on a freelance job, trying to bring in extra money for summer day-camp payments.

The first place, on a dismally litter-strewn street, is $425,000. It has a broken-down staircase, vast piles of clutter, and several missing drawers in the kitchen. That last bit seems especially spiteful. It's like they want to see how much they can insult the buyer and still get their price. A large dog howls ferociously in the yard, prompting Lucy to cling to my leg in terror.

One can only endure so much ugliness before the hysterical blindness kicks in, so we break for pizza. "Can we go home now?" Lucy whines as she pops a blob of cheese into her mouth. "Soon," I reply sheepishly, as I realize this is the closest thing to fun either of us will have all weekend.

In the last few days my belly has begun to bulge, and my energy level is declining in direct proportion. Second trimester is the easiest, my ass. Not in New York City in the summer, not with a fetus who is clearly made of laudanum, it isn't.

The next house is dark, musty, directly on an expressway, and, at $475,000, overpriced. The last place is a little house off Fourth Avenue, asking a cool half a million, which I am looking at simply for comparison. It's adorable, and meticulously staged.

Staging is the fine art of making a home look warm and comfortable while downplaying the fact that anybody still inhabits it. Or as my friend Randall, a decorator in San Francisco, puts it, "You want style but not substance." In a staged home, walls are freshly painted, white. Personal photos and mementos are put away. Clutter is eliminated, and the homey aroma of scented candles wafts through the air.

There are books on how to DIY stage; even the *Idiot's Guide* has weighed in on the subject. Television shows, like HGTV's *Designed to Sell*, hinge on the drama of turning "a tired house into a showpiece." Staging can also help a seller rebrand a home—Randall had a friend stick a desk and a fake phone in her basement, and suddenly prospective buyers were looking at a property with an office.

"It's make-believe," explains Randall. "There's milk in a glass jug, eggs in a bowl, produce is in the crisper, lots of champagne and white wine. You don't have ketchup; you don't have boxes of Cheerios. And the buyer does end up paying for not seeing through someone else's unfolded laundry."

The seller doesn't get off scot-free either. Professional stagers, whether they're full-timers or sidelining designers, charge anywhere from $3,000 to $15,000 or more, but they claim they can increase the value of a property and help move it faster. Realtors are also increasingly moving into staging as a means of driving up the sales price and, ultimately, their commissions.

"If a house is empty or it's junky," explains Randall, "people can't see themselves in it. You want buyers to walk in and think, 'Look how these people have it together; look at the life they lead. Their shirts are perfect and in the closet, they don't have mayo on the table.' They think, something must be great here. They see the books on the little table by the bathtub; they don't see the bath is twelve inches deep. They don't know all the sellers' crap is over at their best friend's garage, that they can't even cook a hamburger in the house because it'll smell bad."

If I were selling, I would, as they say in the Match.com ads, clean up good. Shopping for a house is like dating, minus, unfortunately, the cocktails and sex. If you're not making an effort at the outset, it's not going to get better when you reveal what's lurking in your closet. Yet in this market, you can still make money even if you can't bother to take the dirty dishes out of the sink, empty the litter box, or have drawers in your kitchen. The other day I passed by a house for sale in our neighborhood that didn't have a roof, for God's sake. I peered up through its windows and saw an unmistakable expanse of sky. When I called the seller, he said he was asking $800,000.

I'll give credit to the owners of this little house we're looking at now. They're the only ones who've made any attempt at wooing me, a ploy I always appreciate. The place is clean and fresh-smelling. It's at once inviting and impersonal, like a boutique hotel. It has also been cleverly arranged to downplay the fact that it's essentially a dollhouse.

There's a loveseat in the living room. A café table for two in the "eat-in kitchen." A twin bed with a folksy quilt in the "master" bedroom and a sweet daybed in the second bedroom.

"I want to live here!" Lucy enthuses. Sure she does. It's the perfect size for her and her Polly Pockets. If they tried to bring any real furniture in here, it wouldn't fit. I'm glad I'm not further along in the pregnancy, or I'd take up the whole kitchen.

All of the houses I've seen today will sell, I'm sure, and soon. They will, with work, be right for someone else. It's not insurmountable to replace drawers or countertops, or even to come up with storage solutions. We could live with aesthetic challenges and shortcomings in the right house in the right place, but could we accept a nonexistent roof atop a house we feel nothing for on an ugly block, just to say we own something? At what point is a move a Pyrrhic victory?

I watch Lucy sleeping in her toddler bed now and wonder how she'll fare if and when we ever find a place. Would she miss this little room? Would she even remember it? I moved as a kid; Jeff moved as a kid. People do this all the time, and somehow most of us survive. People like Mike and Debbie.

Debbie was my college roommate and Mike was her college sweetheart. They have two boisterous little boys close to Lucy's age. In August we spend a weekend visiting them in their new house in Media, Pennsylvania.

I loved their old place in Philadelphia, a compact brick row house not far from the 30th Street Station. For a major city, Philadelphia is still a real estate bargain. It also has a troubled school system, a crime rate that's nearly double New York's, and all of the requisite day-to-day hassle that comes with an urban environment. I don't think our friends moved because they were burned out on Philly, though.

Mike and Debbie wanted the life they could give their kids in the suburbs. They wanted the good schools and closeness to Debbie's parents and the swing set in the back and the pretty house. And that's exactly what they got.

When we pull up to their drive, I am blown away. These two people that I once spent Friday nights drinking wine coolers and eating Bugles with are now the proud owners of a beautiful center-hall colonial. It's set back from the street, and empty lots adjacent and behind them provide an expansiveness that only lends to its grandeur. There's an atrium on the side and a fireplace and an attic that's bigger than most apartments I've lived in. Even the doors are strikingly solid and well made. They paid $275,000 for all this, a figure that could make a New Yorker weep. Yet even as Jeff and I linger over coffee in their roomy kitchen and light sparklers at twilight on their lawn, we don't picture ourselves in a story that looks like theirs.

I'm not an urban absolutist. For every attraction of city living, there are just as many arguments for the alternative. It's hard to dispute selling points like nature, elbow room, and less paying through the nose for everything. It's not that our life is quantifiably better in Brooklyn.

What it is, instead, is something my friend Carol casually observed one day at the playground. That afternoon, she had looked around at the abundant chaos around us—the swarms of people, the cars, the noise—and smiled appreciatively. "I love this," she'd said. "I love just . . . stepping outside."

That's it. You can make the best of what's inside four walls, but what characterizes your place in the world is what greets you when you step outside. It's like the old guy I overheard in the deli once. "Leave?" he'd said. "I need my track. I need my bookies." For Mike and Deb and their sons, it's this lawn and this swing set and this hammock. For us, it's the throb of humanity, viewed from a stoop.

I'm scheduled for the sonogram shortly after we return from Pennsylvania; I've been restless and antsy about it for weeks. I could say it doesn't matter what we have, as long as it's healthy, but who am I kidding? I've compiled a lengthy list of semitrendy girl names. I haven't a single boy name. Jeff has offered one possibility: Stanley. I tell him I need to think about it before admitting it's the worst suggestion he's ever had.

I had a dream a few nights ago that I was giving birth. The doctor handed me a baby and told me, "It's a boy."

"No, no, nonono," I'd cried. "That can't be right. It's a mistake. Give me my baby, my real baby."

Which is why this August morning, the day before the sonogram, I'm in a full-blown panic. "What if it's a boy?" I fret into the cell phone to Jeff. "How can I have a boy when I'm having dreams that I'm rejecting my son? How can I have a boy when I can't even think of a name?"

"It'll be all right," Jeff says reassuringly. "This is our baby, and we love it. You're going to love him or her no matter what."

"You better be right on this one," I tell him.

A few hours later Lucy and I are crossing Court Street with our friends when it happens. We don't even notice anything unusual at first, just what appears to be a broken traffic light. As we get closer to the park, though, we realize it's something more. People are stepping outside, looking up and down the street and asking each other the same thing: Are your lights out too? Cell phones start ringing in unison—Margot's sister, Beverly's husband, and Jeff. All the power is out, everywhere.

Nothing to do then but what we were doing anyway. Our children play together all afternoon, oblivious, giggling around the playground till the sun begins to disappear in the hot sky.

It's only when we get back to Court Street that we feel the full effect of being in the midst of a blackout. Throngs of commuters are coming off the Brooklyn Bridge and pouring into the neighborhood. The fancy gourmet shop is unloading its gelatos, and Lucy, Bette, Frederick, and Ashley tear into several extravagant pints of passion fruit Ciao Bella like it's a handout from the Mister Softee truck. Then, improbably, we find Jeff in the crowd, sweaty from an hour and change of walking from the West Village.

When he got off the overcrowded, dangerously swaying Bridge, he tells us, there was the borough president, Marty Markowitz, waiting at the other side. "He's standing there at the entrance to the Bridge," Jeff says, "telling everybody 'Welcome home! Welcome home, Brooklyn!' " He throws his arms out, imitating our leader's all-embracing gesture.

Long after we've trekked home and eaten cheese sandwiches by battery-operated radio and candlelight, long after we've watched our neighbors emerge like fireflies, smoking and eating their Entenmann's crumb cakes on their stoops on the darkest night in ages, the phrase will stick with Lucy. When Jeff walks through the door in the evening, she will stand up and bellow grandly, "Welcome home! Welcome home, Brooklyn!"

The next day there's still no power in large segments of the city, so we'll have to wait and reschedule the sonogram. It still feels like a good day for news, though, so in our steamy, powerless apartment this morning, we will tell Lucy she's getting a sibling. She's been having conversations with my navel for months now, and informing anyone who will listen that she's getting a baby. I've also grown quite a gut in recent weeks, so I figured she was onto us.

When she begins again her game of "Mom's having a baby," this time I tell her gently, "Do you know that we really are having a baby? You're going to be a big sister."

Her eyes widen with delight. "For real and not pretend?" she asks, astounded. "For real," I tell her.

Her face is shining with love. Then she adds, "I just thought you were getting chubby."

My mother calls to make sure we survived the night. The power going off must have profoundly unnerved her. The last few years haven't been the most reassuring of her life. It's hard enough to be a woman who expects a car crash or a kidnapping around every corner. It's harder still when, one cloudless morning, someone flies an airplane into your husband's office building.

My stepfather got out of the North Tower in time. His supervisors had initially advised workers to stay put, but Phil and several coworkers chose instead to walk down more than sixty flights of stairs. Others didn't, or didn't in time. Eighty-four Port Authority workers died that day.

Phil had just reached the street when the first tower fell. He told us later that everything went black; he said he'd never seen such blackness. He stumbled blindly through the streets until he found a door. When he pushed it open, he found himself in a synagogue, full of other downtown workers who'd also randomly, miraculously found that door. That afternoon, unlike several dozen of his friends and coworkers, he found his way home. He took a ferry to New Jersey, clutching a yarmulke as a dust mask over his face.

My mother gained weight and lost sleep. Six months after the attacks my stepfather had a triple bypass. My mother got an Ambien prescription. They put out American flags. They made up excuses not to come visit us.

The electricity in their New Jersey suburb came back up early this morning. "We can handle a little thing like a blackout," I tell my mother. "I was born during one, remember?"

"How could I forget?" she says lightly, and she sounds happy for a while, recounting again a distant November night when the lights went out and I came in. "I thought I was dying. I wished I was dying. Once you were born, though, I knew I loved you," she says. "You were my everything, my whole life." It's the thing she always assures me of, and that much I believe. I was unplanned but I never felt unwanted. My mother didn't have a career or a spouse or even a circle of friends. What she had was me. It's a lot to live up to.

My mom says she waited for my father for years, believing, long after he had gone, that he would return to her. I, on the other hand, always knew that my father wasn't dead, he wasn't lost, and he wasn't coming back, ever. It must have been difficult for my parents, to be so young and completely unprepared for parenthood. Frankly, it was no picnic for me either.

Growing up without a parent is like being born without a

limb. You don't grieve over it; you don't quite miss it. You learn from birth to accommodate. You are, however, defined by it. The thing that you don't have is the thing that makes you who you are.

The autumn before Lucy turned one, I found him. I hadn't ever gone looking for him before, because I was afraid of what I might find. I didn't want to be rejected again; I didn't want to know if he was mean, or dumb. Then one day I looked at the baby in my arms and asked myself how I'd feel if I learned my father had died. The thought that we lived all these years on the same planet and hadn't reached out once for each other seemed like a stupid waste.

I knew a few things about him. My mother had been generous about that. She understood it was all I had, so she gave me her one photo of the two of them together, told me his birthday and my grandparents' names. He left us with crumbs and she shared them willingly.

I plugged his data into a form on a family-finder Web site, paid $80, and two days later had his phone number and address. He lived one town over from my mother. I held the info for a day and then impulsively called.

A woman answered. "Can I speak to Joe Williams?" I had stammered.

"He's not here. Can I leave a message?" she'd replied abruptly, as if I were the telemarketer she surely assumed I was.

"Tell him," I'd said, my words and my heart both crammed into my throat, "tell him that Colleen's daughter called."

There was a silence that lasted roughly as long as the previous thirty-five years.

And then she'd said, "My God. You're his daughter."

He called me back a few hours later. "Hi," he said plainly. "It's Joe." He was genial and guarded, and so was I.

"I just thought you would want to know," I'd said, "that I turned out okay."

"Well, thanks," he'd answered.

Within a few days, a manila envelope arrived, with photos of my grandparents, my aunts and uncle, my father at various ages.

We met up with him and his wife for lunch soon after. He and I look remarkably alike. We both flip to the dessert menu first. For most of my life, I could have passed him on the street and not even noticed.

I didn't ask why he'd left or where he'd been, or if he ever wished he'd done anything differently. I did mention that he owed me a Barbie Dream House, ballet lessons, and a pony.

"I like this girl," his wife had said.

It had gone, I thought, well. They sent Christmas cards, as did we. I wrote in ours that we'd be happy to get together again soon. We haven't heard from him since.

A few days after the blackout, mostly on a whim, I take the stroller out on a Sunday afternoon and push Lucy to an open house in Boerum Hill. Boerum Hill is a short walk from our neighborhood, but it's still considered a rougher patch of Brooklyn. The houses are more run-down; the distance to the supermarket is greater. This is why, I imagine, a two-family house is going for just $700,000.

I walk past a luxury apartment building with a fusion restaurant on the street level. Not long ago it was a bodega selling scratchers and Colt 45. A few yards farther, police cars and ambulances have rolled into an angry throng. The closer I get, the more distinct the yelling, in two languages, becomes.

"It's just another day in the hood," a gum-snapping young mother standing on the sidelines with her baby observes to no one in particular as a squad car rolls away. "Just another day in the hood." Is this really the hood? If so, why is it so expensive?

The house is on a shady street full of attractive, turn-of-the-century buildings. In order to get to it, though, you have to pick which set of housing projects to walk past. A pair of the borough's most notorious bookend the area.

On a warm summer night one year from now, Nicole Sutton, seven and a half months pregnant, will be sitting on a bench outside the Wyckoff Gardens Houses. A stray bullet from a nearby gunfight will strike her in the neck, ending her life and that of her baby. You can put up as many overpriced restaurants or open up lofts on Smith Street, but they'll still always butt against the projects. The projects are always going to be exactly where they are.

My concerns about the location and our inability to obtain a $700,000 home are soon rendered irrelevant, however. Lucy and I walk in, and the unmistakable aroma of a menagerie of dogs, cats, and birds—and their various eliminations—hits my pregnant nostrils so hard I'm sure I'm going to start retching. The floorboards are sagging. There are holes in the ceiling. It is a literal shithole. "I need air," Lucy pleads. "Can we please go?"

When you find a beguiling house that you can't afford, it's depressing. When you find one that makes you physically ill that you can't afford, it's downright traumatic. We race out the door and inhale the car exhaust of the street with pleasure.

Jeff and I have friends who have zero qualms about living in areas they describe as "a little rough." Their lives are different, or their ideas of what constitutes a deal-breaker are. Fair enough.

I don't want sanitized, homogenized, or pristine. Living near people who earn less money or come from other places isn't an issue and never will be. But I won't settle for high crime, failing schools, or noise so bad I can't sleep at night, nor will I kid myself that doing so gives me a measure of authenticity. Because frankly I didn't grow up fatherless and low-income in Jersey City at its seventies-era nadir to just wind up in a wreck in a dubious area that's out of our price range anyway. And I'm way too downwardly mobile to have an iota of liberal guilt about that.

The next week, Jeff and I go uptown for the rescheduled sonogram. On the train ride up I distract myself by reading the paper. There's a front-page story about the fight over the removal of a marble carving of the Ten Commandments from a southern state's supreme courthouse, under the headline "Alabama's Top Judge Defiant on Commandments' Display."

"Do you see this?" I say to Jeff, stabbing the *New York Times* accusingly. "This is why we can never leave New York. It gets weird once you leave the tunnel."

Jeff looks at the paper. "If it's any help," he says, "I wasn't planning on making you move to Alabama."

We walk into the hospital together, and, because pregnancy is all about having somebody sitting on your bladder for nine months, I pause at the ladies' room before we go upstairs. As I'm washing my hands, I remember back to the fortune-teller and New Orleans. Margot says that the plethora of same-sex siblings in our neighborhood is pure urban evolution. The kids can share clothes, they can share a room, and they can keep you living in your teeny apartment a while longer. It's survival of the fit.

As the technician squirts cold goo on my midsection, I tell Jeff, "We're having a girl. I know it," and a few minutes later, an advantageous view of the blurry figure on the monitor confirms it. I see the outline of her pretty little body and feel like I know her already. She's the one who burrowed into our hearts before she was even conceived, the one who insisted upon existence. "Hi, you," I say, and it looks like she's waving back.

Jeff and I get on the train together, smiling shyly at the secret we're sharing. He gets off at his work stop, and I continue on the F line back to our neighborhood. Welcome home, little girl, I think. Welcome home, Brooklyn.

As the kicks in my abdomen grow more acrobatic, the summer languorously winds down. The warm months are supposed to be the best season for real estate. We came up snake eyes.

Friends have been asking if we've checked out Kensington and Midwood yet. To those for whom even Windsor Terrace is becoming prohibitively expensive, the next neighborhood farther out in Brooklyn may be the last refuge. It's a working-class area of small houses, peaceful streets, and, at this untapped stage of the market, plenty of immigrants and no visible hipsters. A work acquaintance suggests I call her broker, and he tells me, "I have one thing you might be interested in. It's a house on Beverly Road for $375,000."

We head out on a blustery early-autumn morning. The subway ride is formidable. My joints are groaning under the strain of the expanding individual under my ribs. Forget about finding a place to have lunch, the options here are near nil.

Jeff, Lucy, and I get off at the Church Avenue stop and walk a few blocks to the end of an eerily silent street. It takes a few minutes, and then the kosher butcher shops and synagogues we passed on the way suddenly make sense. This is a heavily Orthodox neighborhood. It's Saturday. Everybody's inside.

The house belonged to an old Irish couple. The wife's sister, a nun in a navy blue habit, is sweeping the sidewalk when we arrive. Arthur, the broker, has an easy smile and the heft and hairline of a much older man. He leads us around, past the shamrock-themed plates in the china cabinet and photos of the pope on the kitchen wall. It's like stepping into my own home décor past.

The yard is Lilliputian. The front stairs are crumbling. There is a not a goddam thing to do in the neighborhood once you've cruised the Rite Aid. The house, nevertheless, calls to us. Despite its sorry condition, it's full of light, and it's bigger than we'd ever dreamed we could manage to pay for. Three humble yet distinct bedrooms. A dining room with a stained-glass window and Art Deco bathroom. An enclosed porch. There's a tree in the front yard, and the thought of my daughters owning a tree in Brooklyn moves me intensely.

When we talk about it that night, Jeff and I both are roiling with mixed emotions.

"What do you think?"

"I don't know. What do you think?"

"I don't know. It's nice."

"Yeah but."

"I know."

"Exactly."

We wrestle with our ambivalence about that house in Kensington for days. The local public school's test scores are as high as the crime rate is low. The neighborhood is safe. The house has the intangible yet clearly identifiable feeling of a place with a good past.

We sit at the dinner table at night, drawing up a list of pros and cons. The pros outnumber the cons. Yet the agonizing need for a list of pros and cons is, in and of itself, a big fat con. We still don't have much in liquid assets. We would have to either put less than 10 percent down or see how fast we could tap our retirement resources. Oh, and I'm having a baby in three months.

We could explore the neighborhood more; try to uncover its charms. We could find a restaurant or two, talk to more people, walk around at night, all the things serious buyers might. But we don't. The house is doing its damnedest to woo us. Something is holding us back.

"The interior is good," Jeff says. "I like that it's old-fashioned. But for this much money, I'd like a house I really love in a neighborhood where I want to live." It all comes back to our deal. "I could be a deluded fool," he tells me. "Maybe I'm unrealistic or spoiled. We try not to make decisions based on the fear that nothing better will come along, right?"

"Does that apply to real estate?" I ask.

"Beats me," he answers honestly. He looks at the list. "We should take a break," Jeff says, and I unhesitatingly agree. I'm in a last-trimester hell of heartburn and heel spurs, and the days are getting colder. Even if we found the perfect place tomorrow, we wouldn't have the wherewithal to buy our first home right now.

"We liked it very much," I tell Arthur the next day, "but we're not ready." Then I fret that we've blown the only passable thing we've seen in six months of looking.

The leaves float off the trees, and the buttons on my coat strain to fasten around my circumference. Halloween passes, and then my birthday and Thanksgiving and Christmas. The real estate section of the paper gets thinner week by week as we pass through the industry's traditional slow season. We're not going to become homeowners, not this year. Maybe it's just us, but it has been impossible to find a place to live. And I don't think it's us. I think it's this fucked-up town.

When my friend Aaron tells the story of how his family got their house in St. Louis, it's like a beautiful poem. In a foreign language.

Aaron and I were pals in San Francisco, where he played in a band. He's a hardworking parent and a nonmillionaire. A few years ago, he and his wife decided they were ready to buy a home, and they knew they couldn't buy a damn thing in the city. They were also tired of feeling that the quality of life in San Francisco had deteriorated after the Internet boom began to bust.

"We couldn't figure out how to make it work," he tells me later. "Even when we thought, 'What if we live in a transitioning neighborhood in Oakland? What if we go to Stockton?' There was an assumption we would never own a house, and a bunch of factors that could be summed up as 'life is easier elsewhere.' "

They had some family connections in St. Louis, so in the summer of 2001, they went out for a few days to explore. "We came for a week to look at houses," he recalls. "We said, we'll look, and if we don't find anything, we'll rent. We bought a copy of the *Post-Dispatch*, found our price level, and drove around. It was quickly evident where to live."

They homed in on the up-and-coming Dogtown section of the city, an Irish neighborhood that boasts close proximity to a park and zoo—and an influx of young families. "The first house we looked at," he says, "we came back the next day and bought." It's a one-and-a-half story three-bedroom with a basement, front yard, and good back yard. They paid $165,000 for it. In the Bay Area the same year, the median home price was $476,820. And in New York City the same year, you could pay an average price of $205,000—for a studio.

When he got back to the Bay Area to pack up, Aaron says, "I had fun telling people our story. I'd be at a party, and someone would drag me over and say, 'Tell Jim what you told me about how you bought a house.' It was like porn." It wasn't only the price tag that was right. It was the thrill of finding somewhere else that felt like it could be home.

"I used to think, There's no place else I can live; there's no place else *to* live," he says. "Once we moved, I realized there are other places. We're in a house that would be a million dollars in San Francisco or Oakland. There's a lot we could do with that other million. It was revelatory."

I don't see us moving to St. Louis anytime soon, but Aaron makes me believe we could be happy somewhere else. I just don't know where that somewhere else is yet.

I'm more than ready for one member of our family to move, though. My body itself is a home, one whose tenant is reluctant to leave. Two weeks past my due date, I'm lumbering down Court Street and leaving craters in my wake, when I see Ron smirking toward me. "Haven't you had that baby yet?" he chides.

"Can't put anything past you," I grunt, and contemplate wrestling him to the ground and sitting on him.

The next day, precisely four years after Lucy's birth, her sister joins her. The morning is as bright as it is cold, and outside the window the sun reflects brilliantly off the Hudson as I push another New Yorker into the world. I take her tiny hands as she emerges from my body, and pull her out of me and into my arms. "She's here," Jeff says, bleary-eyed and amazed. "She's here." We name her Beatrice, because the name means blessing. A gift from God.

I call my mother to tell her I've had the baby, and her name. "That's different," she remarks dryly. She doesn't come to the hospital, but then, she didn't when Lucy was born either. I'll send my father a birth announcement in a few days. I don't dwell on their absence much, though. I look at this kid in my arms, and it's pretty hard to feel like throwing a pity party.

The first thing I notice about Beatrice is how calm she is. I clutch her close to my skin, and she looks up at me with her wide, curious eyes. They're a strange color—a mix of blue and green and gray, with a few flecks of brown thrown in right at the iris. It's as if all her DNA was vying for supremacy in the middle of her face. I recognize those eyes immediately. They're my father's. They're mine.

The ward is almost empty. Most Brooklyn babies have the good sense not to be born during a record cold snap. We have a room all to ourselves and very few interruptions. In the afternoon Jeff's parents come by with Lucy, who brings me a slice of her birthday cake.

"There you are!" Lucy exclaims as she clambers into the bed with us, as if she and Beatrice were old friends, reunited after a long time apart. She sees nothing else in that room but her sister, the sister she asserted all along she was getting.

I watch out the window as Beatrice's first day fades into night, and the lights of the city across the river flicker on. I can see all the way past the lower tip of Manhattan and straight over to Jersey City, where the big Colgate clock illuminates the hours. As a kid, I was fascinated with that clock. My mother told me it was the largest in the world, and it made me believe my city couldn't be that bad if it could produce something that big.

I look over at it now, as the baby instinctively nuzzles into me. We've been joined together so long, neither of us is ready to let go yet. So we let the night go by together, marking its passage by the same light I looked up to as a child, until morning streaks the skyline.

BACK TO
SQUARE ONE

It's late April. The trees in our neighborhood are heavy with pink and white blossoms. Beatrice is exactly three and a half months old. I am a catatonic, squish-bellied mess.

Jeff and I have barely exchanged ten coherent words since the baby was born. I've started working again and have recently taken on a freelance job. We have no child care—I bang away on my computer at home while Bea sits propped on my lap or naps in the bouncy seat at my feet. The last few cold, isolating months have been like living in the Overlook Hotel, but with more spit-up and less square footage.

Today, however, is our wedding anniversary. We're still not at the point where we can do a night out, but Sharon has offered to take the kids to the park for an hour or two so we can have a brunch date.

Smith Street has changed dramatically during my hibernation. Chic bistros that serve gussied-up meatloaf have sprung up, seemingly overnight, next to superfluous boutiques selling tissue-thin stemware and $15 soaps. But the retail revolution doesn't have a feeling of upheaval or dissent about it, just the indifferent surrender of locals cashing out and rents going up.

Jeff and I go to a fashionable restaurant where we eat overpriced omelets, repeatedly check our watches, and spend most of the time talking about the girls. It may not sound romantic, but it is, deeply. We're thrilled to have a meal in an environment that isn't redolent of Balmex and poo.

We sit surrounded by good-looking people who didn't wake up at five this morning, and their cheery energy is infectious. We talk about spring and the future and plans.

We haven't discussed real estate since we suspended the hunt months ago, but lately, my itch to resume the search has been deepening. It's like childbirth—let enough time pass, and the memory of how excruciating it was fades until doing it again seems like a hot idea.

"Now that the weather is getting warm," I say, "we'll be able to get out more and have fun." Then I mention, hesitatingly, "Maybe, when the time is right, we'll even dip our tired old toes back into the home search."

Jeff also has sufficient amnesia by now—not to mention a growing appreciation for the way one extra female and her accoutrements can make our apartment feel half its original dimensions—to concur.

"Why not?" he says. "It might be easier now that we're not focused on the pregnancy."

That's all the encouragement I need. "Right. And also, Lucy's going to be in Pre-K in September, and Bea will need a day care soon, and I don't want them to start in one place and have to pull out, and my God," I say, "look around. It's getting younger and richer here every second."

I'm prepared to launch into a full-blown stream of consciousness, but Jeff takes my hand and says, gently, "Let's just enjoy our eggs."

As we're leaving the restaurant, my cell phone rings. It's Arthur, the broker who showed us the house in Kensington last fall. "What a coincidence," I say, and Jeff, ever in search of auspicious portents, smiles.

"You said to call if I had something similar to that house on Beverley," he says. "Another place has just come up. Same size, similar layout. They're asking $525,000." In a not especially trendy Brooklyn neighborhood in 2004, you can now pay $150,000 more for a house than you would have six months ago. What will it cost six months from now?

I have a purseful of coupons. I religiously pore over the supermarket circulars every week, basing our shopping lists around what will save us 25 cents. How can I be that person and this one too, the one that doesn't bat an eyelash over looking at a home that's $125,000 above our budget? Is it because 25 cents in my pocket is real—it's seven minutes of clothes dryer time; it's a copy of the *New York Post*; it's something I can understand—and anything that doesn't jingle or even fold in my pocket isn't? Is it that

I can't quite connect the romantic dream of a home with the real money we sweat to earn and save?

"That sounds interesting," I say. "When can you show it?"

Maybe there's a way to make this work. Every time I search online for mortgage information, every time I'm up late at night, watching television with the baby, I see come-ons for "no money down" mortgages. I don't know any homeowner who hasn't put down a substantial chunk of cash upfront, so I wonder who's getting these loans, and how.

The most legitimate form of what's also known as the "100% financing mortgage" is the "80–20." Although it seems at first more complicated than splitting the bar tab at a birthday party, it doesn't sound impossible. The name explains it all—the borrower takes out two loans: one for 80 percent of the purchase price and another for 20 percent. It's taking out a usual-sized mortgage, but also borrowing for the whole of the down payment. The buyer still coughs up the usual closing costs and fees.

I am temporarily lifted by the elegance of the plan. It doesn't appear shady or weird; it's old-fashioned borrowing. For someone with good credit, it seems a viable path to ownership, and getting the most house for the least of one's own money upfront makes a certain amount of sense.

Right on cue, the catch comes in. Lenders get antsy when they see borrowers taking out very big loans with very little of their own money, so they generally require private mortgage insurance, or PMI. The insurance protects the lender in case the person who has taken on the debt can't pay. Most of the time, if you're putting less than 20 percent of your own money down, you will be required to purchase PMI. You'll usually have to keep it until you've paid off at least 20 percent of the mortgage.

There are exceptions. Jeff's grad school friend Chad later tells me about his row home in Baltimore's burgeoning Federal Hill neighborhood, and the 80–20 loan they were able to obtain because of his wife's job. "It was pretty easy for us to get a Bank of America resident physician loan," he says, "which means we don't have to pay PMI. We're probably not going to be here forever, so we weren't going to screw around with having a down payment."

"It was either this or renting," he adds, "and with this, we have the potential of coming out ahead."

For most people, though, the PMI comes with the turf, and the bigger the loan, the higher the PMI generally is. PMI can also run higher for people with lower credit ratings. Rates vary, but they can run to about one-half of 1 percent of the loan. It doesn't sound like much, but for a $400,000 home with no money down, that's an extra $20,000 over the course of the loan.

This being the land where, in 2004, the national debt is hovering around the $7 trillion mark, there's a work-around for the PMI too. Never underestimate our manifest destiny to borrow. A borrower can opt for a "piggyback loan," a second mortgage taken out at the time of the first one. It's basically borrowing on the brand-new mortgage—the one the buyer borrowed to get.

The catch this time is that the second mortgage's interest rate is almost invariably higher than the primary one. It can still work out to a lower monthly payment than a regular mortgage with PMI, but it also means a bigger debt overall, and to a bigger suckhole if the housing market softens or something goes wrong.

It's a debt wrapped in an IOU inside a sea of red ink. It's yet another example of borrowing based on hope—hope of increased earnings and a rising home value.

"Oh Christ," says Jeff when I explain it to him. "It makes me sick just to think about it."

Fortunately, our would-be mortgage broker Roz immediately beats back any notions I might have had about it anyway, because we have almost no collateral. We don't have anything to offer up, not even a car. "Forget it," she says. "No way. No reputable lender would approve this kind of loan for you," she tells me.

She may be vastly misjudging the ethics of her industry. By 2005, 43 percent of first-time buyers will obtain their homes with no-money-down loans.

Jeff and I are not high rollers; there is nothing in our makeup that screams badass, house-flipping moguls. We haven't the gumption to risk what we've earned on the chance of getting a big payoff. We also remember when everybody thought we'd all get rich off the dot-com boom—and look how well *that* turned out. A home is an investment, a potentially lucrative one at that, but it remains for us, first and foremost, the place we want to sleep. And we'd never rest with a loan that would put us in three kinds of debt.

The following Saturday, a family of four takes a trip to Kensington. Bea is snug in the baby carrier, Lucy is reluctantly walking, and the train ride feels even longer than it did in September.

We arrive too early, so we walk around. We prowl the blocks, looking for primitive drawings in windows, scooters on front steps—evidence of other children. We've seen the newspaper stories and heard the accounts from friends of friends that more and more families are moving here; we know the school reports are great.

My feet go in circles as my brain does likewise, thinking: How far do we have to go? How far for a school? How far for a home? How many miles, bus rides? How many dollars? Is it worth it when we get there?

The house is on a tree-lined street near the industrial end of the neighborhood. As we approach, Arthur is already waiting to greet us.

While the other home may have been timeworn and a little shabby, it compensated in character and detail. The place we're looking at now has been renovated, although not well and not in several years. I recognize its fixtures from Home Depot's Don't Give a Damn collection. Those melamine cabinet doors and crystal-shaped plastic faucets have appeared in at least half the houses we've seen. There are no stained-glass windows in this house, no original tiles in the bathroom. It also has a different exposure, so it's noticeably darker, and a concrete front yard where a tree might otherwise stand. We are in the unappealing, $150,000-more-expensive twin of the first house.

Then, as if reading my mind, Arthur mentions, "That other place would have been a lot more work. Turned out it had termites."

Jeff and I exchange similar stricken looks. The baby feels heavy on my chest, and all Lucy wants to do is climb on the furniture.

"The buyers didn't realize it until they were in contract, but they decided to go ahead anyway," he adds.

Just as nonchalantly, Jeff replies, "That would have been disastrous for us."

There's strange vindication in knowing how many more thousands of dollars that house would have cost if we'd factored in the expense of keeping it standing, how much more time and effort it would have required. A nagging part of me wonders if it would have been worth it. It still would have been cheaper than this place, this house we don't even like. And we'd be settled in our bug-damaged home and done with all of this already.

Usually, I'm the one on the ride home trying to talk up some mediocre destination. Not today.

"That house was ass," I say to Jeff. "No ambivalence about this one. So how come I'm depressed?"

"Because we couldn't afford it anyway. Because we're exhausted," he answers, and we sink into our plastic seats.

We chug back into Carroll Gardens, and the rhythm of the train thumps, "Crap house. Crap street. Crap price."

Jeff's cousin Laurie and her husband Jim, meanwhile, have found a place that fits. Jim and Laurie have lived all over the country, from an apartment in downtown Chicago to a 3,300-square-foot home in a suburb outside of Dallas.

"Dallas got us the most house for the least money. It fit into the Texas thing of big and overstated," Jim tells me later. "They put a greater emphasis on appearance than quality there. You don't have the skilled craftsmen. When the wind blows in Texas, you feel it in your house."

They'd been content enough raising their two sons in their big house and their friendly community, but Jim's from upstate New York and Laurie's from the Midwest. They thrive in colder climes, between thicker walls.

When Jim's job with a printing company offered him a transfer to Minneapolis, they gladly went. The family found a newish development in Chanhassen, where they could create a home to their specifications without the intricacies of building from scratch.

"We had a designer help with all the stuff I wasn't good at," he says, "all the plug-and-play elements. When we were done, it was just what we wanted," he says. No saggy stairs. No termites. "We've got it down now to where it's almost no maintenance," he says happily, "because whatever time I'm not spending working is not going to be spent fixing the house." Instead, he and his sons are doing something they couldn't in Texas—the hockey fans installed a rink in the back yard.

It's not the rink or the custom cabinets that matter though; it's the way they feel about the place itself. "I remember the first day I flew from Dallas to Minneapolis, I felt at home," Jim tells me. "For five years in Texas, I didn't. Maybe it's because Minnesota reminded me of where I grew up in Rochester. Culturally, it seemed more like what I was used to. There was comfort and familiarity, and access to natural beauty. It's a clean, wholesome community," he tells me, "a world of tranquility."

Clean, wholesome, and tranquil. Not exactly the first words I'd use to describe New York. Jim's sons will grow up in a green, peaceful town in the middle of America. My daughters will grow up in a bustling city on its coast. Jim and I have planted our families in vastly different environments, but the depth of our feeling for those places, our reasons for being here, are exactly the same. "There's no place else we've ever felt this satisfied and fulfilled," says Jim. I hope that's what we give our children. A place where they can feel they belong.

We're at a barbecue in the Brooklyn back yard of a couple we know through Jeff's work. To our surprise, Bernard and Nancy and their kids are also there. The couple, a hemp-clad pair whose ideologies fit neatly onto bumper stickers, moved to Maplewood, New Jersey, last year.

Maplewood is a pleasant midsized town not far from where I grew up. It has sidewalks and stores and houses close together, and it's on the commuter line, all of which have of late helped it gain heat as the next place to move for families who don't want to move to the suburbs. People keep vanishing from Brooklyn and rematerializing in New Jersey.

We haven't lost too many close friends to relocation, but every now and then someone will begin expressing a creeping exasperation with the subway, with the car alarms going off in the middle of the night, with the rowdy middle-schoolers shoving each other around the sidewalk every weekday at 3 P.M. That's when we know who's not long for these parts. Some of them are renters like us, ones who didn't get in the game when the getting was good, whose options in this neighborhood are as inadequate as ours. Others managed to buy at a reasonable price when the market wasn't this ludicrous. They can name their price, sell out, and get something livable somewhere else.

That's what Bernard and Nancy did. I had thought that their departure would put an end to the incessant bragging about how much they got for their condo—and the disdain for anyone foolish enough to stay in the city—that had been the hallmarks of the months leading to their move. Yet here they are a year later, eager as ever to gas on.

"Hey!" I say with bright hypocrisy. "Nice to see you guys here."

"We're always here," sniffs Bernard. "It takes no time at all to get into the city on the train."

"So you're liking Maplewood," I reply weakly.

"Oh God, yes," he answers. "We got a whole house for what *might* get you a one-bedroom here, and we still had money left over from the sale. Plus, the kids will be going to *good* schools." Unlike city kids, I imagine, whose choices are limited to which gang they'll join. "Everyone is moving to Maplewood now. All the Broadway people live there." Then he throws in, with a hint of not-in-my-backyard menace, "I'm glad we got in when we did, because anyone coming in now is going to pay a lot more. A lot."

"Wow, that's great, and so great running into you," I lie, walking straight toward the beer and cupcakes.

There's a saying that zealotry springs not from faith, but from doubt. Whenever somebody gets that much in my face about anything, I have a pretty good guess who he's really trying to persuade. I'd like to charitably allow that Bernard is being an arrogant hypercompetitive prick to work something out in his own head. That I need to lose for him to feel like he's won.

The thing is, it's working. I feel miserable and sabotaged the rest of the day. I have let a guy with a soul patch and a diamond earring make me feel inferior about my own decision-making.

"Maybe we are stupid," I tell Jeff later, "looking at these dumps we can't even afford. And it's nuts to think we can maintain our situation here indefinitely." I'm starting to get why people get fed up and leave.

A few days later, I meet up with my college friend Tony, an artist who hightailed it out to the Garden State. He says, "Call me when you're ready for me to show you around Montclair."

He loves his town's nineteenth-century houses, its liberal politics, its creative, diverse, academic population. His pride is sincere.

Yet whenever he starts down his geographically evangelical conversational road again, I sense a finger-wagging disapproval of our lifestyle, and an annoying certitude that eventually we'll come off our high horses. "You have the first kid and you think you can do it," he warns, "but eventually everybody leaves. You'll leave. You'll see." Tony makes me feel like a character in a Greek play.

Tony's prophecy is still echoing in my psyche as Memorial Day rolls around. We are going to be at my in-laws in Westchester over the weekend. In anticipation of our visit, I drop a bomb on Jeff. "As long as we're out that way," I say, "let's take a drive to Nyack and see if we can look at houses."

He stares back at me, incredulous. "Let's what?"

Soon after Jeff and I moved back to New York, we spent a blissful wintry afternoon strolling through Central Park. We held hands and crunched through the snow like Oliver and Jenny in *Love Story*, without the inconvenient fatal movie disease, planning the books we'd write and the names we'd give our yet unconceived children in our exciting new life. I can pinpoint the instant it came to a screeching halt.

"Then someday in a few years," he'd said, "we'll probably move out of the city and buy a house."

I stopped walking, the better to provide him the full force of my open-mouthed gape. "We leave the city," I told him, "and I start drinking and scrapbooking. What are you thinking? Once you have kids, it's all soccer games and minivans?"

"Absolutely not," he'd snapped back. "What about driving around through the trees with the top down instead of cramming on the subway? A house with a study and playing tag on the lawn? Quiet and beauty?"

"Someone needs to break it to you," I'd said. "We're not the Kennedys."

Although he's never, in the intervening years, given the slightest inclination that he truly wants to leave the city, Jeff has always held Nyack as his vision of the perfect, Victorian-strewn river town. Creative types, pushed out of the city by the housing bubble, have of late been decamping for its shores in droves. The mayor is currently in hot water for performing same-sex weddings. Also, based on my one prior visit to the town, it has a fair number of muffin shops and antiques. It's quaint. Bedford Falls quaint. A part of me, the part of me that secretly indulges in *Country Living* magazine, responds to that.

"Maybe it's time we branched out," I tell Jeff. "Try on something new."

"It'd be a nice day trip anyway," he replies.

Nyack is becoming pricier every week, but there are still houses to be found for less than half a million if you're up for renovation or a seedier side of town. At this point we expect nothing less. I've been bookmarking Rockland County realtors on my computer, trying to fix my imagination on some slightly run-down but utterly charming turn-of-the-century fixer-upper.

I call a local realtor, who doesn't have anything in our budget in Nyack proper right now. "When are you coming to visit?" Darla asks. "I can show you some houses in Piermont and Congers." I've never even heard of these towns.

"I understand where you're coming from," she tells me. "You have the second child, you're ready to get out of the city." She means it kindly, but I hear the echo of Tony in her words. I hear an admission of defeat.

I know what it's like to be burned out on New York, to want to be somewhere else. I've had that longing for something different. This isn't it, though. I tell her we'll call her from my in-laws'.

A quick perusal of her Web site later reveals the houses in Piermont and Congers are all ranches. I have irrational bias against a ranch. I've lived in apartments for too long. If I'm going to have a house, as God as my witness, I want to have stairs.

On Friday when we arrive in Westchester, I'm starting to feel queasy. That night we take a run to the Super Stop & Shop to lay in some supplies for the evening meal with the folks and to stock up on the mega rolls of paper towels and value packs of meat that you can't find within the city limits.

I'm feeling better as I push an SUV of a shopping cart down a three-lane aisle. Ahhhh, I think, I could get used to this. An on-premises bakery. A produce selection that doesn't resemble something out of eastern Europe in February. I'm lost in a comestibles-inspired reverie when a powdery dowager cuts me off with her cart.

"I'm pushing here!" I immediately bellow, Ratso Rizzo style.

She looks me up and down, and as I feel her boring a hole into the white trashy soul of my being, I add, "You want to get into it, lady?"

I may not be ready for the suburbs yet.

By Saturday morning I'm in no mood for a meeting with the realtor. We don't know the first thing about Piermont and Congers. We're barely pulling it together for Nyack; I can't work up the enthusiasm to envision uprooting my family to a town that's a cipher, not today. My stomach is churning.

"Do you mind if we don't call the broker?" I ask Jeff.

He's relieved. "Let's go to Nyack and drive around," he suggests. "We can go for coffee."

Nyack is no quickie commute. It is located north of the city, between a majestic portion of the Hudson and the high Palisades. People who live there and work in the city have to either sit in traffic or take a commuter train into midtown, and then whatever connecting subway they need from there.

If we lived in Nyack, or Maplewood, or Montclair, Jeff would leave early in the morning and return home later at night. My journeys downtown to see my work colleagues or a gallery show would be severely curtailed. We'd rarely see our Brooklyn friends. Our family life, our marriage, would take place mostly on the weekends.

Jeff and I hop in his mother's car. It's the second time we have been alone together since Bea was born. The day is stunningly clear, and as we drive toward the town, the river sparkles invitingly.

The town is exquisite. It reminds me of San Francisco, with its mountains in the distance and its water and its steep hills and old houses. I am happy to be with my mate, even for a drive. I am looking at pretty streets of pretty houses. I am feeling increasingly, distressingly, sick. The flutters that started again in my stomach this morning have ramped up to a full-blown pounding.

We spot a real estate agency and park for a while to look at the listings in the window and gulp in some fresh air. All of the listings are upward of $600,000. We're not looking to go inside anywhere today anyway. Besides, I am beginning to consider moving on to keening and moaning in pain.

"I don't feel so hot," I tell Jeff.

He shoots a worried look in my direction. From his expression I estimate I look as ravaged as I feel. "Do you want to go home and take a nap?" he asks. I haven't had a full night's sleep in months now. I'm nursing. I'm still dealing with the physical healing of childbirth, the night sweats, and the bleeding erratically at inopportune times.

"No, no I'm all right," I backpedal. "It's nothing. Forget it." I don't want to mess up our day out, our rare opportunity to be alone together and scope out real estate at the same time.

The car climbs a steep street, and I look out the window at an eye-catching teal blue Victorian. Two little girls, a few years older than ours, sit contentedly on the porch swing, a lemonade commercial of childhood perfection. That could be my children there. That could be my house. My stomach feels like it's in a vise. I can tell I'm spotting blood.

A million stupid thoughts fly through my brain. I can go to any other city on earth, in Spain or in China, and get my bearings pretty quickly. Drive me twenty miles outside New York, though, I'm completely overwhelmed. I understand crowding on trains and running to the corner store. Ask me to mow the lawn or drive to the supermarket, and I'm flummoxed.

The other dirty truth is that the farther away from pavement I get, the more outclassed I feel. I don't know if I'm more worried that my kids would be freakish social misfits in a town like this, or that they'd morph overnight into grosgrain-ribbon-wearing little preppies with an interloping ruffian for a mother. I want to go home.

"I've seen enough," I say weakly to Jeff, and we turn the car around. I call my doctor's message service and say I'm cramping and bleeding, and when he phones me back a few minutes later, he says, "Sounds like you should go to the emergency room."

I hate doctors and hospitals. I'm scared they'll keep me there too long, and then they'll chastise me for wasting their time over nothing. My body is also urgently telling me I need to nurse the baby. I crawl into the back seat for the ride back to the folks' house.

I thought Jeff was the immovable one in this relationship. I thought I'd do anything to get the hell out of that apartment and into a mortgage. Then again, maybe not.

I'll never know for sure it if was a stomach bug, a postpartum physical meltdown, simple fatigue, or an epic anxiety attack. I didn't get very sick when we got back to the in-laws' house, but I sure got sick enough.

"Are you bummed?" I moan to Jeff as I curl in the guestroom bed. He lays next to me. "No," he says, "I didn't like it. It was too Main Street, USA, for us."

He's fibbing. I'm letting him. I think he liked it just fine. Had I not had a complete physical breakdown, he might even have, one later weekend, taken a drive to Congers. But he sees me in that hopeless ball, and he knows it's over.

"I'm so sorry," I say.

If someday my children ask us why they don't have a porch swing of their own, I'll have to tell them that their mom spent one day in a bucolic town on the Hudson and started spontaneous bleeding and throwing up. She took it as a sign.

HIGHWAY TO HELL

The plan was to go to one open house this Sunday. The plan was for it to be a quick nip over to Greenwood Heights. I told Jeff, "It's all about exploring our options."

We'll see how we feel about the neighborhood now, even though I distinctly recall standing on the corner of this exact street a year ago, sweaty and lightheaded and guzzling a Snapple and trying to explain to Lucy what we were doing across from a cemetery. This time, thinks the woman who repeats the same behavior and expects different results, we'll feel a connection.

But then this morning I saw a listing for another open house a few doors away, and even though it's out of our price range, what would be the harm in looking? We're not actively looking to put in a bid anyway.

Then Jennifer calls. "Did you see that there's also a co-op showing on Henry Street today? It's a parlor-floor unit and the ad says it needs TLC." It's only four hundred grand, so we'll hit that too. Like a gambler who can blow a fortune at the table with a spin of the wheel, within five minutes I've squandered my family's Sunday. Meanwhile, all those jerks who own property are inside eating lunch.

The homeownership rate in our country is, in 2004, at an all-time high—nearly 70 percent. Homeownership represents security, especially at an otherwise nightmarishly insecure moment in our history. It boosts the economy, it makes Wall Street robust. A year and a half into the war in Iraq, if there's one thing that's certain, it's that you can't have a home front without homes. The cautionary prognosticators say it's a bubble, it's crazy, we're headed for a major correction. But the cost of housing just gets greater and greater, and there's no slowdown in sight. In what George W. Bush refers to as an "ownership society," we are still hopeless month-to-monthers.

Renting can make sense. For those who have a real flair for money, it can be more lucrative to take the amount of a down payment and invest it. And for the many, many of us who don't, it can still be considerably wiser to keep paying the rent you now have than wind up in foreclosure on a mortgage you can't pay.

Yet all traditional logic, all instinct, holds that it's better to own than to rent. Real estate is after all one of life's safest—and often most profitable—investments. In theory, it's an intelligent way of building equity. Housing in Brooklyn has appreciated roughly 20 percent a year for each of the four years we've been in our apartment. It's a challenge not to feel stupid for not having that kind of potential right over our heads.

I have an acquaintance, Adrienne, who's a photographer and flipper. Her husband Todd got the bug when he and his brother bought a co-op near Columbia University in 1996 and sold it just a few years later for $485,000, nearly double what they'd paid. "The same apartment now would be about two million dollars," Adrienne adds, amazement in her voice.

That was around the time she entered Todd's life. They married and bought in the financial district in 2000, a 1,600-square-foot apartment on the twenty-eighth floor. They gut-renovated it and broke a record for the building when they sold it in 2002. "My husband has good connections with contractors, so we're able to work more cheaply," she says. "People who do commercial jobs are a little sloppier, but they certainly still give the look and the sex appeal of a newly renovated, sought-out space."

They purchased another apartment in the building, did a less extensive renovation, and sold it a year later. "Real estate's been a wonderful moneymaker for us," she says. "Post 9/11, lots of businesses weren't doing well. The sale of our apartment kept us living at a level we wouldn't have been able to otherwise."

Then they bought a small co-op on the Upper West Side. "We wanted to gut-renovate it, she says. "We figured the board would be casual. They were not so casual. They shut us down for ten months."

With their month-old baby in tow, Adrienne and Todd decamped to a rental thirty blocks away until the board approved the work they'd already begun. "Half the building were newer establishment and normal," she says, "and the other people who lived in the building forever were typical scared New Yorkers, people who are so paranoid about being pushed out." Eventually, they wrapped up the renovation, and sold the apartment for a tidy profit.

"It's horrible renovating an apartment. We've lived with dust and dirt and stress," she admits. "At the same time, it's exciting and creative. We're stimulated by using that part of our brains; we're stimulated by the real estate market in general." She and her husband are also good at it.

"There was nothing wrong with any of the apartments we bought," she explains. "You just needed to have the vision to see what they could be. We're not at a price point where you're buying views. We were buying well-located places that were ugly. If the space is ample, if there's potential for flow, you're buying the square footage. Certain things will always sell and never soften. There's a reason three-bedrooms will always sell; amazing light and amazing views will always sell." Because, bottom line, "There's a ton of wealthy people in New York."

As we approach Fort Hamilton Parkway, I tell Jeff, "Welcome to the tracks. Let's go to the wrong side of them, shall we?"

"We're not alone," he says, cocking his head toward the street. "Look." I glance down Fifth Avenue. There, marching in our direction, *New York Times* folded under their arms, are an army of our doppelgängers. The men are in baseball caps and corporate freebie T-shirts; the long-haired women are sporting flowered skirts and babies. They all look purposeful. Any illusion I may ever have held of our specialness in the world has just quietly died.

Something has changed in just the last year. The ownership society has become legion. Open houses are crowded and competitive, with brokers entertaining multiple suitors like Scarlett

O'Hara at a party. Just when I thought it couldn't get any more demoralizing.

The first house is $425,000. It has an office in the front that has been painted vivid orange and lime green. Not in a funky, Isaac-Mizrahi-for-Target way either, but an "it seemed awesome in 1972" one. A few coats of Farrow & Ball could easily drive up the asking price, but judging from the clutter, the owners can't be bothered.

The living room is in the windowless middle of the house. When I ask Claude, the barrel-chested realtor, "Can you turn off the overhead lights?" we are plunged into almost total darkness. The kitchen isn't bad, though it's old, and I wouldn't have gone for the lapis countertops myself. The yard is covered in a blanket of Astroturf.

As we head toward the steps, Claude, sweating in his suit and tie, warns us, "The upstairs is small, but everybody on the block builds an extension." I factor how much it would cost to add another room and follow him up the stairs.

Under a low ceiling there are two bedrooms, neither of which could accommodate anything more than a bed.

A half a block away, in a home the same dimensions, a seller has bothered to clean up and paint. They're asking $575,000. In the shuffling crowd we see the same eager faces from the other place. We look like we're on a mass blind date, our faces registering romantic hope and cynical dismissal. Meanwhile, a broker with an anchorwoman's lacquered blond hair and French-tipped nails is scanning the assembly for the ones clocking in with the real thing—connection.

The scene is eclectic-tasteful, with antiques and flea-market finds carefully arranged to look casual. It's gorgeous, and I am carried away ogling stuff that isn't part of the package. Trying to keep Lucy from destroying all of it provides distraction.

That kitchen, with the blue tiles and the white cupboards, and the counter space, is something out of a Julia Child fantasy. And how about the yard? With the little wrought-iron fence separating the patio area from the green. Apparently, a markup of 150 grand can buy you considerable charm. We have to get out before I forget that we don't have that much money and don't even like this neighborhood.

"That place was cute, I guess," an unenthused Jeff says as the four of us sit on the train back to Carroll Gardens. "I can't visualize it without the two hundred people in it."

"Let's just forget it," I tell him.

We get off the F train and plod over to the co-op open house. It's a $400,000, 750-square-foot nightmare.

Irrationally, I'm infatuated. Even more grueling than looking at all these eyesores I couldn't bear to inhabit is finding, now and then, something that really hits me. The kitchen cabinets are dangling precariously from the walls. There are four layers of increasingly horrendous linoleum on the floor. I can tell this because they're peeling up from the corners of the rooms. The effect of all these layers is that the floor is unusually soft. There are no closets, none. It's not an apartment; it's an archeological artifact.

But there are tin ceilings and windows in every room and a common garden. In this microscopic living room there is hardwood waiting to be unearthed, moldings to be stripped and stained. There are white beadboard cabinets in the kitchen and French doors between the master bedroom and the smaller one, waiting for someone to install them. This isn't another crapshack; it's someplace that could be cozy and stylish but still effortlessly comfortable.

Jeff is beelining toward the door.

It's well past lunchtime and we are all ravenous. To hell with shelter; every fiber of the family unit is demanding cheese. We sit in Nino's Pizzeria, and as the first few life-affirming bites of pepperoni hit the bloodstream, I test the waters.

"What did you think?" I say hopefully. "It's in our price range. It's in our neighborhood. Lucy wouldn't even have to change schools."

"That place?" he asks. "It's a disaster!" At this moment Jeff is either deeply pragmatic or profoundly lacking in vision. "No way," he insists. "It's a dump. We'd need to sink another two hundred thousand in to make it livable."

The problems are significant. Its railroady layout and street-level location mean that it would never have much in the way of privacy. It is a spectacular mess. It is also on a beautiful street in the only neighborhood we like, one that is becoming less affordable every time we exhale.

"Maybe," I counter, "but we could fix it a little at a time once we were in. We're not going to get another chance like this, not at this price," I tell him. "I don't get it. How can you not want this?"

"I'm not you," he says, painstakingly sawing Lucy's pizza into squares with a plastic knife. "This is your big security issue not mine, I know you envy our friends who own, like they're smarter or better than we are or something, but the thought of buying doesn't make me feel more secure. It makes me feel less secure."

Marriage? Kids? Sure, he's up for it. But a home? It sounds so *permanent*.

"What if we make a mistake?" he asks. "What if we don't have enough money? What if we're stuck?"

Off the top of my head I'd say we'd be financially ruined and mess up our lives and those of our children. "Then I guess we'd be stuck," I say. His anxiety is legitimate, and contagious as measles.

Searching for a home is getting on a scale and dumping our whole lives on it, standing naked in front of the three-way full-length mirror. We are not the people with the den and the dishwasher and the 2,000 square feet. We are the people whose life savings will take them only a very short distance. Jeff would prefer to look away.

In July, we fly to Rochester to celebrate Jeff's uncle Jim's birthday and to introduce the baby to the upstate relatives. Driving around, Uncle Jim points out elegant homes that date back to the Revolution. We eat lunch in a picturesque part of town where old mills used to operate, right on the canal. We also walk through one of the most sterile downtowns I have ever seen.

At night, we mingle with the relatives under a tent set up behind his cousin Ann's house. Ann and her sister Sue are the siblings I'd like to picture Lucy and Bea growing up to be. They share the natural rapport of two people comfortably distinct yet deeply entwined. They laugh at jokes only the other gets; they finish each other's sentences. Yet despite the fact that I see them once a year, tops, they never fail to treat me like I'm a member of the club. They make me feel like family, which, given my own family, is nothing short of lovely.

I'm considering the contrast on a Saturday afternoon at my

mother and stepfather's house. Eight years ago they left Jersey City and bought a 1960s-era raised ranch on a pleasant street in a non-descript town on the New Jersey Transit commuter line. In Jersey City they had teenagers throwing beer bottles into their bushes and radios blaring under their windows. Here they have a deck and a pool and a "great room."

I take the girls into the guest room to change into their bathing suits. As I'm coming onto the deck, I overhear my mother talking to my mother-in-law.

"I can't believe they're still in that apartment," my mother says. "You'd think after everything that's happened, they'd get out of the city. Go somewhere safe."

After the *everything that happened* that my mother is referring to, a lot of people did leave. Some of our circle bolted within weeks after 9/11. They took off for New England and Pennsylvania. They got away from the memories, found cleaner air and better jobs.

When Peter and Helena watched the towers fall from their window above Johnnie's Bootery, they already had a move to Los Angeles planned for just a few weeks later. "For a few days I felt guilty about leaving," Peter says. "Remember when there was a sense of solidarity for about two hours? I didn't want to be one of those people who was turning tail and running. But I had just been laid off; Helena wasn't working, and I hadn't ever lived anywhere outside New York. It was time."

They lived with their two young sons in a rental for two years. Helena went back to school, and Peter hooked up with the Web site Mr. Skin, helping redo all its content. "There were thousands of new reviews to write, and I was making a lot of money, so we had enough for a down payment."

The Los Angeles bubble was different than its East Coast counterpart. "In New York," he says, "when people find a good deal, they stay put. In L.A. people move all the time. There's a lot of speculation. We bought our house from a friend of ours. I wanted to avoid the brokers, but his wife was into soaking it for as much as possible. There were multiple bids in. The asking was $340,000, and we bought it for $390,000." They got a ten-year adjustable-rate mortgage because, he says, "We have a low interest rate and we get a lot back in taxes, and that money is better off invested. We have a small two-bedroom, and we probably won't stay in Los Angeles for another ten years." For the time being, however, he and his family are living in the house Mr. Skin built.

My friend Andrew took a different path. Andrew is the most genial man I know. He's built like a Viking, with a laugh that could set off avalanches.

In 2000, when he wanted more space and Brooklyn was becoming too pricey, he sold his little co-op in the Heights for double what he'd paid five years earlier and bought in Manhattan's then barely inhabited financial district. He paid $330,000 for a spacious co-op with a long wraparound deck, and put another $100,000 into renovating it.

Over the years he gained a wife and a dog, and more memories than he can shake. Andrew lives a block from Ground Zero.

On the morning of September 11, Andrew was awakened not by the sound of a plane crashing into a building, but the phone ringing. It was his brother, telling him, "You might want to take a look out your window."

Even after the second plane hit, he and his wife Patricia stayed, watching in bewildered horror, too stunned to realize that they themselves would need to leave. That didn't happen until the first tower fell. "It was the loudest sound I've ever heard," he remembers later, "and then everything went black. I thought we were going to die."

They packed a few things, random things—a travel set of Scrabble, clean underwear, and a copy of *The Amazing Adventures of Kavalier and Clay*. They went out into the darkened streets and kept going until the sky was blue again and they arrived at a friend's apartment in Gramercy. Because they were in the "frozen zone," it was a month before they were permitted to move back.

A few days after the attacks, however, they came back to their building to assess the condition of their apartment. They walked back downtown, deeper and deeper into the empty grayness, flashing their driver's licenses past checkpoint after checkpoint.

To their surprise, the electricity had never shut off, so Andrew grabbed a Diet Dr Pepper and inspected the debris on their deck. He found random papers. Bits of plastic. And a clump of blond hair.

The smell didn't dissipate for weeks. Then the tourists started coming, and the souvenir vendors selling "Day of Terror" postcards. "I hated it," he says, "hated it." The human impulse to see that place, to try to understand the unfathomable, makes sense. It just takes a toll when it's right there as soon as you step out the door of your home.

The most genial man I know was depressed for a year. "People get competitive about where they were that day, like the way it's better to have second-row tickets to the game than see it on TV. That's a contest I don't want to win," he says. "I'd much rather have been watching it on television—from Hawaii."

He and Patricia thought about leaving, or even moving to a different part of town, but then she got into a Ph.D. program downtown and they had a good reason to stay. Eventually, it didn't feel quite as awful anymore. One night they strolled home together from a movie in Battery Park, and as they walked past Ground Zero, Andrew says, "I saw a construction site instead of a mass grave."

Jeff and I never once talked about leaving because of 9/11. We're not any braver—or dumber—than anybody else. It's just that what was a very compelling reason for some people to go wasn't any reason at all for us.

If anything, it gave our affection for the city a poignancy it didn't have before. Whenever I look at the skyline now and see that empty space, I can't imagine going anywhere else. How could I tear myself away from all this fragile, wounded beauty?

When Lucy was a baby, we had her in a day care on the upstairs floor of a Brooklyn Heights synagogue. They shut down for a few days after the attacks, and when they reopened later that same week, it was with a pair of heavily armed guards posted outside their doors. The first time I walked past the men and their guns with my toddler and then left her there, I didn't stop shaking the whole way home. Also the second and third time. I had nightmares that bombs were dropping on the city. In the dreams I would run through the streets as *Dr. Strangelove* missiles fell, searching for Jeff and Lucy, crying out their names while buildings tumbled.

On those walks home after drop-off, I would pass posters on telephone poles and in store windows, pictures of smiling faces with the word MISSING above them.

In the window of the flower shop, there was one of a dark-haired young man in a tuxedo. One morning as I walked past, I saw the owner, a fat guy whose cigar smoke obliterated the fragrance of his wares, perched regally outside on a lawn chair. He was talking to a stooped older woman.

The lady pointed at the face in the window. "They hear anything?"

"Naaaaah," he had said, his voice rasping over the word like sandpaper on wood. "He's gone. They're all gone."

Until I heard him say it, I hadn't believed it myself. And I started shaking all over again. The days went by. Posters disappeared from windows. They melted in the rain. They were all gone.

I used to read newspaper stories about bombs going off in nightclubs in Tel Aviv or the West Bank, or in cafés in Sarajevo or Belfast, and think it was insane that anybody who lived in Tel Aviv or Sarajevo would be out in a nightclub or a café in the first place. Why would anybody be dancing in a messed-up environment like that? Now I understand. It's because we keep going. Not because the mayor or the president or Madison Avenue tells us to. Not because if we don't, some undefined enemy will have won. There are days when hiding under a desk sounds like a great strategy. We don't, though, because it's unnatural—not to mention boring. So we make plans for next week and we drink coffee and we keep having babies. Human beings aren't built to hole up. We're built to live. And dance.

A few Saturday afternoons later, remarkably, there's an open house for a rare co-op on our street. The tenants purchased the big four-family from the owners a few years ago and converted it.

It's listed as a two-bedroom and is painfully far out of our range—they're asking $675,000. That's how much it now costs to live on our street, in little old Brooklyn, in the summer of 2004, in a place of roughly the same size and layout as our apartment.

To be fair, it's in significantly better condition than our place, and slightly wider. There's a dishwasher and fresh paint and French doors separating the rooms and promising sweet, sweet privacy. There's a marble mantle in the master bedroom. There's still no outdoor space, no washer or dryer, no super. If we hit the Powerball bigtime, however, we'd jump through fire for it.

The president of the co-op bears our gawking politely. "If you decide to come down in price," I say, "by around three hundred thousand or so, give me a call."

"Sure thing," he says, laughing all the way to the bank.

When we get home, Jennifer and Vincent call us to meet up in Carroll Park. Their friends Clare and Paul are in the neighborhood with their sons, hanging out.

She's a mental health researcher; he's a photographer. They have a toddler and a baby. When they moved here a few months ago from London, they rented for a while in Brooklyn. But Brooklyn was too far from Clare's work, and already too expensive for their budget.

A few years ago, Paul came to New York to cover a story on an accused pedophile priest who had fled from Ireland to the States. The priest was rumored to be hiding out in an Irish neighborhood far uptown in Manhattan, and Paul scoured every corner of the area in pursuit. He never did find the priest, but he discovered a neighborhood. When he and Clare were ready to find a more permanent residence, they set their sights on Inwood.

"Where's that?" I ask Clare, as we stand side by side at the swings, pushing our kids to an endless chorus of "Higher! Higher!"

"Upper Manhattan," she explains. "Around 207th Street."

Manhattan has a 207th Street? I assume she's referring to the Bronx, a borough I know only via its zoo and botanical garden.

"It's near the Cloisters," she explains by way of landmarking. I have been to the Cloisters museum twice in my life. The last time was fifteen years ago, and if you'd told me it was in another state entirely, I'd have believed you. She adds, "There are great apartments up there. And a lovely park."

"Sounds cute," I say. Then it resonates for me. The park. That's how I've heard of the neighborhood. It was in the news recently.

In the late afternoon hours of May 19, 2004, a Juilliard student named Sarah Fox donned her workout clothes, left her apartment in Inwood, and disappeared. Six days later, her strangled, nude body was discovered in the woods.

Eventually, a "person of interest" was identified, a Russian émigré with a wife and young child. Police grew suspicious when he offered them his purported clairvoyant visions and they matched the unreleased details of the crime. He had a past that included violent confrontations with neighbors. There wasn't enough evidence to connect him with the crime, though, and no one was ever charged. The case is still open.

I picture a doe-eyed, short-haired young girl on an idyllic spring day, running in her park. The sunlight playing on the leaves, her hair bouncing. How scared she must have been as she realized she was going to die.

I look at my girls, enjoying a blissful afternoon in their playground. I want them to stay this safe and happy forever. And if there's any way, we could easily spend our lives here. We could wear the identity of a Brooklyn family as easily as we wear the T-shirts that bear our area code.

The next day, we pack up the diaper bag again to look at a $600,000 two-family house for sale by its owner located, for all intents and purposes, underneath the elevated F train tracks at Smith and 9th. Jennifer and Vincent generously agree to accompany us, because as real homeowners they know what to look for.

Jennifer still believes that if we can find a place that generates income and is relatively well priced, we can get a mortgage. I still want to believe right along with her. I am also making one desperate, last-ditch stab at the dream of having a house in our neighborhood. "It doesn't hurt to look," Jennifer says.

The place is solid but crack-house–level grungy. The feral dog in the back howls the entire time, because there's always an angry dog. The subterranean kitchen and living room, strewn with the detritus of last night's dinner, immediately makes me think, This would be the ideal place to die of an overdose.

I hope that we aren't imagination-deficient. We can recognize a place with those elusive good bones when we see it. The question is whether we have the financial and intestinal resources for both a home and a renovation thereof.

When we emerge, Jeff asks Vincent and Jennifer, "What's your take?"

Vincent, ever cheerful, says, "With a hundred thousand or so, you could make that place pretty nice."

The home's eventual buyers will tear it down and build a condo on the spot.

We then head on to the subway and out to an open house for a one-family in Windsor Terrace.

On Friday, I had been walking home from school pickup with Margot and mentioned we were going out here to look at a house.

"Ugh," she had said, rolling her eyes. "Windsor Terrace is dead. You don't want to do that."

Some days I don't know if it hurts more when our friends who are already comfortably settled here enthusiastically encourage us to leave for shoddier shores, or when they turn up their noses at our distinctly down-market prospects. Usually, I keep my mouth shut. But not this day.

"Yeah, well, we didn't buy eight years ago like you did," I had snapped. "So we're not sitting on a million-dollar house like you are now. We have to go where we can afford."

Her face looked like I had just slapped it. "I know," she had said. "It's hard. And I'm sorry."

The closer we get to the address in the ad, the sorrier I am too. Yet again Mapquest has let us down, placing the house a block away from the Fort Hamilton Expressway, instead of where it truly is—directly on it.

"It's like a horror movie," says Jeff. In our case, though, it's not to an Indian burial ground or a pagan sacrifice spot we keep circling back to. "Why are all our prospects always near cemeteries, highways, or overpasses?" Jeff asks.

"It doesn't matter," I tell him. "They're asking $465,000, so it's above our limit anyway."

We enter on the main floor, which holds a minor-sized living room and the house's one bathroom. The broker, a short, stocky woman, doles out fact sheets to the steady flow of visitors. "Think of it as an apartment on three floors," she says.

The upstairs has two little sleeping chambers, separated by an accordion screen. On the other hand, even my husband accedes, "That highway proximity does do wonders for an unobstructed southern exposure."

I totter down a dark, rickety staircase with Bea strapped to my chest and Lucy bringing up the rear. Jeff, our leader and canary in the coal mine, assesses the situation. "The basement is the kitchen," he calls back to us. "The kitchen is the basement." We need only lift our not terribly long arms to scrape the ceiling.

So it's on the expressway and built for hobbits. It's not bad, exactly. Nothing's falling apart. I think it's the best thing we've seen in weeks.

Later our family bakes on the subway platform, waiting for what the Metropolitan Transit Authority lethargically refers to as "weekend service."

"Should we make an offer?" I ask Jeff. "We might talk them down to $400,000."

"You want to pay almost half a million dollars to live on an expressway in a part of town we're not even into?" he asks like I'm the crazy one. "Hell no." Then his voice gets soft, and weary. "Every time we look somewhere else, it's awful," Jeff says. "I don't want to leave our neighborhood. I'd rather be somewhere smaller there."

"Even if it's someplace like those little co-ops we looked at before?" I press him. "We're not getting the brownstone, you know. We can't even get the shitty house under the subway tracks."

"I know," he says. "But I can't keep coming back to Windsor Terrace and Greenwood Heights and Kensington. This is frustrating and gross."

It's only June, and we know what we did last summer. We can spend our weekends traipsing all over our already blazing borough, dealing with uniformly hideous homes on the chance of finding that gem in the rough, this time with the added challenge of our pooping, squalling newest family member. Or we can some up with another plan.

THERE GOES THE NEIGHBORHOOD

The building is still a skeletal collection of beams and rubble and exposed wires, on a plot of land flanked on either side by major traffic arteries. New condos are popping up all over Brooklyn, all promising different nonsense to prospective buyers: "the excitement of the city and the serenity of nature," "luxe and pop," and "modern living in nineteenth-century architecture." This one teases with the lure of sweeping skyline views. Units are starting at around $400,000, and the prospect of anything in our budget that we haven't yet dismissed fills us with wary anticipation. The condo going up by the Brooklyn-Queens Expressway is finally holding open houses. Jeff, Sharon, the girls, and I eagerly hightail our rubbernecking selves over to check it out.

We arrive as the realtor, a rodenty fellow with downy gray hair and pinholes for eyes, is dispensing hard hats and clipboards. "Sign this," he says. They've waivers that we won't sue if one of us dies or is dismembered. "And *they* can't come," he adds, pointing to my offspring. "Insurance risk."

While Jeff stays downstairs with the children and their yet unfused skulls, Sharon and I take the first shift. She isn't actively looking to buy, but as a single woman in possession of a good income, she's the best candidate among us for elevators and stainless-steel appliances. We put on the hats.

"Now we just need to find a leather man and an Indian chief," says Sharon.

The broker herds us up into a group with other people in ridiculous headgear. The first unit he shows us is small but clean and modern. There are two little bedrooms, a tricked-out marble and stainless-steel kitchen island, a quasi-living/dining room, and a deck, the length and width of a newspaper, that seems to float directly above the BQE.

We next move into another, slightly larger unit. The broker stands in the archway between the living room and the kitchen, and begins his pitch. "You could knock down these walls and make an open space for entertaining!"

He says this five times. It seems a shame he feels this way, because the wall probably went up yesterday. I peer out the window, at an onslaught of cars in both directions. The steady whoosh of traffic below has a weirdly pleasant, ambient-noise effect, but I'm not sure I could take a steady diet of it. It's a great place if you're into fumes.

Yet other people on the tour are putting down deposits on the spot. "They're selling like hot cakes!" Jeff observes, astonished, when Sharon and I wend our way back down. He points to a folding table where a crisp young woman from the managing office is handing out paperwork and accepting big, big checks. Jeff shakes his head ruefully. "I thought only homeless people lived on the highway."

Though the building has a swank, yacht-club-like name, after Jeff and Sharon and I have all done the tour, we never call it that again. If you're going to put a building on an expressway, we are going to henceforth refer to it solely as the Meridian.

We had thought, after our expressway excursion to Windsor Terrace a few weeks ago, that we were done with this sort of thing. That night we had talked.

"I don't want to leave Carroll Gardens any more than you do," I had told Jeff. "I wanted space, I wanted a yard, but I want to stay in here more. No more long subway rides. It's Bea's first summer. Let's enjoy it. We'll stick to looking for something like that apartment on Henry Street. It could happen again, right?"

"I feel good about this," Jeff had said. "I feel peaceful. In spite of all the frustration, I want to live in the hood I want to live in."

"Me too," I had replied, and we fell sweetly asleep until Bea squalled for her 2 A.M. feeding.

And that's how we wound up at an overpriced pile of rubble on the highway.

The next weekend, my father and his wife are coming for their first visit to our neighborhood, first time meeting Bea. This is one of my favorite parts of living here—showing off the neighborhood. We'll take them for a walk around the brownstones, out for a slice of pizza you can only get in a great Italian New York enclave.

But by the time they arrive this afternoon, the mercury has climbed to nearly a hundred degrees and our air conditioner has died. They're already flushed by the time they climb the stairs to our airless apartment.

"How is life treating you?" I ask, because small is the only kind of talk I know to make with my father.

"Couldn't be better," he replies as he and his wife shuffle in.

Erica unloads toys for the girls, and Joe Williams is holding an ancient-looking photo album with a velvet spine. "I thought you'd like to see some family pictures," he says, gently placing the book on our dining table.

I gingerly turn page after page of pictures of women in turn-of-the-century garb and men in elegant suits. My grandmother, hair in a 1920s bob and pearls. "This is amazing," I tell him.

"I'm glad you like it, because it's yours now," he says lightly, as if he hands over his heirloom photographs to the daughter he barely knows every day. I can't meet his eyes.

These well-dressed strangers in a book are my family. This somewhat more casually attired stranger perspiring in my apartment is my family. "There's something else," he adds, and Erica pulls a ring out of her pocket. White gold filigree swirls around a rectangle of emerald, set off by two tiny diamonds. "Joe's aunt Hannah left it to me," she says, "but I think she'd want you to have it now."

All I can say is "Thank you."

We walk outside into the raging heat. Erica grew up on a farm. I can tell our neighborhood makes her jumpy, that she's scared of the noise and the sheer volume of people. She is clutching her purse with a kung fu grip, her eyes darting everywhere, as Lucy bounds a few yards ahead. Erica has grandchildren of her own. "Aren't you afraid she'll get hurt?" she asks. "Aren't you afraid, living here?"

I'm stunned to consider the city from her perspective. I'm thinking, you should have seen it thirty years ago.

I look at our city now, bursting with million-dollar condos in neighborhoods where once you wouldn't venture without an economy-sized can of pepper spray, and I doubt the new inhabitants have any notion what it once was like.

There was a time in New York when the city didn't have this careless expectation of wealth and commerce. It didn't look like downtown Disney then. It was more like *Taxi Driver* meets *The Warriors*.

I was too young to appreciate the worst of it. Times Square in its sleazy depths, Alphabet City and Harlem when the mention of their names alone could inspire shudders of fear and revulsion—these were things of my childhood. My excursions into the city were of a mostly cultural nature then, and my exposure to filthy subway cars and crime waves was limited. I was eleven in 1977—the summer of Son of Sam and the big blackout that turned New York into a looters' paradise. Suffice to say, in those days you didn't move anywhere with the immutable assurance of inevitable gentrification. You didn't look on the map and calculate how long before the baby strollers and coffee bars moved in. You watched as people died off or moved the hell away; you held your breath as gangs moved in. There goes the neighborhood, again and again and again.

I don't take that for granted. I don't assume that housing bubbles or the upwardly mobile yen for Whole Foods is perpetual.

I only have the hope that we will find a good place somewhere, and that it will sustain us.

"No," I tell Erica. "I'm not afraid."

Not of crime or recession, anyway. Things are changing rapidly in our borough these days. There's a battle going on right now for its soul. On the one side are our borough president Marty Markowitz and the developer Bruce Ratner. Together they want to reinvent the downtown with a new sports arena and a vast, ambitious housing development. They vow the Atlantic Yards project will bring jobs and revenue into the neighborhood, promising to build moderate- and lower-income housing along with the luxury high-rises.

On the other side of the fight are the residents whose homes and businesses would be swallowed up in the new wave of building, the ones who insist the plans will not adequately accommodate the lower- and middle-class families who live in this dense neighborhood. Under the current plan to spiffy up downtown, when the government takes over private property for public use, it's known as eminent domain. Ideally, it's supposed to make a neighborhood more useful for everybody. Realistically, the potential infusion of wealth to the area and the helplessness of those left behind in the real estate gold rush becomes more and more glaring every day.

At least this boom doesn't have a body count.

When I first started attending my all-girl Catholic high school in Hoboken, the mile-square city still resembled the rough world *On the Waterfront* had depicted. I took the bus every day from my street corner to the Erie Lackawanna Terminal, and walked the rest of the way to my school. Some of the streets were beautiful, with elegant nineteenth-century brick houses. There were also rotting docks and crumbling tenements.

The new wave of early-eighties affluence was pushing its way into the town, propelled by the city's easy access to Wall Street. If you were a landlord, perhaps looking to convert your property into condos, Hoboken was a potential gold mine. There were just a few problems getting in the way—rent control, nearly nonexistent vacancy rates, and tenants.

On October 24, 1981, eleven people, including seven children, were killed in a suspicious fire on 12th Street. Throughout the early 1980s, other fires continued to blaze through the city at an alarming clip, gutting the old tenements and snuffing out the lives of their inhabitants. Hoboken earned itself the dubious nickname Arson City.

The smoldering apartment buildings came down; pristine condominiums came up.

That was when I met Carmen. We sat next to each other on the first day of high school and remained at each other's side the next four years. She's my oldest friend and still one of my best, a woman with the same long beautiful hair and generous, uncynical spirit that she had in ninth grade. Carmen's family came from Puerto Rico in the 1960s with almost nothing, and they lived in the Hoboken projects until Carmen was thirteen. That's when they bought the small house on Monroe Street where her mother still lives.

Carmen's a mother of three now herself, working for the government and living in rural Maryland. Earlier this year she and her family moved to the home they plan to spend the rest of their lives in.

"The market was so hot, there were no houses," she tells me later. "We looked for years. I looked at places the owners wouldn't even clean, let alone fix up."

Eventually, instead of waiting forever for the right house to come along, she found a parcel of 8.6 acres for sale not far from her older daughter's school. Then she looked around and found somebody to construct her dream home on it. "It was cheaper to build than to buy," she explains. "But the further north the builders were, the more they cost. There were differences of $200,000 in the prices we were quoted. It had nothing to do with quality; it had nothing to do with the lumber or the windows or the paint. I picked the best guy, but because he was from southern Maryland and not Anne Arundel County, I paid less." Their land and the house combined cost $546,000.

My friend lives in a 4,000-square-foot home with a 2,000-square-foot basement. I get excited when I see listings in our price range for a quarter of that size. It must be pretty splendid to have all that room. It must be nice to have a big custom-designed kitchen and a den and a deck and five bedrooms. Then again, it must also cost a bundle to heat and cool it, it must be a full time job to clean it, and the taxes on all that acreage must be through the roof. I imagine that great space, like great beauty, can be both a blessing and a curse.

The house didn't start out so expansive. "I started with a three-thousand-square-foot home," Carmen says. "Then I started wanting the porch to be six feet as opposed to four. Then I wanted the kitchen to be a little bigger, and that added four feet to the house. I picked a plan that added stairwells. Every time I did something, it added something to the house." It's more than she ever planned on, but it makes her happier than she'd imagined. "It's a great house," she says proudly, "and I picked out every single thing in it." She sounds happy and rooted.

I, on the other hand, have been scouring the real estate listings, seduced by the promise of anything in our range in our neighborhood. How disappointing is the process? Like when you hear the opening bars of a song you think is "Super Freak." And then it turns out to be "U Can't Touch This."

We look at a ground-floor duplex on Court Street for $375,000. The main floor is one room with a kitchenette the width of my body shoved into a corner. There is only a slit of a front window, but it's still brighter upstairs than down. There, we find two sad little bedrooms in a windowless basement, and a boiler between them. It has a certain bunker-like chic, minus the canned goods, automatic weapons, and cyanide tablets.

We see another, for $425,000, on the ground floor of yet another building directly on the Brooklyn-Queens Expressway. The living room is paneled in an indefensibly hideous wall of mirrors. The undersized second bedroom, the one we'd ostensibly put our children in, faces straight into the flow of traffic.

It's not the apartment for us. This is the skank pit you retreat to after the divorce, the apartment where you have a leftover sub for breakfast and Klonopin for dinner, with an inappropriate hookup for a chaser.

"I'd like our next place to be better than what we have now," Jeff says sadly as we walk home. "It's horrific to see how little a tremendous sum can get you."

Sisyphus has nothing on us. "Do you think we're any closer than we were a year ago?" I ask him.

"I don't know," he replies, "but we're not there yet."

Outside the city, friends like Carmen are buying property and building big houses to their exact specifications, fresh clean slates to write their family histories on. Closer to home, developments like the Meridian are springing up, luxury condominiums with their granite countertops, dishwashers, and slim little decks.

My building has an old soul.

Every time I come home, I look to the top of my building's façade, where a date was carved a century and a half ago. It staggers me every time I see it. This building gives me connection, not simply with people or even place, but with the past itself.

I sometimes try to visualize how it used to be laid out—before the bathroom was added, and the heinous drop ceiling was put in. A boarded-up door to the hallway shows where another entrance once was. Before or sometime after, the building was surely a one-family. The living room looks out on a tar roof that covers an addition built on the unit downstairs, probably in the fifties when the neighborhood was at its greatest pitch of uglifying improvements.

When the building is quiet, I try to hear the echoes of all the people who've passed through it. The small family, like us, who lived in our apartment immediately before we moved in. The brood that walked through the big wooden doors the first time. Sheila from upstairs has told us tales of the sailor who used to live in our apartment, a dapper dresser who brought back exotic gifts from his travels.

I imagine all the mothers before me, for over 150 years, stirring pots and mending clothes and reading stories and tucking their offspring into bed at night, as I do now. I remember when Lucy was a baby, burning up with a fever of 106 degrees, and agonizing until she was well and strong again. How many other mothers tended their sick children here, and with how many different outcomes? We stretch out across time toward each other, linked by these walls and every mundane and extraordinary thing that's occurred within them.

I think of the families that sat at their dinner tables worrying that the South would truly secede. I think of the names on the World War I monument in Carroll Park and wonder if any of those men slept here. I picture the astonishment of a family flicking on their first electric lamp. I see children gathered around a rabbit-eared television set watching an astronaut walk on the moon. And I think of someone who will come after me, and if she'll ever imagine the woman who sat on her couch on a bright September morning while her baby slept, watching a deluge of white dust and debris rain down with such alarming suddenness that she thought, for just a moment, that it was snow.

It is a day like that one, warm and blue, when Erica calls. We must be getting more relaxed with each other, I think, for her to phone unexpectedly, and I ask how she's doing. "Not so good. Joe wasn't completely honest when he saw you," she says. "There's a growth in his kidney. He has to have surgery. He doesn't want to."

Well that's exasperating.

"You know Joe," she says, but I don't. "Stubborn. He hates doctors. Says he doesn't feel sick."

"Tell him we've only started to get to know him," I reply, "so he can't do anything stupid like die."

There's anxiety in her voice. "I'm trying to get him to go for the operation. He'd have to go to Columbia Presbyterian. Is that anywhere near you?"

Columbia Presbyterian is in Manhattan, on 168th Street. It's nowhere near me. "Not far," I say. "Tell him I'll see him there."

A few weeks after our conversation, I arm myself with a September issue of *Vogue* that weighs more than my baby and take an extraordinarily long subway ride.

When I go to see my father, he's still in the post-op ward. I feel like a phony as I approach the nurse's station. "I'm here for Joe Williams. I'm his daughter," I unconvincingly declare.

Yet the woman in teddy-bear-festooned hospital garb appears to believe me. She doesn't demand I summon forth a childhood memory of dancing on Joe Williams's shoes, or ask what his favorite color is, or require any other evidence of daughterhood that doesn't exist. She just points me down an aisle of groans and mechanical whirrs.

He's got the easy job; he can call me by name. When I speak of him, to my daughters or friends, I refer to him by his full name. First name alone seems somehow disrespectful, and any version of "Dad" is unthinkable. This is what Lucy calls him now too. "Is Joe Williams coming to visit again?" she'll ask.

Mostly, though, I go to pains to not have to call him anything. It's like when you forget someone's name. You'll get in his face and look him in the eye to ask a question, relying on signal rather than direct address. Whenever I call, I usually get Erica, and ask her to put "your husband" on. I try to make it light and natural, but I cringe every time. He just identifies himself to me as Joe. It's as if I happen to know an older couple, who we see once in a blue moon and whose house we've been to a single time, one of whom happens to have given me half of everything that I am.

The post-op is very stuffy and hot, and sweat streams down my neck as I gingerly peer through a curtain. He's flat on a stretcher and looking like a very old man as his doctor monitors his progress.

He looks up at me and gives a weak smile. "Heyyyyy," he exhales in a heavily sedated burst of air. "This is my daughter," he tells the doctor, who nods pleasantly.

"And your wife was here before," the doctor says.

"Right," my father replies, wearily. "I got one of each."

I am thirty-eight years old, and this is the first time in my life my father has ever acknowledged me as his child. It could be the assload of anesthesia he's coming down from doing the talking, but his frankness startles me. His daughter. His one.

"I brought you a slice of chocolate cake for later," I murmur. He's half asleep already. "I'll let you rest now." I give him an awkward peck on the forehead, and I go, not knowing if I'll ever see him again.

Reluctant as I am to assign pat explanations for anything, I have asked myself again and again over the years if I'd be this obsessed with getting a home if my parents hadn't been such utter strangers, to each other and to me. I usually swat the idea away like a pesky insect. I don't think this deep need of mine is just to create something I never had. I did receive sufficient love and attention as a child to not be that desperate.

It's not that family history doesn't matter. It's just that even pigeons know to build a nest. It's instinct, which is right now gasping under the weight of housing appreciation and rising mortgage rates. And what I am fanatical about is efficiency and intelligence.

With every connection Jeff and Lucy and Bea and I form, every friend we make, every day that we live and rent in that damn apartment, our roots grow deeper. They never grow stronger, though.

We're paying out so much money every month and not building any equity on it. Our rent could rise capriciously or we could be turned out, like we were in our last place, and we would have nothing to show for the years we've been there. It gnaws at me that our lease is month to month. It feels, for a family of four, too damn flaky, and it doesn't take a student of introductory psychology to figure out it's driving me crazy.

I walk outside the hospital and look down the street. A busy strip of Broadway, with grand old apartment buildings right near the river. Washington Heights, I think. I should check out the listings for this part of town. Then when people ask how we'd discovered the neighborhood, I could say, "It's an interesting story."

A few days later, my father is home. His wife calls to say he's recuperating well. Then the weeks slip by, and we realize they've gone off the grid again.

We're progressing in other ways, though. In September, Lucy starts prekindergarten at the public school down the street. A few years ago, we were getting pinched, sympathetic nods when we told people where we were zoned. "I hear that's okay," they'd mutter pityingly.

Then two years ago a dynamic principal and troupe of go-getter young teachers came in, right as the progeny of the neighborhood's recent, more prosperous arrivals reached school age. Real estate ads starting touting our school in their come-ons. Which, to a public school parent already living in the zone, roughly translates as, "In your face, world."

Lucy's teacher is young, attractive, and plays guitar. Her class is a rainbow coalition of African-American, Latino, Caucasian, and Asian kids, and the school's test scores are fantastic.

Bea, meanwhile, has started at a day care three blocks away. The head teacher is a Turkish woman who plays belly-dancing music along with the usual mix of Raffi and the Wiggles. The kids are sweet-tempered and beautiful.

We careen through the whirl of autumn, with school and work and parties. Without even trying, we let the weekends go by without looking at apartments. I still diligently peruse the real estate pages and craigslist, but the pickings are meager and our stamina is likewise.

We have other, happier things vying to occupy our thoughts of late anyway. Before we know it, the holidays have blitzed past us. We've been planning their shared birthday party for weeks. Lucy is turning five; Bea is turning one. We'll have two kinds of cake and all kinds of nutritionally vacant stuff like Chex Mix and little hot dogs that the parents will enjoy even more than the kids. We'll dance to our Dan Zanes albums and play hot potato.

Two days before the party, my mother calls to say she can't come. "We've been trying to get together with some friends, and Sunday is the only day they can make it," she explains.

Goddammit, she always does this. The last time was Halloween, when we'd made plans to go the children's parade and have cupcakes afterward, and then she called to say that she wasn't coming after all.

There are two possibilities here. Either she's so stressed at the thought of the party she just can't do it and she's making some face-saving excuse, or she really would rather see her friends. Either way it stinks.

It seems to me that my mother has a problem with crowds and parties and driving into the city. I can't say for sure, though, because she'd never admit it. I get excuses instead. I get last-minute cancellations and long silences between phone calls. I get wondering if I made her angry, if I'm being punished. I get no answers.

"When were you going to tell me?" I ask.

"I guess now," she replies.

I know things are stressful for them. They've been dying for my stepfather to take an early retirement, grab the pension, and get the hell out of Dodge since even before 9/11. In the ensuing years, their desire has reached a fever pitch. Their nice raised ranch in suburban New Jersey is littered with copies of *Where to Retire* magazine. Graying boomers, both of them, they are part of a new generation of potential homeowners—the ones looking for somewhere pleasant and affordable to spend what may wind up being the next thirty years of their lives. Developers from Las Vegas to Vermont are scrambling for a piece of their pension dollars. Mom and Phil talk of going to Delaware, where the property taxes are lower, or down south, where land is cheap. They don't have a plan yet. Just a melancholy sense of needing to move away from it all.

I never expect much. I invite my mother and her husband to our celebrations, and if they come, they come, and if they don't, I'm not surprised. Yet no matter how low you set the bar, your family can still let you down.

On Sunday we have our two kinds of cake and our game of

hot potato and the mayhem that's only possible when you cram a dozen kids into a small apartment. It's a rousing, rowdy success, and when it's all over and the wrapping paper is in the recycling and the girls are passed out in sugar shock, I stand next to Jeff over the sink full of dishes and break down and cry.

A few weeks after, it's the glistening alabaster morning after an overnight snow. The weekend in Miami with my college roommates that I've planned for May seems a million miles away. Bea is at day care, but Lucy has the day off from school, so I take my firstborn to Central Park to see the Gates.

For two brief, stunning weeks, the artists Christo and Jeanne-Claude have flooded the landscape with a sea of hundreds of tall portals, each topped with a billowy saffron-colored panel. On this starkly sunny morning of bare trees and sugar white ground, my little girl is running through an Orange Julius–colored park. I feel as buoyantly happy, as bathed in beauty, as Lucy is.

My phone rings and it's Jeff.

"You have to see this," I tell him. "We have to come back this weekend before it ends. It's incredible."

"Maybe," he replies. "Listen. I just got laid off."

This is what a swift, unexpected punch in the stomach feels like.

His company hasn't had a great year. They're eliminating forty jobs in several departments. It's nothing he did, it's nothing anybody did. It's business.

I'm instantly seized with remorse over the bottle of water I bought us on the way over, mentally speed-calculating what expenses we can eliminate. We don't use a babysitter; we hardly ever eat out. We could pull Bea out of day care, but how would I get any work done? I have a part-time job and haven't had a raise since the dot-com crash. What we've saved in the last two years for a down payment wouldn't get us through too long a lean time.

"It'll be all right," I say gently. "We'll both freelance more. We'll move our health insurance over to me, and we'll be okay."

I'm silently panicking, though. I say nothing to Lucy, and we go pick up Bea and go to a birthday party that feels like a migraine waiting to happen, on an afternoon that seems to last as long as the *Lord of the Rings* trilogy.

When we're home a few hours later, I check my email. My company is having a staff meeting in San Francisco next week, can I attend?

When Jeff walks through the door that night, we just look at each other stoically for a long time, the children chattering between us.

"Eventful day," he says.

Later that night I tell him, "I don't want to leave you now. And even though they'd be paying, I'd still have expenses. Plus, I'm still nursing. It's the stupidest time ever."

"You should go," he says. "It'll be good for your career. You'll see some friends. When are you going to have another chance to get away? It's not like we're going to have any big vacations soon."

The next day, as he's cleaning out his office, Jeff gets an email from a colleague at another publishing house. They have an opening for an on-site copywriter for children's books, of open-ended duration. Does he know anyone?

Jeff recently finished the second copywriting job of his life. He types back a reply: "I can start right away."

On Sunday, Jeff, Lucy, Bea, and I are most assuredly not

going to any open houses. We will not be going to any for a while. We can't get a home while our cobreadwinner is marginally employed.

We are going instead to Central Park. It teems with people, but it doesn't feel crowded; it feels like a party. We hoist our daughters on our shoulders so they can touch the panels as they wave in the wind.

"I guess it's about moving through one thing into another," he says.

"Works for me," I tell him.

Then I throw a breast pump in a suitcase and go to California. When I return, Jeff starts his new assignment. The pay is higher than at his old job and he loves the work, but he gets no benefits, no paid days off, no promises the job won't end tomorrow, and we count our blessings that he has it.

The days warm and lengthen, and I head down to Florida to see where a different family has forged a home. Debbie and I are visiting Jill in Miami.

In college, Jill, Debbie, and I shared a ramshackle trinity house in Philly, where we sat on furniture from their parents' rec rooms and complained about guys. Eventually, Debbie married her junior-year boyfriend. I found Jeff. For years we couldn't understand why Jill couldn't find the right man. Finally, she explained it was because there wasn't one. Then she married Michele.

Michele is a firefighter and a former lifeguard. Jill is a children's speech therapist. When I arrive at their condo, I see shelves lined with books on rescue techniques and learning strategies. Of all the couples I know, they're the one that's doing the most tangible good in the world.

They bought their place for $145,000 when they moved from Philly in 2003. It's moderately sized, in an unassuming complex. "We didn't buy too much house," Jill says modestly. "It's not worth it. I don't mind." It nevertheless has two bedrooms, two baths, and a deck that overlooks the canal. As I languidly paddle about the heated pool, I think, *These women have found a little bit of heaven.*

The next day we go to a beach party swarming with the tannest, most beautiful women I have ever seen, rubbing belly rings against each other to the strains of "Don't Cha." Debbie and I are attired in similarly dorky inner tubes and Lands' End tankinis.

"If anyone asks," she says, "you're with me."

After the party, Jill's friend Alice takes us over to see her new condo. The unit is still deep in the midst of renovation, so it's an explosion of tarp and plaster. But the building itself, with its cool and velvety lobby, has the luxuriant feel of an old hotel, and the swimming pool overlooks the ocean. It's devastatingly gorgeous.

In a few months, the dust will be gone and her belongings will be where exposed wires now hang down from the ceiling like tentacles. And that's what matters to her.

"More than equity, more than making an investment, your home is where you live," she says. "If you're not going to be happy when you come home at night, what the hell else does all that other stuff matter?"

I've never regretted any of my wanderings or exploits, any of the places I've temporarily nested. But if we'd stayed put and aimed our incomes toward a mortgage years ago, Jeff and I too would have a home, something besides canceled rent checks to Gina.

Someone in the building has written her last check to Gina.

Isabel is a warmhearted schoolteacher with a big smile and a Ph.D. in progress who lives in the studio apartment in the attic. We're crazy about Isabel—she babysits sometimes and brings Spanish food from her father's import business frequently. We cook dinners for her in our little kitchen, chopping vegetables on our cutting board propped over the sink, and we lend her books. She has lived in the building since well before we arrived, and would stay longer if she could.

But Gina's son Carlo needs a place to live. He lost his job a few months ago and has been living downstairs with Gina, her daughter Francesca, and her granddaughter Mikayla. The situation must be getting to everybody, because Gina gave Isabel word a few weeks ago she'd have to find somewhere else to live. There's no place affordable in the neighborhood anymore, especially for schoolteachers with student loans to pay off. Isabel knows, she's looked. She's found an apartment in the unassuming Riverdale section of the Bronx.

"I just wish this weren't coming at the end of the semester," she says. "It's hard to study and pack at the same time." I look at her things on the sidewalk, going into the U-Haul.

"We'll keep in touch," I say.

"You bet," she says.

And I never see her again.

I thought nobody ever left this building. Sheila and her mother have lived upstairs for thirty years. Sheila is a big blonde and her mom Marilyn is a big redhead. They conduct their conversations with Gina by yelling downstairs, and Gina replies in kind by yelling up.

Oblivious to modern security and the broken lock on our

building's front door, they leave their door open all day. A procession of friends and relations stream in and out, bearing cannoli and Parliaments. They have the nephews and cousins and uncles over for huge Italian feasts on the holidays; they have a big screaming fight about once a week, and they smoke around the clock. They have the vocal chords to prove it. They're also two of the kindest women I've ever known. They start their sentences with either, "Sit down. Can I get you anything?" or "I'm going out. Can I get you anything?" Sheila has, over the years, offered to take me to the hospital, sign for my packages, get me out of jury duty, and watch the kids in a pinch.

Gina, meanwhile, has never raised our rent. We, reciprocally, ask for as little as we can, calling only when the ceiling falls in or the water stops running. In the winter, we keep a space heater going during the day and wear extra sweaters. When the light in the hall goes out, we replace the bulb. We don't make waves, because Gina could get a lot more for our place than the $1,800 a month we're paying. Or she could decide to let Francesca and Mikayla have their own space. This apartment where we maintain the illusion of home is, after all, rightfully hers.

I once could convince myself we stayed here because we were waiting for something better to come along. Now I realize we're stuck in this erratically maintained rental because there's nowhere else to go. I want to leave this apartment. I don't want to be asked to go.

Jeff has been at the new publisher a few months, and he's happier than I've seen him in his career ever. Maybe now things are turning around for us, maybe now it's time.

"Don't freak out," I tell Jeff—an unpersuasive opening gambit if ever there was one—"but if things are holding steady at your work, we could think about looking around again."

"Sure," he cheerily replies. Man, he must really be liking that job.

There's only one nagging sticking point. In the last five years the median sales price of a home in New York City has appreciated 68 percent. In the half year we haven't been home-shopping, prices in Brooklyn have leaped in Superman-style bounds. We're never going to catch up.

THINK OUTSIDE
THE BOROUGH

My friend Jane inspects my pink-streaked limbs and furrows her brow. "A shrink would have a field day with that," she says.

"No shit," I answer. "I'm immolating myself to get out."

From the elbows to the wrists, my arms are marked with a series of flat, angry burn marks. Our kitchen is so small that our garbage can is propped practically right in front of the oven. If I'm cooking on the stovetop, I can wedge myself in. When I open it, though, to roast a chicken or bake a pie, I have to come at it sideways and curve toward my target. I frequently miss the mark, and wind up searing myself on the oven rack.

Jane's last straw was laundry. She doesn't even have it that bad—she has a laundry room in her building. "I'm tired of sharing my clothes with strangers," she declares today over pork sandwiches at Cubana Café as her baby naps in the stroller nearby. "I came downstairs one afternoon, and one of the neighbors had taken all my wet clothing out of the dryer so she could use it. That was it," says Jane. "The switch was flipped." She and her husband started arranging his job transfer that day. "You know what it's like," she tells me, reaching across the table to hold my scarred wrist. "I know you know."

Of course I do. Who cares about crime or terrorism? It's the dirty grocery stores next to the overpriced cheese shops, the lack of storage space in our apartment, the bored dads reading *Barron's* by the monkey bars that chip away at my fortitude. It's the catch-phrasey way realtors are now touting Boerum Hill, Cobble Hill, and Carroll Gardens as, cripes, BoCoCa. It's the constant class-consciousness, the haves so conspicuously amid the have-nots. It's the nonexistent middle ground.

New York City has the smallest middle-income population of any metropolitan area in the country. Only 16 percent of the city's families here have a "middle" income—one that comes within 20 percent of the city's median (just under $50,000 a year). In 1970, close to 25 percent of the city's population fit into that bracket, and half the city's neighborhoods classified as middle class. By 2000, only 30 percent of them did. The few remaining middle-class nabes, like ours, are at their tipping point, easy prey for either poverty or gentrification. My demographic is diminishing faster than the polar ice caps. We've become like Douglas Adams Golgafrinchams, castoffs in a city comprised of the very rich and important, and the very poor and useful.

But they're not going to get rid of us that easily. I can't help thinking we still need each other, our cities and our average folks and our phone sanitizers. I won't surrender the urban territory entirely to the Wall Street traders and models and tourists. Those people can have their share of the city; they're part of the glamour and the commerce of Gotham. I just want cities to belong to families and students and immigrants too. If all a place has inhabiting it are people so rich or too poor to go anywhere else, the whole social ecosystem goes out of whack.

Besides, why should we have to leave to get good schools or affordable housing? We build these cities, we work in them, in the hospitals and the police stations and the restaurants. It's not the millionaires who are its administrators and musicians and teachers. So who deserves Shakespeare in the Park or the Barneys warehouse sale or stellar takeout more than we do?

Yet when I walk down Smith Street one morning and see a handwritten scrap of paper stapled to a streetlamp that reads TOWNHOUSE FOR SALE. ASKING $1.2 MILLION as casually as if it were an offer for free kittens, I know something's got to give.

The *coup de grâce* comes a few days later. There's a woman in our neighborhood Jeff refers to as my nemesis. We're in similar fields and with offspring close in age, but we're barely acquainted. Yet I have never once run into her that she didn't seem in a terrible hurry to get away.

At first, I chalked up her avoidance of my friendly waves and noncommittal "How's it going?" salutations to maternal preoccupation. Eventually, I observed how she'd stiffen at my approach, as if I were going to hit on her, ask for twenty bucks, and tell her about Jesus. I concluded, perhaps unfairly, that it had to do with her far-more-pedigreed background and socially ambitious circle. I, after all, am the bedraggled, sweat-stained creature whose children never fail to pitch a magnificent fit whenever the woman comes within a block. Unrefined and unruly, that's us.

Normally, she's not enough of a presence in my grubby milieu to make a dent on my psyche. On this balmy evening, though, the girls and I have detoured on our way home from the playground, past the disaster co-op with the hideous floors that I fell in love with a year before.

I never told Jeff how I hadn't ever let it go. I masochistically staked it out, long after he had utterly dismissed it. I continued to go out of my way to walk past it as long as the FOR SALE sign was in the window, then when the dumpster parked in front and the debris of half a century began appearing on the curb, as workers with dust masks trailed in and out, until one day a pair of crisp curtains appeared in the window.

Now I know who they belong to. On this night, there she is, coming in with her children, key in hand, to that place I'd wanted to call my own. She spots me half a block away, and, trapped, gives a halfhearted wave. I smile placidly, as if it weren't the most shocking thing in the world that this awful woman is occupying my home. She scurries inside, and I immediately become acutely aware of how oppressive it truly is out. I plod the rest of the way home, pushing the stroller like it's a boulder, bring my children inside, and throw up.

Jeff and I have scoured from Brooklyn Heights to Sunset Park. We've pushed the limits of what realtors broadly refer to as Park Slope, from the noisy streets of Prospect Heights to the South Slope to an ever-extending border of the furthermost reaches of Windsor Terrace. We've been priced out of neighborhoods we wouldn't dream of inhabiting, places where the presence of gorgeous nineteenth-century brick homes is mitigated by the fact they currently serve as drug houses and squats.

You can think you have your life all mapped, but life will prove otherwise. My friend Kate is finding that out too. She recently bought her first home. It's not what she thought it would be.

I met Kate in a writing workshop several years ago. We bonded over after-class coffees and gossip. She was as proud of her Japanese heritage as she was of her small-town Midwestern upbringing; she threw the most elegant parties and rode a motorcycle. I thought she was outrageously cool.

Kate spent most of the past decade living in China with her boyfriend, a high-tech executive. Two years ago, in rapid succession, she got married, got pregnant, and watched her marriage crumble to dust. By the time her son was born, her husband Connor had already moved out.

She moved back to the States and stayed with her in-laws in Naples, Florida, while the divorce was going through. For months Kate coexisted uneasily with her quasi-family: her child's grandparents, the mother and father of the man who left her. She was eager for a place of her own.

Her husband, meanwhile, had been enjoying unprecedented career success. He returned home and bought a house on the canal for $3 million.

Because she had only worked sporadically during her years of travel and motherhood, Kate couldn't obtain a home alone. Before the divorce was final, Connor amicably agreed to cosign for a mortgage. She had to go through the ruse of being married to get away from it.

She is newly single; she has a toddler; she's never owned

property on her own before. She's pissed. "Connor got a house with a boat and a beautiful view and mango and orange trees," she tells me later, her anger still flaring. "All this was the life I was supposed to have. I couldn't handle him having a better place than me."

So she has just become the owner of a $600,000 home in one of Naples's gated communities.

"That's what you want in Florida where there are kids," she says, "and I knew if I had to sell it, I could, because it's a neighborhood attractive to families."

A laundry list of unexpected costs quickly starts to mount. "In Florida everybody has a pool," she explains, "so you have to hire a pool person. You have to have the landscape person. You're paying homeowners' fees to be in this gated community." She has done well in the settlement, but not that well. "I got a crumb of what he's worth," she concedes, "and I bought a house that was way too expensive. I was so out of it because of the divorce. I was totally uneducated."

She has done this, she knows, as a consolation for what she doesn't have. "I had looked at condos, but I wanted a house. If I were in a condo," she says, "I would have killed myself. I could at least think, I wouldn't be in this family community if I weren't really a family. The house is the ideal. It represents all the things I lost."

We've lost too. "Like it or not, Brooklyn's jumped the shark," Jeff admits one dreary Sunday as he looks up, hopelessly, from the real estate section, where a house on an edgy street with "some details" and needing "TLC" is listing for nearly $4 million. "It's like we're trying to make something fit that doesn't fit anymore."

So we've started looking again. This time will be different, though. This will be our summer to check out vistas beyond the 718 area code. We don't know where we'll wind up; we only feel increasingly aware we can't buy anything here.

In my zeal for a project, I research other areas that might fit our criteria—resolutely urban and diverse, but relatively safe and family-friendly. My mission takes next to no time, because the number of places that potentially fit the bill is close to nil. I narrow it down to three contenders: ethnic, accessible Jackson Heights, Queens; bustling, park-laden Inwood, Manhattan; and, God help us, familiar, lower-priced Jersey City, New Jersey.

While we're trying to just check out another side of the river, Quinn is moving across the country. She's a friend from the early dot-com era in San Francisco, where we rode out its headiest days together. Her body is a gallery of beautiful tattoos, and her mind runs in lines equally sharp and elegant. She met her husband on-line and worked with him at a Web community.

Then when the industry started going bust, they both lost their jobs, changed careers, and moved from the Bay Area to a town she refers to as "nowhere, outside San Diego." They bought a place, then it burned down in a California drought. They lived in a trailer, they had a baby. They had almost no child-care options. It was a bleak time, to say the least.

Now they've had it with their "something out of *Deliverance*" SoCal lifestyle, and her husband has a chance to run an East Coast branch of his father's business. They've bought in Harrisburg, Pennsylvania, another big, rapidly changing American city where, as Quinn puts it, "You can find an abandoned building that's a flophouse and go two blocks and find a farmer's market." When she tells her story later, she makes it sound both shockingly simple and wrenchingly difficult.

"We came for a weekend," she starts. "We had looked at places online and had a realtor take us to a bunch of houses. We found one we loved, but the inspector dinged it right away. Then as we were driving around, we saw a FOR SALE BY OWNER sign. We set up an appointment, saw it, and bid on it." Now she and her family live in a 2,200-square-foot 1900 brick house with a mix of "the best of all worlds, with charm and all new everything," a house that cost, in 2005, $165,000.

"We could have bought a crappier house for seventy-five thousand dollars," she continues. "We saw one we liked that was in the process of being rehabbed, but we would have had to wait five years for the neighborhood to turn around."

For seventy-five thousand dollars in Brooklyn, she could get about three years of private school tuition, or a down payment on a pretty nice two-bedroom condo by the waterfront.

Because their house was relatively inexpensive, they could buy it before they sold their California property. This turns out to be fortunate, because it will take them almost a year to unload it. "We were trying to sell land in the mountains," she says later. "We kept getting into fights with the county. They try to make rural land fit into suburban permits." She's happier now, settled in her new home and her new town. And, she says philosophically, "It's where we could afford."

As our family is still trying to figure out where we can afford, we're grappling with the possibility of starting over in the place it all began. We're heading to the city of my birth.

I think there are two kinds of people in the world. There are those who have warm, fond memories of the place they grew up, and who want to give their kids the same happy childhood they had. Mike and Debbie, who now live five minutes away from Debbie's parents, are like that.

Then there are the rest of us.

I have friends from all over, from Brazil and France and Japan, from small towns in Ohio and Oregon. The phrase "I had to get out of my hometown" is our communal mantra. The difference is that for me, the Promised Land was in my sightline.

When I was little, I could look out my bedroom window and see the tips of the Twin Towers. It was a short ride to them on the PATH train, but I can mark my childhood by the number of times I went into the luminous world across the river, to eat in a restaurant or go to a museum or shop at Macy's. When Jeff asked me once, early in our relationship, how far away from New York my hometown was, I told him the distance. I said it was light years.

People in other parts of the world think nothing of driving an hour just to buy groceries. In New York, if you live off your friends' nearest subway line, or anywhere that involves crossing a park, a body of water, or from east to west, you will never ever see them. The PATH train takes all of fifteen minutes to deposit a traveler from downtown Jersey City or Hoboken to the West Village, but New Jersey is a whole other state, so its mass transit system qualifies as foreign.

We make our outing to Jersey City on a cloudless summer Saturday. Riding under the river on the PATH today, it still seems like a journey to another world. The station even smells different than the subway, and its unique pungency assails me with a wave of memories: standing on the platform in intoxicating adolescent anticipation of hanging out in the West Village; crowding onto early-morning commutes into Midtown; kissing Jeff goodbye at the station after our early dates; and always, always, the bittersweet rumble of the train pulling me back to Jersey.

Though my old neighborhood, a working-class enclave of vinyl-sided houses and run-down discount stores, is starting to attract professional, priced-out Gothamites, I am dead set against even looking in Jersey City Heights. In my mind, if I move back to exactly where I clawed my way out of, I haven't gone anywhere in my life at all.

We are here to explore the neighborhoods of Paulus Hook and Hamilton Park. All I know of the area is the stalwart Newport Centre Mall, the self-proclaimed "premier shopping destination in Hudson County." It was built in the eighties, when the rapid gentrification of Hoboken appeared to bode well for its neighboring city. Instead the stock market crashed, the recession hit, and the mall and its adjacent high-rise condos sat largely dormant in the middle of a barren stretch of ugly land by the Holland Tunnel. In my early adulthood, I would occasionally nip over to the mall to shop at the Gap or catch a movie for less than the price of a Manhattan ticket. It was a fucking no-man's-land.

But 9/11 was good to Jersey City. Several lower Manhattan businesses relocated there while downtown rebuilt, and the housing crunch created an instant demand for residential space. Shiny high-rises rose up, boasting killer views of Manhattan and speedy access to it. Meanwhile, the nearby brick row houses, once a dilapidated stretch near a venerable park, were being snapped up by savvy investors and turning the neighborhood into a contender for the next hot Brooklyn knockoff. The irony of looking to my hometown for a glimmer of resemblance to my current one is not lost on me.

We emerge from the bowels of the station and I feel my chest tighten. I haven't been here in ages. I don't have any remaining family in Jersey City, and it's not as if there are a whole lot of other compelling reasons to go back.

A few years ago I took a day off to venture over to the old neighborhood. I was looking for what is flippantly referred to as closure. I'd never loved that house or the neighborhood, and I felt no sentimental longing to return and wax nostalgic over smog and graffiti. Yet something had compelled me to return, to walk some of my old routes again and shake myself free of the past.

That had been what I had done. I strolled down Central Avenue, virtually unchanged since my childhood, with its dusty card shops and bakeries full of plastic-tasting confections. I walked through the park that I'd walked through to school and to mass six days a week for years. I saw Auntie's house, its pink-flapped face now covered in nondescript beige siding. I walked down the block and up the back alley to peer into the yard of my very first home, the home I hadn't seen since I was seven.

It was significantly tinier than I'd remembered, but well tended. Auntie's rose of Sharon bush still bloomed in the back. I went around to the front and stood there, lost in my thoughts, until a young African-American man appeared on the porch, looking puzzled. "I used to live here," I said weakly, and headed back to Journal Square and the train that would take me home where I belonged.

Now I am in another part of town, with virtually no history, no baggage. Nevertheless, seeing the Manhattan skyline from the other side feels as familiar as an old blanket, and just as suffocating.

We head first to the freshly developed side of the neighborhood, where sleek office buildings, quaintly cookie-cutter townhouses, and skyscraping condos have risen up where once nothing had been. It is clean and eerily sterile.

"Is this it?" Jeff says as he stands like the Omega Man in front of a bank of high rises. Empty storefronts at the ground floor of brand-new buildings boast of the banks and day spas to come, but the essentials of affluence are already in place.

We eat lunch at a sushi restaurant and amble around afterward in the shadow of a new Starbucks. There's hardly another soul around. We sit at the riverfront gazing at the skyline while Bea, her chubby legs as unsteady as a fawn's, chases her sister around a meticulously spaced arrangement of saplings. This is my hometown, version 2.0. This is weird.

I'm not a snob. I pride myself on being the woman that Springsteen and Bon Jovi sing about, a broad from Sinatra country. We're not in some leafy Princeton suburb here. That's why it's a bit of a shocker to accept that condos on this waterfront are currently going for upwards of a million dollars. A million dollars. To live in Jersey City. I'd think seven figures would get you a tonier zip code than my old one. This neighborhood didn't even exist a few years ago. I look up at the looming high-rises, with their beautiful views of the city across the river but so little of substance right outside their doors. The waterfront is so clean and new it hasn't had time to get any scuff marks. At these prices, I doubt it ever will.

We didn't come to this side of the neighborhood to scope it as potential habitat, though; we just wanted to enjoy the view and see how the town has changed. It was a way of easing into the whole idea of Jersey, starting out in a spot we knew we wouldn't nest. Now it's time to move over to the grittier side of the street.

A few blocks away, the area around Hamilton Park is obviously decrepit and undeniably attractive. The main drag of the neighborhood is another riff of the same dull strip we've encountered time and again, in Kensington and the South Slope, a battered gauntlet of drugstores and Chinese takeouts. But off the main drag, it's an open-air lab study on neighborhoods in flux. There are neat brick houses with fresh paint and potted flowers in the windows next to crumbling buildings with broken banisters and piles of garbage. There are yuppieish looking fathers hoisting babies, and cold-eyed teenagers loudly swapping expletives.

We pass a house that I've made a note to check out. It's currently on the market for $375,000, a steal for a brick two-family. It's compact and well maintained, a place that would easily fetch seven figures in Brooklyn. A thirtyish blonde appears at the front door, and the timing seems too good to not speak up.

"Excuse me, is this your house?" I ask timidly. "I saw the ad on the Web and would like to talk to you about it."

Her mouth opens, but no sound comes out. She just stands there a bit, gaping.

"I live upstairs," she says finally. "They're selling? The house? Nobody told me."

"I probably have the wrong address," I bluster, knowing full well I don't.

She looks up and down the street. "Whatever," she shrugs. "You looking to move here?"

"We don't know," says Jeff. "What do you think of the area?"

She's not selling, so she's not invested in painting a rosy picture. "I've been here a year," she says laconically. "It's a pretty good block. There are other families," and here she waves a hand at my children, "like you." I'm not sure if this is some code for—sssshhhh—Caucasian or what, but I let it slide.

Then she gestures in the opposite direction and adds, "But a few of the people here have some *domestic issues*, and it gets loud. I had to call the cops at four this morning. Again. It's not me I'm worried about," she explains, "but when they start fighting in the street, I'm afraid for my car."

I'm instantly relieved. "We don't have a car," I say brightly, as if the screaming and the fighting are totally doable. "Thanks!"

We wend our way next toward Hamilton Park itself, a once-elegant square that still bears vestiges of former beauty. As long as I can remember, its reputation for drug traffic has been its claim to fame. On this Saturday afternoon, however, it's inviting, unthreatening, and full of people. Suddenly, out of nowhere, a passing cloud erupts into a rainstorm. Nobody has an umbrella, and everyone ducks under the gazebo to wait it out. We're young, old, light, dark, up and coming, and down and out. All we have in common is that for this one afternoon in our lives, we're all looking for shelter in the same place.

Jeff and I don't need to say very much on the way home. "Jersey City wasn't bad," I tell him.

He finishes my sentence, "But we didn't connect with it."

The city has indeed changed, but I guess I haven't. "No," I say, "we didn't." Against all evidence, we're still holding out for that magic rush of attraction, still believe that we'll know it when we find it. I'm so tired of waiting, though.

In August, we visit Mike and Debbie and their sons in Pennsylvania. There's a shock waiting when we arrive. Their charming center-hall colonial is much the same, but crowding next to and behind it, encompassing as much of the adjoining space as possible, are three recently built, great big houses. They've been selling for $600,000 and up.

Debbie says her new neighbors are friendly, which is a good thing when you're living right on top of someone.

The next day Jill's parents, who've known me since I dressed like a lost member of the Human League, want to throw us a little party. They live just a few miles away, so we gather at their home along with Deb's parents for fried chicken and some swimming in their pool. The kids splash around exuberantly while the elders sip their beers and make plans for their next vacation.

Debbie, Mike, and their kids are already talking with Deb's parents about going to Ireland next summer, with Jill and her wife Michele and Jill's parents and sister. They sit around together, easily talking of the future and travel and togetherness as if it were the most natural thing in the world. There seems to be no effort, no falseness to their familial ease. Neither of my parents is talking to me lately. I feel uneasy and uncomprehending. I spend the afternoon hiding in the pool.

I'm standing on the deck with my sopping limp hair and my hideous Lands' End bathing suit when Debbie's mother stops to put her hand on my shoulder. "Your girls are beautiful," she says with a warm smile. "I hope they turn out exactly like you."

"Ha!" I say self-consciously. "Two more women in the world! Like me! Ha-ha!" I repeat.

Debbie's mother looks me directly in the eyes. "Mary Beth," she says, "I'm paying you a compliment here. Take it." Then she walks away, striding confidently toward the bucket of chicken. I meanwhile am rooted to the spot. I can't move, because if I do, I'll run after her and beg her to put her hand back on my shoulder, to give me, for a little while longer, that feeling that I'm all right, and that it's all going to be okay.

A week later it's the hottest day in New York City in four years. Jeff and I have, uncharacteristically, been up late the night before, celebrating his birthday a mere six months after the fact. The girls have been awake since the first light of day, which today occurred somewhere around 5:30 A.M. The subway isn't running into Manhattan from our stop, so we have to detour more deeply into Brooklyn in order to catch an uptown train.

As I feel myself deliquescing onto the stifling subway platform, I glance at my mate, who looks completely fed up before we've even embarked. "Is this our stupidest plan yet?" I ask, while Lucy tugs on my skirt for attention.

"Probably," he sighs.

We have come to experience Inwood, a traditionally Irish area that has more recently become home to a booming Dominican population. If you ride in a yellow cab sometime, you will find pasted in the back a map that ends above Central Park. I've seen real estate ads describe Inwood as "twenty minutes from the city," a disarmingly modest claim for a Manhattan neighborhood. No wonder I've always assumed that after Harlem, the island is over and you're in the Bronx. In fact, the city stretches on for another hundred blocks or so.

Coincidentally, Inwood made the papers yesterday. There was yet another story in the *New York Times* on rising real estate prices, and which neighborhoods have appreciated most. The neighborhood at the top of Manhattan was at the top of the list, with housing prices that have escalated 295 percent in the last five years. Two hundred and ninety-five percent. It's funny, because that's a little out of sync with what's happened with our incomes. Yet even at this leapfrogging level of appreciation, it's still way cheaper than Brooklyn.

I have already taken my investigations as far as possible online. I've posted questions on a neighborhood discussion board and been greeted with an outpouring of helpful advice on everything from street safety to where to get coffee. I have methodically scoped out the school reports. I also went on urbanbaby.com, where the harpies were quick to dismiss the "glorified ghetto" where the locals are "pigs," the schools are "lousy," and the whole area only in Manhattan on a "technicality" anyway. The snob scorn only makes me intrigued. Even the locals refer to it as "upstate Manhattan."

Besides, Jennifer and Vincent's friends Clare and Paul say they're happy in Inwood. We've seen them a few times since that initial meeting on the playground last summer, and they're the sort of smart, pleasant family we'd want as our neighbors. They may be onto something.

So off we go, crossing our fingers that this destination hasn't yet turned into a commune for hedge fund managers. The train at least is air-conditioned, and Beatrice helpfully nods off as soon as we're in motion. Lucy, similarly lulled, rests her head on me, too droopy to complain of boredom.

We watch the stations roll by. Jay Street. Fourteenth Street. Columbus Circle. 125th Street. Dyckman. Sixty minutes later, we're at the 207th Street stop, the end of the A Line.

As we step outside onto Broadway, the heat hits us like a hair dryer on high, and we instantly resolve to make getting out of it our first priority. I look around, at the dollar stores with plastic bowls and boxes of soap splayed out on the sidewalk. There's a liquor store, and the EZ Credit pawn shop. Also, anachronistically, the eighteenth-century Dyckman Farmhouse, a white-gloved old lady right next door to a tattoo parlor.

For all the inherent grimness, there's a strange beauty here. The intersecting streets are dramatically steep and offer seemingly endless vistas. In the distance, I can see Fort Tryon and Inwood parks rising in the hills, walls of greenery adding drama to grit. The Cloisters, a reassembled hodgepodge of medieval abbeys, is here too. This place is special.

We had called Clare and Paul this morning to say we were coming, but they had plans for the day and couldn't get together. They did nonetheless recommend a place for lunch, so we drop into a casual bistro called the Garden Café. It's a cinch to find because there's nothing else remotely as upscale on this end of Broadway.

If you wanted to cast the *Inwood: It's for Everybody!* propaganda film, you could round up the clientele. A Latino family with a preschooler and baby are laughing with the grandparents. Two older African-American men are deep in conversation. A twentysomething couple who look like they rolled in from bed are gazing at each other. An elderly white woman sits primly alone. Here we are, representing the aging, uselessly liberal-arts-educated breeders.

We crowd around our precariously small table, and within minutes we're tucking into pancakes and grilled cheese sandwiches. I study Jeff as he takes in the jazz music in the background, the art on the walls. He's not shutting down. He's warming up. He looks relaxed.

I am less so. I look at all the families here, and feel a sudden pang for my own, or what's left of it anyway. I haven't seen my mother since Memorial Day, when we had all gathered at my in-laws' for a cookout.

It should have been a minor blowup. Lucy was acting out, pulling a toy out of her sister's hand, and I told her to be good. My mother had done the indulgent grandmother thing. "Lucy, tell your mother you *are* good," she'd said.

I'd retorted, "Can you not contradict me here, Mom?"

She looked cornered and embarrassed. She took a second to compose herself. Then she picked up her bag, said goodbye, and left.

I waited for both of us to cool down. Then I tried calling, but the phone rang and rang, as it does when Mother is avoiding someone. I remember whenever she'd have a spat with a relative or acquaintance, and the sight of her sitting in the kitchen; serenely listening to the insistent clamor of a phone she had no intention of picking up.

Eventually, Lucy got a card thanking her for "all the fun" they'd had together and signed "I love you best of all." Finally, a few weeks ago, she called, offhandedly asking what was new and how the girls were.

I decided that was good enough, and put Lucy on, to tell her about camp and swimming and her baby sister. When I got on the line again, Mother sounded sated. "You have no idea," she said, "how incredible it is to have grandchildren. You can't imagine the love. It's so different than what you feel for your own child."

Something about those words, coming after ignoring us all summer, incensed me.

"It's hard for me to believe you," I shot back, "when you don't show up for Halloweens and birthdays and you walk out of cookouts and don't call us for weeks on end." The line grew silent. "You can call anytime you want," I continued, "you can see us whenever you want, but I want you to understand this. I don't trust you."

"Okay," she answered dully. "Okay." She hasn't picked up her phone since. I'd assumed she'd never cut me off. I thought I was holding four aces—Jeff, the girls, and myself. But what good is a winning hand when your mom walks away from the table?

We're putting down our forks, and Beatrice is indicating she's revving up for her daily postlunch meltdown. Jeff tosses a few bills on the table and says, "I'll take her out. You and Lucy relax and settle up."

A few minutes later, we exit from the restaurant and Jeff is moving toward us, sweaty but smiling. There's a real estate office on the corner. "I was looking at the listings in the window," he tells me, "and one of the agents came out. She wants to talk."

We weren't prepared for this. "This is only an initial reconnaissance trip," I tell Lara, the soft-spoken Russian émigré behind the desk. We're upfront about our situation, our pitiful finances, but we're trying not to pull the entire sorry history out of our asses for her. She is unfazed. She picks up a set of keys and steers us out the door.

Lara leads us around the corner and through Isham Park. It's lush and full of stairs. As Jeff gamely hauls the stroller up a seemingly infinite number of landings, rivulets of perspiration pour off his forehead. Lara meanwhile tells us all about the area. Yes, she lives here herself. Yes, she likes the parks and the mix of people. Yes, she feels safe here. Yes, there are lots of families. I find myself nodding. Yes. Yes. Yes.

By the time we're at the top, I feel like we're in the clouds. Actually, it's an imposing array of co-ops known collectively as Park Terrace. The buildings are large and brick. The streets are leafy and shady. Broadway and the rest of the city sit below us on the right as we walk, and the river and Inwood Park peek through on the left.

We enter a tall apartment building, solidly built and riddled with Art Deco details. We get out even higher up in the air. Lara opens the door to the unit, and . . .

It's charming. I've seen so many eye-searingly ugly places over the last two years, I'm blinking in disbelief as I wander the rooms. It's not big, not as big as our place now, for sure, but it's a good size and intelligently laid out. And it's in a prewar building. The word "prewar" is to Manhattan what "brownstone" is to Brooklyn, the real estate equivalent of Viagra. Guaranteed arousal. I'm getting flushed. Is it hot in here, or is it me?

Actually, it is hot in here. It's 100 degrees outside and the windows are closed. I've been so swept up in the apartment—its sweet if run-down bathroom with a window (an unheard of luxury), its cleanly designed eat-in kitchen, the two real bedrooms with two real doors, the sunken living room and separate dining space, the unobscene $360,000 price tag—that I hadn't noticed we're all about to faint from heatstroke. It's a good thing that it's a sauna in here, or they might have to call the cops to get me to leave.

We walk out into the blazing sun and lazily saunter down to Seaman Avenue. There before us is Inwood Park. On the sprawling ball fields, ten Dominican teams are playing five games of baseball. Beyond them lies the only remaining bit of real forest in Manhattan, a revelation I find spectacularly romantic. A person can walk into it and forget this is the city in about three minutes.

We gaze together at the place where the island ends and the Hudson and the Harlem rivers meet at Spuyten Duyvil Creek. There is a salt marsh here. And there are caves, caves right here in New York City, where Native Americans—and homeless guys—used to live. A few blocks away there's an intersection of Seaman and Cumming, and the twelve-year-old boy inside me could move here for that alone.

I look over at Jeff and I know. It's happening. We're falling for this place. Jackson Heights will have to wait.

Every time we've ever looked farther out in Brooklyn, it's felt like a loser move. Why would anyone leave the prettiest, smartest part of town, after all, unless you couldn't cut it there? Traipsing through open houses out by cemeteries and expressways, I've always felt I was wearing my defeat on my sleeve.

But if we were to leave for Manhattan, even the godforsaken end of the island, that would be perfectly understandable. You can't argue with it. You found a place? Yes, it's in Manhattan. We're moving to Manhattan. How do you do? I live in Manhattan.

I feel like a schoolgirl doodling hearts in the margins of my notebook. Mrs. Mary Elizabeth Manhattan!

Obviously, I've never lived in Manhattan. I never felt any burning desire to do so either. I still can't for the life of me imagine us as upwardly mobile Upper West Siders, or artsy Tribeca millionaires, or postpunk gentrifying East Villagers. I can, however, all too easily see us here, kicking autumn leaves in the park and having perfect dinner parties in our small yet sensible prewar for our professorial neighbors, gossiping about the co-op board and commiserating that we have to go all the way to Fairway to get decent groceries.

There is a rock in that park that bears a plaque commemorating the spot where Peter Minuit allegedly purchased the island of Manhattan. This area might be favorable for real estate bargains. We just have to hope developers will start calling it SpyDy, and we're golden. We descend back into the subway. Glittery lettering on one side of the station proclaims "At the start . . . ," while across the way, another perspective is offered: "At long last . . ." We are starting here. At last.

SHE STOOPS
TO CONQUER

There's an upside-down bottle of baby aspirin on my desk. If there are no atheists in foxholes, imagine how few you'll find in housing bubbles. St. Joseph, the patron saint of homeowners, has of late become superhot. The Internet is lousy with "St. Joseph kits," cheapie boxes of Catholic tchotchkes designed to bring blessings to those looking for a real estate deal. While it's heartening to think that there are other people out there as desperate for a thaumaturgic intervention as I am, jeez, it's sad. Believing that a figurine and a prayer card are going to snag you something in this economy.

Still, a little insurance couldn't hurt. I'm named after the guy's wife, after all. That's got to be some kind of in. Our neighborhood is riddled with statues, mostly the Virgin and her Italian compagnos St. Anthony and St. Francis. One more figure would have plenty of company. Yet the prospect of going to catholicsupply.com and purchasing one of those kits, spending money and admitting even to myself that I am that superstitious, strikes me as too weird and backward. I am also creeped out by online promises that "We sell these by the case to Catholic realtors!" So I decide instead that I should smuggle Jesus' step-dad into my home in a more innocuous guise.

I go to the Rite Aid. There, in aisle three, I find my saint right there on the box. Even if he can't help me find a home, he does promise to help fight off a heart attack, which, given my stress level lately, is good news.

I don't hide St. Joseph in the medicine cabinet, though. I've read that you're supposed to bury him up on his head in your yard, because traditionally, history's most famous foster parent works mainly for those trying to unload a home. (Even among the saints, it's a seller's market.) Since at our rate I'll have grandchildren and a steel hip before I have a yard, I set the bottle upside down next to the computer, right near where I make my phone calls and compulsively read craigslist. It's all very feng shui by way of Catholic mysticism with a detour to Batshit Town. If my carpenter friend is doing any work, so far he's keeping it on the down low. But I'm hoping this pull we're feeling toward Inwood means he's bringing us closer to home.

The neighborhood has real promise for us, and Jeff and I are determined not to lose our momentum. When we go out to my in-laws' in Westchester the weekend after our initial recon, we see an opportunity for a more extensive survey of the area.

Jeff's parents want what most parents want for their children and grandchildren—to see them secure and happy. When he tells them, "We've been looking into moving further uptown. Maybe we could borrow the car to explore more?" they are psyched.

The folks are reasonably familiar with the neighborhood—it's not far from where my mother-in-law used to work. They're also pleased at having us potentially moving closer to them. It's a short drive from Westchester to northern Manhattan, and the possibility of less schlepping to see their granddaughters appeals.

"Take the Henry Hudson Drive," Jeff's mother says, tossing him the keys. "And when you're ready to make an offer on something, let us know how we can help."

I love having them on board for this. Loath as I may be to believe that God plays favorites, the two of them do seem especially blessed. Perhaps it's because they met in seminary that they live a life that can only be described as divinely serendipitous. They'll need a new boiler, but then an investment will come through that pays for it exactly. They found their splendid house during a casual drive through the neighborhood. Things seem to fall into place for them. I like to think that if they want something for us, they can work mojo that even St. Joseph can't.

Early on this late summer day, Jeff and I drive around, cruising and circling and doubling back around a fifty-block radius. I know there are dodgy side streets and noisy neighbors and crime here. I know that we're seeing it on Sunday morning when the potential weirdo element is low. Still, gosh, it sure is nice. We drive through Fort Tryon Park and squint as the sun reflects off the river. We pass a school and I wonder if this is where we'd send our kids. Would this be my grocery store? You, walking down Broadway with the paper, would you be my neighbor? Are you a psycho or a Ph.D.?

We can feel the season changing, the sun hanging a different way in the sky, the air not yet turning cool but promising to. How many ways can we mark time? I haven't seen my mother since Memorial Day, and it's been almost a year without a peep from my father. My babies have grown in leaps just from the start of summer. Bea has more teeth and Lucy has two loose ones. Life is changing and I want things to change for us. I want to be able to say "Let's go home" and mean it.

"It's different here," Jeff says, "but different good. I could do this." He's never said that before. It's not unconditional love, but there's potential.

We have a good enough feeling that a few days later Jeff meets with our accountant to get a clear sense of our finances and possible down-payment picture. I was supposed to be there too, but Lucy is home with an ear infection, so I'm doling out penicillin and running an all-day *Wizard of Oz* festival instead.

Our accountant makes me tense. When I'm around him, I feel judged for how little I make, ashamed that I'm not performing up to expectations. The last time I was in Laurence's office, he bluntly demanded to know why we weren't saving more. I told him it was because we weren't earning more, and I felt thoroughly mortified about it.

I'm cranky and edgy all morning; between the feverish child and the whole unceasing trying-to-uproot-our-lives thing. The ring of the telephone doesn't make it better.

"We may have to wait a while," Jeff says gently. "Laurence says that most co-ops will ask for twenty percent down, and we don't have much liquidity. He thinks we should try to put a thousand away every month for a year."

"Well that's bullshit," I whisper as Lucy naps, "because housing is going up faster than we can keep up. Does Laurence know that? Does he read the papers? What good does it do to save $12,000, even if we could, which we can't, when a place that's $350,000 now will be $70,000 more in a year? Did you tell him that interest rates are going up? Did you tell him to go blow himself?"

Jeff informs me he did not.

Then I can't talk anymore. "I have to go," I say, and I hang up and put my head in my hands for a long time.

It's not that I think buying a home will make us happy. I do believe it will make us more secure. And the thought of not having that security makes me sad. A home is not like wine. Its intrinsic merit does not increase with time. Its value is whatever the market says its value is. Part of the terror and the thrill of real estate is how much of it rests on the "bigger fool" theory. You buy at a certain price, then you find the sucker who will buy it from you at the most obscene markup. Then that person can turn around and do likewise. None of the houses in Carroll Gardens have changed radically in the last three years. The perception of their worth, however, has, to our utmost exclusion.

"It's never going to happen," I say dejectedly to Jeff that night as we curl on the couch. "We're giving Gina over $20,000 a year to pay off her mortgage. We're living in her house; we have to tell our kids they can't play in her front yard. I want our money to be going to us, to our home. We have nothing."

Finally, he speaks. "I guess I didn't think of it that way. I thought you save up and buy when you're ready. The bubble makes you rethink the idea. Everything's moving further and further away faster and faster. And we're watching it happen."

The next week, Sharon calls to say that she and her upstairs neighbor are combining forces for a stoop sale on Sunday. They are motivated by the fact that one of the city's biggest real estate firms is having an open house for the monstrous condo that's going up down her street, and, as Sharon explains, "I want to know which member of the Strokes is moving to the hood now."

When, four years ago, Jennifer and Vincent bought the three-family brownstone where Sharon also resides, they paid $780,000. A year and a half ago, developers bought the sixties-era eyesore a few doors away that was going for a million. Then the buyers razed it and for the past year have been banging and clunking around the clock to build something new.

It now vaguely resembles the other structures on the block, in that it's brown, and stone. The McLoft also has enormous windows and imposing silver columns. Henry James has collided with the *Enterprise*. Sharon and I stand outside with our jaws slack. "Who designed this thing?" she asks. "Mies van der Douche?"

Although the building, which now has a European name and a Web site, is still very much a plywood-enclosed husk, units are officially on the market. The top floor is going for $1.2 million. Most of the other units come in at the million-dollar mark, but a 675-square-foot one-bedroom can be snagged for half that price.

Sharon reasons that the foot traffic to gawk at the open house can only help her move her castoffs. She puts up a yellow sign on Court Street, halfway between the subway exit and the new building. "Here to buy a million-dollar condo?" it reads. "Perhaps you'd also like my used dishes."

The girls and I come over for the afternoon, toting some barely used books and baby clothes. We're presumably there to help, but really we're in it for the freak factor. The locals provide plenty, including the old guy who pokes hopefully at my cleavage and asks, "How much for that?" and the woman who tells us she makes wedding clothes. For dogs.

Our attention is mostly on the people wandering in and out of the building. "I don't know how long we are for this street," I sigh as an impossibly well-oiled couple in complementary shades of Gucci glances at us and promptly retreats back up the street. "We're white trash, and everybody sniffing around is Euro-trash."

Eventually, Vincent and Jennifer, bursting with curiosity, go over to check out the property. Their cover story is they want a pied-à-terre for his parents. They return a few minutes later with a thick folder of floor plans and prices. "They've already got offers on the one-bedrooms," Vincent says, dumbfounded. Then he adds in a confidential hush, "You know, Ava died." I'm drawing a blank who Ava is.

"The old lady across the street," he says, pointing to a massive structure twice the size of his brownstone. "You'd always see her outside sweeping."

"That's too bad," I say, pausing a beat before adding what I know he's waiting for. "So what's happening to the building?"

Jennifer is trying to be dignified. "A woman has *died*. Vincent, this isn't right to talk about."

He and I shrug. "I'd like to sell this place and buy that," he says, eyeing the building with the same appreciative twinkle that old guy had when he surveyed my rack.

I feel sorry for the old ladies of Carroll Gardens. The minute any of them gets a cough, you can almost hear our speculative palms rubbing together in anticipation. Last year the woman who ran the produce stand around the corner from us passed away. Josephina was built like a fireplug and always threw an extra plum in my bag, "for the *bambina*."

Besides the vegetable market, the building has a takeout coffee shop and apartments on the upper floors. After Josephina died, the building went on the market for over $2 million. On this sunny weekend day, it's still empty, but the FOR SALE sign is gone. In time, it will become a real estate office, with other $2 million properties listed in its windows.

We're doing a brisk stoop sale business when a khaki-wearing poor man's Jeremy Piven bounds energetically from the condo. He looks dismayed at our assortment of fondue sets and Pez dispensers, and the sight of Lucy in ornate sunglasses and me in a $5 pink wig.

"You should give me a cut," he huffs, "because I own that building."

We have spent the afternoon depreciating property values. Which, given how the last few years have gone, is rather satisfying. Sharon and I immediately begin making plans for the next open house. They involve radios, lawn chairs, and wine coolers. Sadly, our plans never come to fruition—almost all of the units go into contract the first weekend.

I have been feeling particularly class-conscious ever since Lucy started kindergarten a few weeks ago. Her school has lost its Title I funding this year because not enough underprivileged kids go there anymore. What's the side effect of an influx of wealth? Your school relies on parents to supply basics like paper towels and markers, and the music programs you had last year are no longer available.

In their stead, a stream of transplanted young Manhattanites and their helicopter moms whirr around the schoolyard. I watch newcomer parents converge in a clusterfuck of anxiety and fret that their Fletchers and Bathshebas aren't being challenged enough by the kindergarten curriculum. The moms who grew up in the neighborhood, meanwhile, clump together at the gate and smoke. Across the jungle gym, the two tribes eye each other suspiciously.

"If the parents want extra programs," says a reed-thin woman who swapped her Greenwich Village condo for a brownstone, "why don't they do what we did at Ajax's old school and have every family kick in two or three thousand dollars at the beginning of the year?"

I am standing outside at morning dropoff with several other demographically challenged parents. A strangled sound rises unbidden from the back of my throat.

"I mean, it would be voluntary," she hastens to add.

Later, I'm in the park with Geri and our spawn. I'm talking about the weekend and the million-dollar condos and the fancy new crop of families at the school. "What is happening here?" I ask. "I feel like we don't belong anymore."

She shakes her head in disgust.

"I have a friend who just bought a little condo on the other side of the Brooklyn-Queens Expressway in Carroll Gardens West," she says, "across the street from the place where they sell live poultry. The guy's a big shot, and you know what he sees when he looks out his window? Chickens running around with their heads cut off."

I'm nodding in sympathetic exasperation, and then I find myself off on a rant against rich people and their designer diaper bags that starts from my toes and gushes forth like a Vesuvius of resentment. "These douchebags come in and ruin everything. What is it?" I ask. "Why do they make me so crazy?"

Geri, with all the wisdom of the Dalai Lama if he'd grown up over a bar in New Jersey, fixes her gaze on me. "Do you know any rich people?" she asks.

I ponder this. I have a suspicion a few of our friends are wealthier than they let on, but actual, three-kids-in-private-school, wheeeee-I-have-so-much-money rich? "A few," I tell her.

"They're all assholes, right?" she replies. I have to admit she has a point there. "You don't get rich enough to buy a house in this neighborhood today unless you're fucking people. So when you see somebody pushing one of those $800 strollers, you know it was paid for by fucking people. That," she says with a flourish, "is what you hate." I'm sure there are very decent people with expensive strollers out there, but I find Geri extremely validating.

Our family is on the A train again, en route to an appointment with Lara the broker. "I want my borough back," Jeff says.

"That's why there are five," I tell him. "One of them's bound to pan out."

The last time we were here, Jeff and I zipped around in my mother-in-law's car on a sunny Sunday, listening to the radio and feeling good.

Today, I am less certain what we're doing here. Lara shows us two apartments in Park Terrace. Dark. Tiny kitchens. Grim. We know the drill. The pizza we have for lunch, however, is as good as anything I've ever tasted in Brooklyn. Afterward we take the girls to the park, where they run around giddy at the novelty of a simple expanse of grass.

"If we could have this," Jeff says, "it might be worth it. We could have picnics. We could build snowmen here in the winter." He is open to the possibility of a place with some wide-open spaces. I am ready to claim considerably less.

A few weeks ago, I bought a latch lock for the bathroom. It's simple enough to brace my feet at the door to keep out wandering offspring and distracted spouses if I'm sitting on the toilet, but an uninterrupted shower has, until this point, been impossible. One short trip to the True Value and four dollars later, and I have bought back some measure of my modesty.

The bathroom is, in other people's homes, a sanctuary. In ours it's an asylum. It's the room Jeff retreats to when he needs to do a freelance job and I'm dying to watch a movie. He hauls in a TV table, puts down the seat, and gets to work. It's where I go to break down when it all gets to be too much, this stupid window-less room with an unholy water stain on the ceiling and a ghastly brown linoleum floor. During the girls' birthday party, when I got a work-related call, I flipped on the vent and threw my weight against the door, bravely attempting conversation while fighting off a hoard of five-year-olds with full bladders thumping on the other side.

In 1950, the average American home was a modest 983 square feet. In 1970, it was 1,500 square feet. Today the figure looms close to 2,500 square feet. I don't need my own wing. When I cruise through New Jersey, I shudder at the houses on steroids dotting the landscape. I see circular drives and enormous windows, revealing the chandeliers and grand staircases you can see all the way from the turnpike. They don't look like homes. They look like somewhere to have a prom.

But the limits of our space, the blatant absence of privacy, they're the things that make me feel small and self-conscious when our friends with real homes come over. Beatrice sleeps in the crib an arm's length away from our bed. Lucy is a few feet farther away, in her 8-by-12 room with no door. We have four human beings vying for space in this tight yet wide-open unit.

"I feel like we live in the illegal alien apartment," I grouse to Elinor one afternoon while our daughters play Barbies in Lucy's bedroom. Elinor's apartment is even smaller than ours, but at least she has only one child. She and her husband are contemplating having another, but it's complicated.

"I have to ask myself questions I never would if we had a house," she whispers. "We have so little room now," she says, and a trace of anguish crosses her face.

We're ingenious IKEA addicts, and we're both prisoners of our good rental deals. We have plenty of company. There's the couple we know in a tiny one-bedroom who sleep on a futon while their twins share a loft bed. There's the family who moved the fridge to the living room to make space in their cramped kitchen. There's the divorcee who lives with her mother in the apartment she grew up in. In other cultures theses arrangements are what pass for efficiency and intimacy. This, by the way, is why we couldn't cut it in other cultures. We all stay because we can't afford to buy and we can't bear to leave. But who among us would mind not having to hide in the toilet for a few minutes of time alone?

On Monday, I call Roz, the mortgage broker. The last time

I spoke with her, I figured our search would be challenging but not interminable. I thought she'd be helping us put together a mortgage in a matter of months at the outside. That was two years ago.

I update her on our lives and savings and tell her, "We've zeroed in on a neighborhood we like. I think we'll be able to make an offer on something soon. Tell me what we need to do."

"I'd recommend doing a no-doc mortgage for you," she says. I have never heard the term before. No-doc I learn, is short for "no documentation."

If subprime loans are the catnip of borrowers with spotty credit, no-docs—and their slightly more forthcoming kindred, stated income low-docs—appeal to people with good credit but fluctuating income. That's why they're also called "Alt-A loans"— alternatives for people with A-level credit.

Lenders, as a general rule, want to do business with people who draw steady paychecks from a verifiable employer. Jeff has lost a job in the past year, freelanced, and is now working as an in-house independent contractor. I have a half-time job and I freelance. We're financially stable, but on paper, we appear all over the map.

Where there's money to be made, however, the lending industry will find a way. With the particular form of no-doc Roz recommends, we wouldn't have to provide the banks with the cruel minutiae of our careers, just our incomes and credit history. In exchange, we'd likely pay a slightly higher mortgage rate. It's a lending version of "don't ask, don't tell."

Historically, no-docs have been popular with the self-employed and the wealthy who prefer to keep the details of their financial dealings private. They've also become yet another fiscal back door for would-be flippers looking to gobble up property and turn it around fast. There's less information buyers have to reveal, ergo fewer hoops to jump through. Little wonder they're also referred to as liar loans.

I am choosing to look at this as the industry's way of giving those of us who aren't traditional nine-to-fivers a shot at home ownership. If we do it right, it'll all come down to what we have in the bank, which still isn't all that much. Roz also tells me we should aim to put 10 percent down. No less, because most co-ops and condos won't accept it, and no more, because we don't have it. The median first-time homeowner down payment this year, meanwhile, will be just 2 percent.

"I don't like to waste my time," Roz declares in a firm tone, and I can feel breakfast rising in my throat. Then she adds, "I don't think I'm wasting my time with you. I wouldn't talk to you if you couldn't do it. You can." I don't know what will come of any of this, but it occurs to me that this woman may have changed my life.

A few hundred miles away, Cynthia's life has changed too. Cynthia has hair the color of honey and a meltingly sweet southern accent to match. We met a decade ago in California, where her quiet, confident intelligence distinguished her within our aggressively hip, attention-seeking nouveau-media community. We continued the friendship when later we both moved to New York. Her heart, however, never strayed above the Mason-Dixon line. A few years ago, she moved to New Orleans.

I had been spending the weekend with the in-laws when the clouds gathered in the Gulf. Over the next several days, I watched, like everybody else across the world, the levees break, the decimated Crescent City. The human loss, the psychic toll, is incalculable. In the largest redevelopment project in United States history, however, the profit margin for developers is already being added up.

For the last five years, Cynthia has lived in a rental in the Garden District of New Orleans, in a big house with two other families. She had already safely evacuated when Katrina hit. Her house wasn't damaged, though it was looted. She has somewhere to return.

The city sustained damage to 80 percent of its housing. A lot of Cynthia's friends who've cleared out aren't coming back. For now, she's just driving. She stays in Oxford, Mississippi, she spends a few days staying with a group of friends; she goes home to Charlotte, North Carolina, for a while. She is putting, as she says it, "thousands of miles on my car." She doesn't know yet what her city will be when she gets back there, but she's determined to go home.

This morning I feel embarrassingly blessed to live where we do, to have a roof over my head at all. On this particular Saturday there could not be a better place on earth. The humidity has lifted and the sun has come out. My hair has even stopped frizzing. Buoyed by the splendidness of the weather, Jeff and I decide to take the girls to Coney Island.

Development is rising here in Coney Island, and Brighton Beach too. Here at the farthest reaches of Brooklyn, the last stops of sand and freak shows before the ocean, there are fancy condos going up. If even this is becoming another bastion for millionaires, maybe Manhattan really is the affordable alternative.

We eat hot dogs at Nathan's and ice-cream cones on the board-walk. Lucy and I ride the Wonder Wheel, and shriek in delight as the hundred-year-old contraption swings us precariously over the amusement park. I ride the Cyclone. It's scary and thrilling and too expensive and madly addictive. I do so appreciate an obvious metaphor.

I'm gazing at the ocean when Kate calls. She's in town from Florida with a friend and wants to know if I'm free to join them for dinner tonight.

Kate has had it with her life in Naples. She has thrown a fortune into renovating and upkeeping her $600,000 house, but couldn't bring herself to buy furniture, or pots and pans. She's still reeling from the devastating impact of Hurricanes Wilma and Rita. The real estate market is taking a huge hit, and she is finan-cially in way over her head. All she knows is that she badly wants out.

A month ago Kate was apartment-hunting here, but she real-ized she hated the thought of raising her son in New York City. Then she went to visit a friend outside of Burlington, Vermont. She's buying a house there instead.

A few hours after wiping ketchup off my shirt on a beach with its own sideshow, I'm at a swank Asian fusion hot spot in Chelsea. Kate is a food writer, so dinner is on her, which allows me to enjoy the tasting menu without fretting over blowing my kids' college funds on nut-crusted halibut. I swan in, and the waiter tells me, "They're drinking champagne and you have to catch up." Which I promptly do. We eat oysters adorned in foie gras and figs. I feel sparkling and sophisticated and terribly well connected as the kitchen keeps sending out caviar-flecked treats.

"I'm moving to a foodie town, a smart town," she says. "I think it'll be good."

Later, we wind up at the less-than-accurately-named Princess Lounge, a dive bar on a seedy alley in Chinatown, where we reminisce and pour out tales of our children's adorableness.

"It's good to see you," she says, and we say our good-byes on a crowded street.

"I'll visit when you're settled, I promise," I tell her, and give a parting hug.

The San Gennaro Festival is still in full swing in Little Italy, and though I should sensibly grab a cab or at least head toward the nearest train, I don't. Instead, I let myself melt into the throng, breathing in the reassuring din. It's Saturday night and the streets are teeming. People heading out, people heading home, people sitting and eating cannoli.

There's a scientific concept known as "intermittent reward." Given the choice of getting the same payoff consistently or taking the risk of losing for an occasional prize, however meager, our brains are wired to light up over the thrill of uncertainty. It's what makes us throw our money away on slot machines and scratches. It's what makes us obsess over the flame who snubs us for weeks and then shows up unexpected at the door. It's what makes us try and fail and try again. It's what happens when you ask yourself for the thousandth time why you put up with it all, and life answers with a night like this one.

I ride home in a packed subway car long after midnight. Later, as I drowsily head into the bathroom to brush my teeth, I look out the kitchen window. Across the yard I see the flickering blue light of a television screen through another window. When my daughters were newborns and I would find myself up at exotic hours, it comforted me to look outside and see taxis rolling by or to hear the distant drone of trucks. Whatever hour I'm awake, I'm never alone in my wakefulness. I flick off the light and head to bed. I'm lulled to sleep by the sounds outside, and I'm happy knowing that, even after I drift off, someone else will always still be up, taking care of the city for me.

ARE WE THERE YET?

We get off the subway at the A Line's penultimate stop, a dingy hole with brown water seeping onto the tracks, and find ourselves a bleak corner on the grungiest, grayest afternoon in weeks. Seeing Inwood today is like waking up next to someone for whom the morning light does no favors. The neighborhood I remembered as bright with promise now wears the grime of disillusionment.

Our mission is to look at two open houses: both the same street, but vastly different sides of it. The first place is on the eastern side of Broadway, where the condo we're headed toward is listed as a "real two-bedroom" for just $340,000. "It has a Jacuzzi," I mention to Jeff, although neither of us has ever expressed the slightest preference for aqua jets.

"Jacuzzi?" he repeats. "For 340? Christ, how shitty is this neighborhood?"

I check the address again, as we cross block after block farther away from the hubbub of Broadway, passing a corner where a steady throb of bass pulses out of a storefront emblazoned with a sign that reads CAR MUSIC.

The closer we get to the number on my paper, the more populated the street becomes. The scene is loud, louder than I'm used to even in car-honking, no-YOU-shut-up Brooklyn. We are in the neighborhood that leads the city in noise complaints. Inwood outdecibels even Times Square or the bar-dense Lower East Side. Maybe it is noisier, or maybe its newer denizens, perhaps staid nerds like me who work at home all day, just gripe more?

We walk past families sitting out, music pumping from radios propped in apartment windows. Adolescent boys are slouching in doorways; old ladies are keeping an eye on grandkids. I feel eyes on me.

I remember all the times I've seethed at the sight of a perfectly highlighted investment-banker wife cooing to her Sophia or Olivia at the park. All the times I've stewed watching an Oilily-bedecked toddler getting her ass dabbed with a Mustela baby wipe, like it's a problem for me if the nanny speaks to the kid only in French, or her diaper satchel costs more than a Birkin bag. All the times I've hated somebody for moving in on my turf. What's to stop anybody from seeing us the way I do the well-heeled arrivistes in my neighborhood? It's the same dynamic, just an economic tier lower.

We are the interlopers here. Over 76 percent of the residents of this neighborhood speak a language other than English at home.

Almost half the total population are immigrants. We are the ones the realtors try to seduce with tales of the yoga studio and the farmer's market, the ones who'd been discouraged from this side of Broadway when Lara warned, "European people don't live there."

I'm looking at my girls and praying nobody is resenting them just for being with me. A woman in a lawn chair seems to read my thoughts. She sighs extravagantly as we walk past. *"Qué linda,"* she says, smiling broadly at them and giving me a much-needed shot of welcoming reassurance.

As we pass crumbling buildings with misnomers like "Regal" or "Towers" on their façades, Jeff is growing more miserable with every step. We're getting closer and closer to the screech of the elevated subway. "Every time," he groans. "Every single time. We're either by the highway or a graveyard or the friggin' train tracks." Just shy of the entrance to the 1 train, we find our destination.

The realtor, a scrawny white guy who looks barely out of his acne years and wastes no time bragging about his place in Harlem, leads us into a darkened hallway and sheepishly points toward the stairs. "The elevator isn't working today," he says. This, we know, means the elevator doesn't work, period.

We carry the stroller up to the unit's door, where a crucifix still hangs. Inside, the confined quarters are illuminated with every one of the owner's light fixtures. This is what realtors do when a place gets no real light of its own. I amble over to the windows, crisscrossed in bars. The living room overlooks an airshaft. The bedrooms face an alley. On the one hand, there probably isn't much street noise. On the other hand, there's a high risk of existential despair. Maybe I'm making snap judgments about the place, but who has time for any other kind?

I peek in the bathroom, and there, in this very small, very dark place in this crummy building that boasts "low maintenance," is the Jacuzzi. It's strangely touching. Someone, at some point, decided that bars on the windows and broken elevators be damned, at least at the end of the day, the family could have bubbles.

I gaze at the mementos scattered around the apartment, the vinyl-covered couch, the pictures on the walls. My decorator friend Randall would have a heart attack over how artlessly unstaged the joint is. I pause at a photo of a smiling teenager, her arms slung around her parents on graduation day. I wonder where they are all going now. I hope it's somewhere better.

Back at the Garden Café, I am picking at a sandwich and feeding Beatrice her French fries and wiping up a slew of spills. "That was one depressing apartment," Jeff mutters.

I shrug back gloomily. I don't want to talk. I don't want to talk about the fact that my parents won't speak to me. I don't want to talk about what a bust today has been, an hour on the subway to see our one prospective neighborhood dimmed in this low-rent light. I want to crawl into this plate of fries and never come out.

Instead, we trek off to the second open house, this time on the western side of the street. It's around the corner from the A train, and while the street lacks the beauty of some of its park-hugging counterparts, it seems quiet and nondescript. The broker buzzes us in, and a blessedly functional elevator whisks us up several floors.

We enter, and my mood lifts so fast I might have to chase after it. The apartment is smaller than our current place, but we knew we were in for that. What excites me is the beautiful condition of the place, how airy yet cozy it feels, the spacious kitchen, the way the girls are running around the place like they already own it.

"I like this house!" giggles Lucy, as she and Bea dart through the kitchen into the living room. This is it. This is the one.

Sanjay, a pencil-thin dark-haired man of about forty in an impeccable suit, hands me a sheet with all the financials. They're asking $379,000, and the maintenance is a reasonable-for-Manhattan $625 a month.

The top of the page has the names of both the realtor and a local financial company. When I later check the mortgage broker's Web site, I note they offer mortgages for "100% financing, low or no documentation products, less than perfect or perfect credit!" How generous that they've included, as an afterthought, even prospective homeowners with unblemished credit.

What interests me most about the sheet Sanjay has handed me are the jarringly different numbers on it. There are six different mortgage scenarios, and accompanying figures for the alleged monthly output for each. There's the 3-year adjustable rate mortgage (ARM), the 5-year adjustable rate, and the 30-year fixed. Then there are the figures for the same three time spans with the "interest-only option." To sweeten the bottom line even further, the final line of each calculation reflects the "after tax deduction monthly payment." Not what we'd be paying out each month, mind you, but what it'd average out to after our taxes.

Sanjay points to the lowest number on the page. With a three-year adjustable-rate mortgage and an interest-only loan, our "after tax" monthly payment would be $1,700. We pay $1,800 in rent now. "You can see, it's very good," he says invitingly, as we lean our heads close together to look at the page. A few lines above, I can see that the pretax deduction estimate for a 30-year fixed is $2,680—almost a thousand dollars more a month.

Interest-only loans can be a great option for some people. We know couples who have them and are perfectly happy with them. It just depends on what you're looking for, where you see yourself and your money down the line, because they can also be a big pain in the ass.

IOs, as they are sometimes familiarly known, are not mortgages. They're loans tacked on to mortgages—usually shorter-term, adjustable-rate mortgages—because those tend to have lower interest rates. When you take out an IO, you leave the principal balance untouched and pay off only the interest for a preset amount of time. Because you're not paying off the price of the home itself yet, the monthly payment is lower. But if you choose to bulk up and pay off some of the principal as well, nobody's going to stop you. This is why IOs can work well for people whose incomes fluctuate. When they're flush, they can pay more, but the expected monthly expenditure is relatively low.

They can also work for people who don't intend to be in their homes very long and expect the value of the property to increase appreciably. A buyer could, in theory, get more home for less initial investment, then leverage it into bigger and better. There's a difference, however, between what people expect and what they wish. That, my friends, is the stuff that housing bubbles are made of.

Interest-only loans have skyrocketed in the last few years. In 2001 they accounted for less than 2 percent of all home loans. In 2005 they will tally closer to 30 percent, and in places like San

Francisco the figure will rise to a staggering near 70 percent.

Here's the rub: Mortgages are generally amortized so the borrower pays off some interest and some principal with each payment. With the schedule of most mortgages, the borrower is mostly paying interest for the first few years anyway. It's only over time, as the interest gets paid off, that the proportions start to shift toward the principal. In other words, when you're right out of the gate, the difference between an IO and a conventional mortgage may not be that significant. The total amount the buyer winds up paying over time with an IO, when all that interest is racked up, however, can be. Another thing, one not mentioned in the exclamation-point-riddled Web page of our potential lender, is that if in three or five or ten years when it's time to refinance, interest rates have risen and income and property value haven't kept up, borrowers can find themselves with much bigger payments than they bargained for.

It didn't get that bad for Carmen's sister Marie and her brother-in-law, but they did pay a price for their exuberance. A few years ago, armed with a budget of $600,000, they decided to build a home in the suburbs of Washington, D.C.

"They ended up with an almost million-dollar home," Carmen tells me later. "They went in, and these sales people were saying, 'You have to have the brick on the outside and the professional kitchen,' telling them, 'We'll get you this interest-only loan.' They had a team of people to suck them in, and they were intimidated and they thought, I want to be a part of that."

Then Marie lost her job. "They couldn't afford their dream house anymore," recalls Carmen. "They were paying five or six thousand a month, and she was pregnant with their second kid.

They had depleted every single bit of their savings and were living off credit cards."

"They had to get out," she continues. "It took them forever to sell the house. Then they moved and bought the world's smallest house, completely overpriced, for $555,000, because they just got frustrated."

Although they're getting back on their feet now, stories like Marie's give me the chills. If disaster can strike people in million-dollar homes, how vulnerable are the freelance-hustling, layoff-prone like us?

I'm unpersuaded by Sanjay's tear sheet of risky financial plans. The co-op itself, however, refuses to be argued with. The floors are shiny and the walls are freshly painted. A nearby empty lot means the view isn't much but the light is unobstructed.

"We should take this," I say to Jeff. The look on his face isn't the naked terror I've seen at other open houses, but it isn't the gob-smacked ardor I'd been hoping for either.

"It gets light, it's not a bad amount of space," he says. Then he looks around, and slowly nods.

I want to skip out the door. We've found our home, with a sureness we both felt without even having to say it. We head to the subway on the corner, and across the street I spy the Fine Fare. This will be our supermarket now. On the roof, two life-sized plastic steers are gazing out placidly. Between them, there is a plastic chicken of equal size. We are moving to Inwood, land of unspoiled forests and monstrously large poultry.

The next morning, as we're getting ourselves and our girls out the door, I say to Jeff, "We should call the realtor and make an offer today."

He looks at me as if I've asked for his bone marrow. "I don't know," he stammers. "I have to think about it more."

Good Christ, what is there to think about? We've been going around on this for two and a half years now. We've found a place. We can afford it. We need to get in there before somebody else does. Before the stars tumble out of alignment.

Jennifer sometimes tactfully observes that Jeff's "restraint" tempers my "enthusiasm." This may be Jennifer code for "two kinds of crazy." We need to, for once, be the same kind of crazy.

That night, when we both have had more time to ponder, we try to figure out our future.

"It's not pretty like here," Jeff says, "and I'm freaked out at the thought of leaving Brooklyn." I think he'd be content to stay in Brooklyn, flimsy roots and all, indefinitely. "Being in an affluent environment, I feel affluent," he admits. "Like I'm in the club. I feel more privileged here, like these are my peers."

I, on the other hand, feel more miserably like an interloper here all the time.

Then he adds, "I thought we could do better. I guess I have to let go of my will. If we want to own, we have to be realistic. We have to lower our standards."

I don't mind resetting my dreams, but it breaks my heart to see him not get his.

It helps a little that the Brooklyn we fell in love with is disappearing.

You expect that gentrification will bring the swank shops selling rock-and-roll onesies. You don't expect that they'll be bracketed by an outcropping of brand-new Domino's and Rite Aids. The pizza place on the corner, the brick-oven establishment with a statue of St. Joseph in the patio and cheese so good it should be designated a controlled substance, is going out of business.

The owners could continue to put their sweat and their muscle into churning out some of the borough's most sublime pies, or they could do exactly what they are doing—renting the space to Dunkin' Donuts and getting more money for less work. They will be two doors from the small, independent neighborhood dough-nuts-and-coffee place.

I'd heard the rumors bubbling up for days, heard the owner's sincere denials. "We're going to be here for a long, long time," he'd told me as I picked up a large half-plain, half-ham. When the buzz didn't die down, I walked in one day with the kids after school and said, "Come on, Mario. You know us. Tell us the truth."

He looked up at the ceiling for a moment for his reply. "It's true," he said quietly, quickly adding, "It'll be nice. You'll have doughnuts and coffee and everybody will hang out here just like they do now."

Lucy had burst into tears. I had lost my appetite. It wasn't long ago I was despairing that the borough was becoming a mall for millionaires. Some days when I look around, it just feels like a mall, period.

And while the real estate boom is crazy enough in Carroll Gardens, nowhere in Brooklyn has change come as dramatically as it has in Williamsburg. My friend Enrique lives there, in a great rental on a nice block. He discovered the neighborhood when he worked there in the early nineties, and moved there in 1996. He had lived in other neighborhoods, but, he explains later, "In Manhattan I lived in an eighty-unit building and didn't know my neighbors, and Park Slope was all strollers, lesbians, and Dalmatians." So he moved where the rent was cheap and a bunch of his friends had already migrated.

There were hookers on Kent Avenue, muggings at gunpoint "where the big condos on the waterfront are now," and meatpacking plants on North 6th, "with the guys hosing down the blood off the sidewalk in the morning, and the bars open at 6 A.M. packed with meatcutters covered in gore." It was also, he says, "the first small town I'd ever lived in that I didn't want to leave."

"It was somewhere you moved because there were people you knew," he says. "People would ring your bell because they saw your light on, and say 'Come on, we're going out,' and you would go." He went to warehouse parties where Yo La Tengo would be playing in the meat locker, and old-fashioned hootenannies where he'd hear "The Star-Spangled Banner" played on a blade of grass. "It was neighborhood, it was community," he says.

That sense of community didn't always flow omnidirectionally, however, especially toward a guy with Enrique's Middle Eastern features. "Years ago there was a bar that was old-school Polish," he remembers. "I went in one day for cigarettes and to use the bathroom, and they took one look at me and said, 'Get out, nigger.'" He pauses, the word crackling in the air between us.

"And as these two guys were throwing me out the door, they said, 'Don't ever come back,'" he continues. "I told them, 'The next time I come in here, I'm going to burn this motherfucker down.'"

Then came the hip little bars and funky shops and the condos. Flash forward ten years. Enrique's wife tells him her friend's band is playing at the same bar. "I told her what happened, and I said, 'I can't go. I made a solemn vow if I ever came back I'd burn that place to the ground.' She told me, 'Dude, those guys who did that to you are all dead. That bar has bands playing there now.' "

Enrique is the last guy on earth to get misty-eyed about the heroin trade or racist bullying, but he does admit, "I lament what I thought was a great neighborhood. Now it's bespoke suits and water taxis. It's like a joke. You see the kids with skateboards and their Brooklyn Industries T-shirts getting out of Jaguars with their parents, going in the real estate offices on the weekends. They say they're putting 80,000 new housing units up. That confuses me. There's one train into this neighborhood. How are they doing the sewage? The water? The parking? People see this as a destination now. For us, it was a place we created."

Now it's time for my family to create something too, somewhere else. I have to believe this co-op in Inwood is the compromise we can live with, and maybe the adventure too. "We like the place, and we like the neighborhood," I tell Jeff as we wash the dishes. "Did you notice the dishwasher? If we have a dishwasher, we're going to take all that time we spend now cleaning plates and utensils, and put it directly into fucking."

The next day we make an offer.

I'm still trying to understand how anyone ever manages to make this profound, life-changing financial leap. Our bookshelves have become lined with guides—*Home Buying for Idiots, Mortgages for Dummies, Real Estate for the Remedial*. We've been practicing what to say.

We bid low, because as Jennifer says, what have we got to lose? "We are interested in the property," I say smoothly to Sanjay. "We'd like to offer $345,000."

The realtor could not be more offended if we'd urinated on his mother. "This unit is already reduced," Sanjay insists. "You cannot offer that." Bitch-slapped back, we offer asking, and he says he will communicate to the seller.

Before we get an answer, we have to first fill out financial forms we can barely comprehend to prove our fiscal worthiness. It doesn't matter that we're attempting to get a no-doc mortgage; the co-op itself can request whatever financial information it desires before accepting our offer. We painstakingly tally up our every cent, our monthly expenditures, everything we have in the world on one page.

By Friday, Sanjay is saying that the seller is having another open house that weekend, but he'll call next week to let us know. I'm trying to go with the attitude that if it's meant to be, it will happen. Really, though, I'm ready to vomit blood.

On Tuesday, Sanjay calls. "Mary," he says, though I hate being called Mary and never identify myself that way, "Mary, I'm happy to tell you they've accepted your offer. I'm messengering the contract to your lawyer today. Please send it back with the down payment as soon as you get it." I'm dumbstruck.

"Guess what?" I say when I give Lucy the news. "It looks like we're going to move to that nice apartment!"

Lucy can detect mixed emotions like other kids can sniff out the nearest McDonald's. "No," she replies casually. "I don't want to."

"It's the place we saw the other week. You liked it," I offer by way of persuasion.

My kindergartner gives me a look that suggests she's weighing the possibility of litigation.

"Okay," she counters, "we can move. But only if I can keep going to school here."

I'm not sure I'm up for another negotiation this week. I'm also a little distracted. It's a school holiday, so there's no time to do anything. Also, my cousin Tara sent an email this morning asking if we're going to Massachusetts to our Aunt Peggy's funeral. That's how I learn she died.

It's so sudden and we have no time to make travel or child-care arrangements, so my family is grieving two hundred miles away while I'm stuck at home, feeling ill at ease.

When I call the house and speak to my cousin Cam, he tells me, "We talked to Phil this morning. He said your mother was out of town." She's not going to be there. If she called or sent flowers, she hasn't done so by the morning of the services. It's reassuring knowing it's not just me.

That night, Tara's mother, my aunt Bridget, calls. I think we both need somebody to talk to, somebody who remembers. The thing about having a family in which nobody speaks to each other is that you have nobody to reminisce with. So we chat a while about long-ago Thanksgivings and car trips, and then she says, startlingly, "You know what I think our problem is?"

"No," I tell her. "Please, help me out."

"We were never allowed to express anything when we were kids," she says. "We were never supposed to fight. So now, we don't talk."

All that stuff they never worked out eventually exploded in adulthood. Right on their own children. It's such a cliché, I could laugh.

"I suppose all families are like this," she muses.

"No, they're not," I answer, "that's what makes it so crappy."

Not that I'm a stranger to ignoring what's gnawing at me either. I've been prone to bouts of such severe abdominal pain recently that I find myself doubled over and crying just walking down the street.

The day after our offer on the co-op has been accepted, I'm staggering down Smith Street with the girls, too consumed with agony to take another step. I'd been to see the doctor two weeks before and had been dismissed with a "simple cyst." This doesn't feel simple. I call again.

"I'm doing surgery Friday," my doctor says, his tone as light-hearted as if he were hosting a barbeque. "Why don't you come to the hospital and we'll do a laparoscopy?"

My weekend plans now include bandages and morphine.

The next day Sanjay calls, looking for the contract and the down payment check. When I tell him I'm having an operation, he takes it as an affront. "You and your lawyer are not perform-ing your fiduciary responsibilities," he continues. I'm guessing he's talking out of his ass. Our lawyer got the contract a whopping one day ago.

"Mary," Sanjay says, "I am within my legal rights to request that paperwork."

Go nuts, Sanjay, I think, because before I can sign this contract, I have to deal with the death and the kids home from school and the family weirdness and the operation.

"I'll be in touch after my surgery," I say as I rummage through my purse for Extra-Strength Tylenol.

Because it's an outpatient procedure, I assume this will be a cakewalk. I've given birth, twice, after all, how hard can it be?

I plan to breeze in, have a little anesthesia and internal tidying up, and float home in a cab as if I'd come in from getting a haircut.

Jeff has a better idea. "Take a few days to stop being so damn stiff upper lip," he says. "Accept some help." So we call in the troops. Jeff will stay home to take care of the girls. Jennifer will come over with Harry to distract and entertain them. Jane and Sharon will do shifts with me at the hospital.

I'm so scared the night before I can barely touch my dinner. I try to call my mother, but no one picks up the phone. The next day at the hospital I sit in the waiting room with Jane and her baby for hours on end, trying to get someone to greenlight poking me open.

I go up to the front desk and say, "How's my paperwork?"

The woman at the desk looks at me blankly. "We can't get authorization because there's no record of you with Empire Blue Cross." I tell her my insurance isn't with Empire Blue Cross. She says, "Ah." This goes on every hour or so until nightfall.

Eventually, more than twenty-four hours since my last morsel of food or drink, a nurse beckons me into a back room to have my blood drawn. I watch a needle go into my arm, and fill with dark liquid. Then I stand up, sway, and burst into hysterical, inconsolable, attention-getting sobs.

You'd be amazed at what throwing a fit can do to speed things up. I am escorted to triage, where I change into a paper gown and cry nonstop in an uncontrollable gush. When I'm finally so weak with fatigue and hunger I haven't the energy to continue, Sharon takes the next shift. She swiftly takes charge, promptly demanding to a passing orderly, "Get this lady some happy gas, pronto."

As a fresh-faced intern obligingly jabs an IV into my arm, Sharon tells me about a book she's reading about souls and fate and all that. "The author says," she explains, "that before you're even born, you pick your parents. You choose the people who will lead you to your destiny."

"That's the most depressing thing I've ever heard," I mumble, "because if that's true my judgment was suspect before I was even conceived." Then I wobble into the operating room. The bastards didn't even give me a gurney ride.

If you pick your parents, that would mean I chose two people who resolutely did not choose me. It would mean that my presence is one big "Up yours," because what I need more than acceptance or even love is the satisfaction of just being here. That sounds about right.

I lay on a table while a gentleman I'd swear identified himself as Dr. Drunk prods me with head scratchers like "Who are you?" and "Why are you here today?" while I slip further and further away. I'm guessing he wants the short answers, but it's a good moment for me to think about it nonetheless.

If you choose your parents, it means my girls chose us. Lucy has said as much. She told me once that she and Beatrice knew each other before they were born, in heaven. "I got to be born first," she explained, "so I could tell you to have her." What if she was telling the truth? If our children chose us, how can we ever live up to everything they deserve?

Then I tumble into unconsciousness.

The next day I'm still coming off the morphine and tanked up on prescription painkillers. I awaken in the morning to stumble through the motions of getting my children's breakfast on the table before passing out for several hours. I awaken again, briefly, when Jeff brings the girls home from school. I smile weakly at them at dinnertime, too nauseated to eat, and go back to bed until the morning. I can safely write off "junkie supermodel" now from my list of potential careers.

At some point during my recuperative day, though, I am dimly aware of the phone ringing. It is Sanjay, calling to inquire why we haven't yet sent back the contract. He informs Jeff that because we've been so troublingly slow, the seller has left him with no choice but to hold another open house this weekend.

"That's understandable," Jeff answers frostily. "We'll call you next week when my wife is back on her feet."

I've been consumed with the desire for a home for so long. Now we have an accepted offer on a place, and it's rapidly slipping through our fingers. Maybe it's the elephant tranquilizers, but I can't give much of a damn. Sanjay's increasing impatience is setting off alarm bells, albeit through the cottony fog of surgical recovery. We are living in a seller's market, even this far uptown. And if he's trying to apply scare tactics, he's picked the wrong doped-up prospective homebuyer.

By Sunday the medication has worn off, the scars have stopped oozing, and I'm primed for another double shot of co-op shopping. Sanjay wants to see other people? You don't play a game like that with any woman who's ever been single in New York City. I can circulate too. I snap open the weekend real estate listings, and think, It's go time, pal.

In my pathological checking on craigslist and the *Times*, I have seen the name of one particular local realtor coming up again and again. Their firm has a particularly intriguing listing that's been running for several weeks now—a "nicely maintained" two-bedroom across the street from Inwood Park for $369,000. Though I don't know if we're a financially desirable enough family for this place or anything else the brokers have, I give them a call.

A woman named Karen answers the phone. I quickly spill out our particulars, especially the fact we can only put 10 percent down. This eliminates a good portion of co-ops, which usually require 20 percent or more. Still, she says she can show me the place by the park. "The light isn't bad, but I wouldn't describe it as bright," she says. She also has another listing that might work and invites me to come up.

I gaze out the window at our perfect brownstone street. It seems silly to be trying so hard to leave a place other people dream about living.

Elinor and Roger have figured out how to have the security of home ownership without forfeiting their sweet rental deal. They've bought a house in the Catskills with another couple. "We paid cash," Elinor says in amazement as we line up at school pickup on a blustery October day. No broker fees, no co-op costs, no battling it out with other bidders, no freaking out over interest rates—just a straightforward, drama-free transaction. They'd barely started looking.

"I found a 'For Sale by Owner' for eighty thousand dollars on craigslist," she says. "We drove up and that was that." It's a weekend and vacation place, it needs some fixing up, and it will be shared with its two other new owners. Still, I am agape at the ease of the process. "It's such a relief," Elinor says. "I feel like now we know we're going to stay here."

They've got it all now—the city apartment, the country home, and on a middle-class income that's close to ours. For the forty grand that is barely enough for a minimum down payment on a small apartment somewhere, they are full-fledged property owners. Maybe they have the right idea.

Mostly out of curiosity, I do cursory online exploration of properties upstate. It's not that a house in the Catskills wouldn't be charming, but it's not what we're looking for now. We don't even own a car. I have a phobia of bears. We're not looking to share with another family. I am also not as enamored of our apartment as Elinor's family is of theirs. I'm in fact often fed up with it.

Our lawyer, Sean, asks Sanjay to send over the last few co-op board meeting minutes, and we get a truncated version that looks like it has been blacked out by the CIA a few days later. "That's weird," Sean deadpans. I like Sean. We found him through a friend when we decided a year ago that we should be responsible adults and make a will. In the eighties, Sean had a punk band called General Tso What. It's not the only reason we chose him, but it's a plus.

All during the week, Jeff and I read over the co-op contract, and we don't sign it. Sanjay meanwhile keeps hectoring us to send it back, his tone more truculent with every voicemail. Every time he mentions due diligence or fiduciary responsibility, our feet get a little colder. "There is a rumor that prices are dropping," he says menacingly into the voicemail, "but certainly not for units in up-and-coming areas like Inwood."

I think the market's slowing down a little, but I
going to collapse.

He calls to say they're having another open house.

"You're free to offer the apartment to other bid
because it's my understanding that he is. I've watched
were selling their apartments entertain multiple offers
accepting one. As far as I can tell, everybody's a big tea
thing actually gets done.

Why then is Sanjay pushing so hard? Right now, o
losing this apartment is roughly on a par with our fear
that contract.

I arrive in Karen's real estate office on a gray Saturd
noon. Karen's got perfect long straight hair, and the open
someone who clearly didn't grow up in New York. She's
hands with a demure-looking woman with a baby carria
woman and her husband, it turns out, have lived in the ne
hood several years, and just purchased a new place to acc
date their growing family. "It's fantastic here," the woman t
before sailing out the door. "They'll have to drag me out."

Karen, meanwhile, takes her key chain and walks me t
Seaman Avenue. The first apartment is a little above our
range at $425,000, but the maintenance is so low it might wor
a good space, with a brand-new kitchen and two remarkably
proportioned bedrooms.

I'd given up on my daughters ever sleeping in anything
bunk beds, sharing anything but a broom closet. When I thin
them inhabiting a bedroom they could both truly fit into, I
myself welling up. But the building is one of those old U-sha
structures. The living room and kitchen look out across a d

courtyard and directly into another apartment. The layout is so tempting, but my gut is saying no.

We then walk a short distance. Karen is giving me all her experiences with the schools and the parks and sports and safety as we enter an Art Deco lobby. It's another prewar building, converted to a co-op in the eighties. Some of the old renters still live in it. Karen pushes an elevator button and leads me to the other apartment.

The photos on the Web site had shown it still full of furniture, but the place is bare now. I enter through the small dining nook and peer into a kitchen that is full of white cabinets and has Wedgwood blue walls. Next to it, there's a tiny bedroom that still has a child's shelf and baseball stickers on the walls. Deeper into the apartment, one stair delineates a sunken living room. Off the short hallway, there are a cheery master bedroom and old-fashioned-looking bathroom with a pedestal sink and black and yellow tiles. I look out the window, at the end of the island of Manhattan. If I stuck my hand out, it could be in the Bronx.

I take it in. Cute kitchen, sensible layout, a budget-friendly $369,000. The master bedroom and the smaller one are far enough apart, and they both have doors. Visions of marital pleasures, not to mention naps, dance through my head. It feels very small though; the light is not great, and the view across the street is of another apartment building. In the second bedroom, I whip out my tape measure. It stops short at the 7 ½'-by-11' marks. Yet there's something charming about the place, something that makes me feel this one has a good soul.

"The owners left the city when they had their second child,"

Karen tells me. That's what I've always heard people do. Yet there are more children living in New York City now than ever before. I do wonder where we will put all of them. And their Polly Pockets.

Karen and I go outside again, and this time I see what I had forgotten to pay attention to before, the thing that had intrigued me most in the ad. That big beautiful park is right there, with the marsh and the trees and the Spuyten Duyvil Creek, at my feet when I leave the building. It's spectacular.

I like Karen. I like her ten times more than Sanjay. "I'll call you this week," I tell her.

"That'd be great," she replies. "I'd like to meet the rest of your family. I'll let you know if anything new comes in too, because there's a bid in on this place, so I don't know how much longer it'll be on the market."

It's okay. It was pretty, but I guess it wasn't meant to be. It was, however, good enough to give us the confidence we need to do what comes next.

"Will you be mad or let down if the Sanjay apartment doesn't happen?" Jeff asks me that night.

"I thought it was the one, and it's hard that it's not," I tell him, "but it isn't, is it?"

"It's embarrassing to back out now," he says, "but it's the right thing to do. We can't take this place. All the signs are telling us to walk away."

On Monday, Sanjay calls Jeff. "The seller was expecting the contract by now," he says, his irritation oozing through the receiver. "Usually, the turnaround is less than a week, and now it's been two. I'm under pressure to have another open house this weekend. If we do, there's a good chance we'll get offers above the asking price. But if you can get the contract to me by 5 P.M. tomorrow, I'll call it off."

"We understand your position," Jeff replies, "and we've decided to withdraw the offer. We're sorry for the inconvenience."

"What?" Sanjay sputters, his fury undisguised. "Why?"

Jeff tells him, "Our reasons are private." He doesn't want a sales pitch; he doesn't want pressure. He just wants out.

The next day Sanjay's boss, Alfred, boss calls Jeff at work. "I need to know what happened," he says.

There is not much Jeff recoils from faster than an ambush. "It's a private decision," Jeff reiterates. "We don't want to give our reasons." Inwardly, he can rattle them off easily—the death in the family, the surgery, the growing concern that something here was not okay. We know we made an offer and backed out, which is a pain for the seller. We are not the kind of people who make a habit of disappointing others. But hey, they kept showing the place and we didn't sign anything.

"I'm within my legal rights to ask you to provide a reason," the broker sallies back. There's something so bullshit about this, so high-pressure and frantic. It's threatening and weird and Jeff has had enough.

"No," Jeff tells him, and he hangs up. This marks the only time my husband, who could pleasantly while away an evening with a telemarketer if given the opportunity, has ever hung up on anyone.

"That felt very freeing," he says when he calls me to tell me the latest. He sounds like a condemned man who just got a reprieve from the governor. He didn't really want to move anyway, I think.

We are back to having nothing for all our efforts, yet I too feel strangely like fate has handed me a gift in the form of an invasive, painful procedure. If I hadn't had surgery, we'd be fully in contract by now. We would, I feel certain, be making a huge mistake.

SHOULD I STAY
OR SHOULD I GO?

The next weekend our whole family schleps back up to Inwood to meet with Karen. She has four apartments in our price and needs range, and wastes no time hustling us off to them.

The first is a big, airy corner apartment in a large building on 204th Street, listed for $399,000. The bathroom is skuzzy, and the kitchen cabinets have been repainted so many times they refuse to shut. It's nevertheless light and lovely. It's also at a busy intersection across the street from a run-down–looking apartment building. I smell noise.

The next two apartments are across the street from each other, right on Isham Park, both also $399,000. The first has a heart-stopping view from the living room and no visible defects besides a semigaudy, overmarbleized bathroom.

The next is intriguing. "The price has been reduced," Karen tells us, which means it's been for sale a while. The small kitchen-dining area boasts a new stainless-steel fridge and dishwasher, but one significant shortcoming.

"Where's the stove?" asks Jeff. The owner, who Karen tells us "recently renovated," must have realized that you couldn't fit both a person and an oven in the narrow kitchen, and had gambled that no one would catch on about the missing appliance. We measure where the oven would go. We would have to stand to the side to open it. I envision more burns on my arms.

On the plus side, it has a half bath off what would be the girls' room. The apartment is in spectacular condition, except for the stove thing. It's impressive.

The last place Karen shows us is the little apartment by the park again. As we walk down toward it, Karen says nothing about what happened with the bid that was in on it when we last spoke. Clearly, the owners are still open to other offers.

Everyone is tired by now and dying for lunch, but we allow ourselves to be charmed. Jeff looks at the step leading into the sunken living room and dryly remarks, "Look. It even has a downstairs."

We're walking through empty rooms, as we have a hundred times before, and there, in the narrow passageway to the bedroom, a surge of anxiety wallops me. This is happening. We're going to do this. Not in the speculative, open-house-crashing way we have before, but the pack-up-your-boxes-and-change-your-phone-numbers-and-transfer-your-schools-and-say-goodbye-to-friends kind. I am at the level of panic Jeff's been riding for about two years now. Oh shit.

"Look at me and tell me," I say to Jeff. "Could you live here? Here? *This* one? Could you live anywhere other than where we are? Could you move?"

This man who has been hyperventilating all along doesn't hesitate.

"Yes," he says gently. "Wherever we go, it'll be because it's the right one. We'll put our things in it, and we'll hang up our pictures." He puts his arms around me while the girls shriek in the living room, bouncing off empty walls, and I feel safe and reassured. "Our family will be here, so it'll be our home." Something has changed in him. He's there at the place where it's okay.

We walk out with our girls and cross into the park. A few leaves are still clinging to the trees, glints of gold against the silvery shimmer of the river.

By Monday, Karen informs me there's an accepted offer on the second co-op we looked at, so we home in on the other three. Jeff says, "I'm drawn to that little one on Inwood Park. I got a good feeling in there." I agree, but then we start talking about the stoveless one, because what it doesn't have in appliances it makes up for in beauty and additional toilets. "I want to be open," says Jeff. "I want to move on."

During the week we hear from our Brooklyn realtor Vivian. "I have a two-bedroom co-op with exposed brick and a laundry room," she says. "They're asking $600,000." Two years ago she still had co-ops going for $400,000.

"Can't do it," I say.

I ask Karen if she can show us Stoveless Place, as we've been referring to it, one more time the following weekend. "We liked all of the places you showed us," I tell her, "but had a pull toward that one. Even though in my dreams I'd prefer a bigger kitchen, when I think about three females and one more bathroom, ahhhh."

We decide to bid $370,000, to give wiggle room for negotiation, and troop the family uptown once again.

A lot depends on what the maintenance would be, and the interest rate we can snag. We've been diligently saving and earmarking money we'd planned on using for the kids' college and our retirement, but there are still a lot of question marks. As Jeff says, "Just because we have almost $40,000 for a down payment doesn't necessarily mean we can buy a $400,000 place."

Two months ago Roz told me she could get us about a 6 percent rate, but I know other banks have been offering between 5.5 and 6.5. If we assume we're putting down $40,000 and have then a $360,000 loan, we could wind up paying around $2,275 a month, depending on the rate, plus maintenance. It's a huge leap from the $1,800 we're paying now in rent. If we're able to lock in a 6 percent interest and get the seller down to $370,000, our monthly mortgage goes down to closer to $2,000. Nice difference. The rate, that question mark, is a huge sticking point.

When we see the apartment again, we are enormously torn. I have spent the week mentally moving our furniture around within it, picturing the morning light coming through that bedroom window. Now, in addition to the AWOL stove, the main bathroom has been ripped up. The toilet is gone, as is, cryptically, the shower curtain rod. In their stead is a pile of rubble. "I can't imagine what could have happened," Karen says apologetically, "but I'm sure there's an explanation."

Our real estate spidey sense is tingling. We came to make an offer today though, and by God, that's what we're going to do.

Last night an early-December snow blanketed the city, and the girls are jumping out of their skin to go out and play in it. "I'll let you two talk alone," I say to Jeff and Karen, and take the girls outside.

Lucy is by my side as I push the stroller out the main doors, and I feel like I already live here. This neighborhood, glinting in the snow, is ours. We go into the park, tossing snowballs and making angels in the cold white powder. I look up at the building with the little blue kitchen and say a prayer we made the right choice.

Then I see Jeff charging through the drifts. "It's done," he says. "Now she's going to give the offer to seller, and we'll see."

We go to an Irish bar called the Piper's Kilt that promises "Irish nachos" and Guinness on tap to have a cautionary celebration, and we wait. And wait.

When I don't hear back from Karen by the middle of the week, I call her. She sounds guarded and reserved.

"The seller says she's dumbfounded at your offer," she tells me. Though Karen doesn't come out and say the woman's rejected it, there's not a lot of encouragement in her voice when she says "We'll let you know."

I then tell Jeff our seller's reaction.

"We bid well within reasonable range," he reminds me with the crisp authority of one who has skimmed a few Wikipedia entries on negotiation. "The apartment has been on the market awhile and the seller has already had to come down. We've seen comparable places for our price, and it sure looks like the market is slowing down there. So the seller was offended? That pisses *me* off."

I on the other hand am trying to be Zen, figuring if it's meant to be, it'll work out, and if it isn't, we should keep playing the field. I go on craigslist, as is my uncontrollable wont, to see if anything else interesting has come up for sale in the past few days.

There I find our stoveless, ripped-out-toilet apartment. Not once, but several times.

It's listed, interestingly, not at the asking price of $399,000, but at $11,000 more. It's listed again a few lines down for $15,000 more. All in all, a variety of classifieds for the same place, ranging from $410,000 to $450,000, are sprinkled across the page. They feature photographs—some of which, like the off-kilter shot of the overhead light fixtures, appear to have been taken from the floor. One of the listings even includes an offer to throw in a free plasma television at closing. The ads all include a cell-phone number. It's not Karen's. In a fit of pique at the insult of our bid, the seller must have determined to unload that apartment, and for more money, even if it killed her.

I forward the listings to Jeff. "I'd rather have a toilet than a plasma TV," he muses, "but that's just me. Especially because this whole situation's so full of shit."

Then I call Karen. "What's going on here?" I ask her. "Why is the apartment all over craigslist?"

She is taken aback. "I hardly ever look on craigslist," she says. "It's not us."

I hear her fingers drumming the keyboard while she checks the Web, and then I hear her take a deep breath. The seller was trying to broker a deal without her. "I'll have to call you back," she sighs, adding in an off-the-record sotto voce, "because my mother said if you can't say anything nice about someone, don't say anything."

My friend Andrew's reaction is more direct. "That is psychotic," he declares, cheerfuly aghast. I'm at a Christmas party in his apartment, a block from Ground Zero, numbing myself with nog.

He and Patricia have had their fill of New York and the emotional weight of their location, and are ready for something new. They have put their apartment up for sale and are moving to Los Angeles. They keep their home in ready-to-show condition at all times. They leave it every Sunday morning, with their dog and soon their infant son, for hours at a time while the broker conducts open houses. They will, over the next few months, have eight sets of people make offers, all of whom will gnaw at their time and resources and seven of whom will back out. They will eventually fetch $955,000. It's a good deal for this part of town now, largely because the building doesn't have a concierge, health club, or parking. It does, however, have a river view that wasn't there when Andrew bought it.

Over the days that follow Andrew's party, the craigslisting mania from our potential seller does not abate. It's the week before Christmas, and she appears increasingly eager to sell—and not to us—before the year is out. She's provided no counteroffer to us, no flat-out refusal either. We just want an answer.

My response to the suspense is to stand out in a blizzard with an Allen wrench, dismantling furniture.

There's a dearth of closet space in Inwood. I've always assumed that when and if we ever move, the garment rack that has graced our bedroom for the past several years will continue to be the sartorial eyesore of our décor.

On this weekend morning, things are looking up. For starters, the woman next door has died.

The news comes as a shock. Regina was older but not old, and she hadn't even appeared sick. As I peer out our window, I see family members cleaning out her abode. They're overseeing a procession of boxes into a moving truck while hauling other items unceremoniously onto the curb.

Among them are two white laminate wardrobes.

At what point is it not vulturelike to swoop in to take them? More importantly, how are we going to get them up the stairs? I spend hours silently contemplating strategy before I approach Jeff on the subject.

"They look like IKEA—how heavy can they be?" I say.

As the sky turns from heavy gray to ominous white, we park the girls in front of a Winnie the Pooh movie and head to the sidewalk. I am trying to affect an indifferent, these-are-my-wardrobes-and-I'm-just-bringing-them-in demeanor as I gingerly tip the first one toward my spouse. "Got your end?" I ask as he grunts under the strain of weight and wobbly workmanship.

I'm only slightly embarrassed when Gina's son Carlo and his girlfriend step out of the front door to witness the spectacle. Fortunately, no one has to explain the allure of the curbside freebie to a fellow Brooklynite.

"Good score," he observes appreciatively, and then unhesitatingly he hoists the side I've been weakly dragging, lending an extra set of arms to the enterprise. Large flakes are starting to flutter down on us.

A few Advil-inducing minutes later, there is a wardrobe in our bedroom, and Carlo and his girl are on their way to dinner. The snow is coming down more heavily now, and the streets are already coated.

"I guess we'll have to be happy with one," Jeff says.

"That's what you said about our children," I counter, rummaging through the toolbox. I bring the Allen wrench and a plastic bag out with me, and as the flakes descend and day turns to night, I take the wardrobe apart piece by cold, wet piece, bring it up the stairs, and reassemble it in our bedroom. Crappy old garment rack, your days are numbered. We may never get an apartment, but we have, at last, a place to hang our hats.

On the Thursday before Christmas, Karen finally calls back with a reply about the apartment. "The seller will accept her full asking price," she says, "and you would need to defer on receiving the paperwork for a month while she ties up some loose business ends. She says she's replaced the toilet but she won't put in a stove." Karen sounds mortified to communicate all of this.

Jeff and I have agreed that whatever she comes back with, we will say we need time to think. We read that in a book somewhere. "We'll let her know," I say. For the first time in this two-and-a-half-year process, I am relishing a moment of power.

A few days later we're clearing up what looks like an explosion in Santa's workshop in our living room.

"She's waiting for a higher offer, that's obvious," says Jeff.

"She might get one eventually," I say, "but not from us. I've been thinking, maybe we go back to the place on the park again. It's looking like our best option."

It's Christmas night, and Sharon and the in-laws have just left. When my mother begged off coming to Thanksgiving, we figured it was pointless to invite her for the yuletide.

I feel guilty about how not guilty I feel about this. It's easier than waiting for the next letdown or freeze-out. I can understand the sadness in my mother, the disappointment that her life didn't turn out the way she'd planned. I can imagine all the pain behind the silences and the staying away. But I can't fix any of it.

We're too preoccupied to give my family psychodramas much thought anyway. During the dead week between the holidays we mull over our reply to the seller. Jeff and I come up with several colorful endings to the sentence "You can tell her . . ." Most involve stuffing and shoving and sometimes ramming sideways.

By the time I call Karen, however, we've settled for "You can tell her no thank you."

Karen takes a pause to form her response. "Yeah, I think . . . uh, let's just say I don't blame you," she says finally.

"We'll call you in January," I tell her. "Jeff and I have been talking, and we'd like to look at that other place one more time."

Jeff and I have by now considered that the craigslist seller's mind may have been a few points below prime. There is nevertheless regret and frustration and some weeping over yet another loss.

"I feel more and more like we will never have it happen," I email Jeff. "I need to just friggin' let go."

Mostly though, we believe we've dodged yet another a $400,000 bullet. Which almost immediately sends another one whizzing right for us.

The last few days of the year are slipping into oblivion when we get an unexpected email from Sanjay addressed to "all interested parties on the listing." The place we backed away from in October is still up for grabs, and they are dropping the price to $340,000. "Consider this insider news," it reads. The email reeks of desperation; the fact Sanjay would even communicate with us after our bad ending last time makes it even more pungent.

Yet do we scoff and run away? Do we recall what a nagging pill Sanjay was to us two short months ago? Do we think, wow, why can't they unload this place—do the walls bleed or what? No, we don't. We are amply demoralized from the crazy craigslist experience to say foolish things to each other like "Maybe this is how it's meant to be," and "Wouldn't it be weird if after all the running around, we got the place we bid on before?" This is the kind of bonkers forgetfulness that leads people to hook up with bad exes and make unnecessary movie sequels.

On some level we do realize we might be deranged, so we decide to try to start the year with a semiclean slate, to put all our actions and major decision-making on hold a few weeks to recharge our batteries.

The holidays and the crushing last few home-searching months have wiped us out. After the girls' birthday in early January, Jeff is fulfilling the dream of a lifetime and visiting friends in Hawaii for a week. All I want is to see him come back happy. Only good things on the horizon.

We agree that when Jeff returns we'll look at our two remaining contenders again and make an offer on one. "They've both been listed for months," Jeff notes. "We'll do another trip with tape measure in hand after I return. I feel pretty safe deferring a decision till then."

"Have a good vacation," I tell him, "and take your mind off everything but having fun."

I sail through the first few days of solo parenting with aplomb. The girls are remarkably well behaved, and the weather isn't even too miserable. I spend my free moments obsessing about the two apartments. Both have their charms and drawbacks.

The Sanjay place is nearer the subway and the layout is sexily sensible. It's cheaper and has a lower maintenance. It's also on the less desirable block, lacks any detail or personality, and has remained on the market an eerily long time.

The other place is right on the park, is in good shape, and has an intangible allure I can only chalk up to its karma. It's also smaller, darker, and, at $369,000, would entail monthly payments much higher than we're straining to pay in rent now. What must it be like to have a lifestyle where you don't have to make excruciating trade-offs?

By midweek I decide I need to explore one more neighborhood to purge the indecision from my veins.

Washington Heights is the area of Manhattan directly below Inwood, slightly farther downtown. It's still mostly a lower-income immigrant neighborhood, but slightly more upscale, slightly more expensive than Inwood. Ronnie Spector, Julius Irving, and A-Rod all hail from this part of town, and the neighborhood featured prominently in the film *Mad Hot Ballroom*. More recently, gay men who've been priced out of Chelsea and Hell's Kitchen have begun flocking to it, which is good enough for a woman who gauges a neighborhood's desirability by the size of its homosexual population. So I call a local realtor and tell her I want to get to know the area better.

I meet up with Marina at a coffee shop on an icy morning when it's pissing rain. Unfazed by a deluge of biblical proportions, she leads me through the streets, shouting above honking horns and thunderclaps. She tells how she moved here from Israel twenty years ago, how this is her favorite neighborhood in the city. "We're getting more of *this* lately," she says, pointing warily toward a new, French restaurant, "but it's still a good place."

She charges down Fort Washington Avenue, the neighborhood's nicest commercial and residential street, until she stops at a gorgeous corner building. She shows me a unit that is $380,000 and much too small. The bunk bed wouldn't fit in the little bedroom. Our dining table and the couch couldn't both fit in the living room. I know it's too small, even in my most blue-sky interpretation of the space.

But what's outside the window is tempting. From there, the world looks like I've always imagined it would to someone living in a real New York City apartment. It's an experience I've never had firsthand. I've lived on the main drag of Hoboken; I dated Jeff in the East Village when it was frequently on fire; I've done seven years in brownstone Brooklyn. But this bustling street, these tall, Beaux-Arts apartment buildings? This feels strangely glamorous, quintessentially Manhattan. My alternate-reality self, the one without a mate and kids and all their tangential accessories, could prosper here.

Others who've lived here certainly have. We're a few blocks from where the man who controls every home-buying American family's fate grew up. This is Federal Reserve chairman Alan Greenspan's old neighborhood.

I have over the course of our home search developed a symbiotic relationship with the Fed. I can be innocuously walking down the street or pouring a cup of coffee, and suddenly I can practically feel the rates creeping up my spine.

While housing costs have been leveling off somewhat this year, interest has been steadily rising. On this January morning the Fed is not yet nearly finished with its dance of escalation. Ultimately, between 2004 and 2006, the Federal Reserve will raise interest rates overnight seventeen times. Seventeen times. Overnight. Banks will have no choice but to follow suit, in a torturous dance of escalation.

People who got their adjustable mortgages when rates were at all-time lows three and five years ago probably didn't gamble on that. A lot of them can't shoulder it either. Some of them were probably greedy. Many were probably ignorant. But almost all of them just wanted to have a house. When I think about this later, when I think about this ideal of the ownership society, how it's been peddled so seductively and is coming due so cruelly, when I think of so many people losing their homes and with them their dreams, it makes me very, very, very angry.

"This place is too small," I say, and Marina quickly ushers me to another apartment right downstairs.

The next place is an attention-getter straight out of a Woody Allen movie. I promptly fall for it—the big, cluttered eat-in kitchen with a dumbwaiter, the soaring windows looking out onto a widow's walk, and a hallway so big the owners are using it as an office. It's not even overpriced, but at $425,000, and with a steep maintenance of $1,200 a month, it's out of our range. "It's too expensive," I say, and out we go back into the rain.

"I have something else I can show you," Marina says. "It's going into contract for $400,000, but you might want to see it in case something similar comes up."

Looking at a place that's in contract is like going on a date with someone who's engaged. It's about 90 percent pointless and heartbreaking. And 10 percent dangerous fun.

She leads me to an old building near Columbia Presbyterian Hospital, a place I haven't been since my father's surgery. The hallway is ill-lit, run-down, and the-first-five-minutes-of-*Law-and-Order*-caliber bleak.

The apartment is in an awful condition I've seen before. The walls are peeling, the ceiling has a hole, and floors are warping. Yet all those horrors only add to its spooky allure. It's right on the river, and the windows offer a sweeping, unobstructed view of the stormy waters.

The space is so big—bigger than anything I'm used to looking at these days—that I have to remind myself it's a structural disaster to prevent doing something messed up like making a counteroffer.

Picture it. Looking out the window and seeing the river. Not just the skyline, not the bridge, but that unforgettable gray water against the gray sky. If I'd come here on a sunny day, with the light bouncing off the flaking plaster, I'd be less moved.

I don't want to get in a bidding war; I couldn't even if I did. The people who bought this place have a lot of work ahead of them. And they will have scored a beautiful deal. "Let me know if anything else like this comes up," I tell Marina as she ushers me outside.

Nothing fit today, nothing was right. It may be bad rainy-day luck, but I know for certain we won't live in Washington Heights. On the subway platform I am wet and bedraggled and tired and have wasted another morning of my life. There's a guy with a horn, and he's playing "Que Sera Sera." I break into a smile and hum softly to myself. Whatever will be, will be.

The next afternoon the girls and I drop by to visit Jane and the baby, bearing cookies from the Italian bakery. The heady scent of anise floats up from the box as we dive in. Powdered sugar is falling down my front.

"I've got news. Barry's transfer has finally come through," she says excitedly. "We're moving to Chicago in May." She'd been talking about leaving for months, but now it's here.

I think the move will be great for them, and I'm heartsick they're leaving. The irrational part of me tends to assume that even if we go away, everything else will remain the same. Our friends will still be there, immovable as the brownstones and the plaster Virgin Marys who guard them.

Old friends pack up, new people come in. Even the Virgins on the half shell are disappearing. That's life. Everywhere I've ever gone, I've found friends—at a class or in a work cubicle, down the hall or at the playground. Then they moved, or I moved, and sometimes we stayed in touch and sometimes we didn't. Some departures are harder than others, though, and this one is hard.

On Friday I am reflexively checking craigslist to see if there are any listings or open houses, because even though I'm already up to my emotional eyeballs in our two contenders, why limit myself?

I see one that catches my eye. The number of rooms isn't listed, but the price, $370,000, leads me to believe it's in our spatial ballpark.

The broker answers right away. She tells me it's listed as a "plus one," which is realtor speak for "almost nonexistent second bedroom." I tell her it's okay, we like the area, we want to buy, we have two young daughters who'd be sharing a room.

Then she does something that no realtor, of the 8 million or so I've encountered thus far, has ever done. She tries to talk me out of it.

"Then this place is the wrong size for you," she says. I speculate she's got a bigger place she's trying to pitch, angling to get us to spend more money. It's unlikely though, because the next words out of her mouth are, "You might handle a place that size for a short while, but not long. You put your kids in an apartment that tiny, they'll grow to hate you."

If she has other apartments up her sleeve, I never hear about them, because this is where I abruptly say "Thanks anyway" and end the conversation.

That bitch. Some total stranger on a phone, who doesn't even know me, who doesn't know my daughters, is going to tell me how my children are going to feel in ten or twenty years? What's best for them? What, because we're not moving to New Jersey our kids will hold a grudge? Goddam asshole.

Yet I can't shake her words from my head. They rattle around, bouncing off similar sentiments we've heard over the years, until they become a deafening, guilt-tripping chorus. "Children need a yard," my mother had once tsk-tsked me. "There are no good public schools in the city," a fellow parent had offered before evacuating for the burbs.

It's possible that not giving our kids a yard doesn't automatically make us selfish, bad parents. It also doesn't mean we have any semblance of superiority about living in the city. My God, look at us. We're not exactly riding high on our trendiness.

I'll show them all. I'll get an apartment—an itsy-bitsy one, and it'll be great. My fingers fly across the phone receiver, and I've got Karen on the other end in an instant.

"You know my husband's been out of town," I begin. "He gets back Saturday and we want to look at the apartment on the park again. We don't want to wait, we want to get this all wrapped up soon."

Karen does not, to my surprise, suggest times to get together Sunday. Instead she says, "About that. They've gone with another broker. We don't have the listing anymore. I think the price may be going up."

In the cartoon version of this scene, this is where the little apartment sprouts wings and flaps away until it, along with the last remaining shards of my optimism, evaporates with a decisive poof.

Karen then tells me the place on 204th is still available if we're interested.

"I can't make an offer on our fourth choice," I say. "I'm sorry."

"We'll keep working," she replies, "and you and your lovely family will find a home here." I hang up and miss Jeff so badly I don't see how I'll possibly survive the twenty-four hours until he gets home.

I scour the *Times* online listings. It doesn't take long to see it. An open house, Sunday, for the apartment. Our apartment. It's $410,000—$40,000 more than the old asking price.

The co-op has been on the block since the owners moved in August, and they have been carrying both mortgages all this time. When I think back now on all my dealings with Karen, I suddenly realize her laid-back style, the one that's been such a refreshing change for us, is probably less appealing to the sellers. The place has been listed on her firm's Web site, but there have been few open houses, no craigslistings. The sellers must be going nuts, especially because in the last few months something has changed.

Existing home sales are declining. Prices are still going up—

but not as much. Between 2004 and 2005, the median cost of a single-family home in the United States rose 12.2 percent, a twenty-six-year high. From 2005 to 2006 it inched up only 1.3 percent. It's the lowest gain since 1968.

It's easy to look for signs and portents; it's easy to spin. You can find somebody to say the bubble is bursting. You can call it a related blip. You can find markets in places like Arizona and Florida where housing is depreciating at a scary clip.

You can as easily find someone to say that the bottom line is that housing costs are still rising. You can say that a co-op is not a single-family house, and this is New York City, its own special wonderland of insanity. The owners of that little apartment on the park will still no doubt fetch more than if they'd sold last year. But as far as escalating costs go, they picked a lull in the market, when appreciation has slowed down to non-off-the-chart levels.

That's why they've switched to one of the city's biggest firms, the same realtor that sells luxury condos on the Lower East Side and brownstones on the Upper West. They're making a bold, increasingly common gambit—taking a property that isn't selling, and instead of marking it down, polishing it off and raising the price. Makes it instantly appear more desirable.

It's the smartest thing the sellers could do. I'm, however, not the seller. I'm so blindsided, so incensed at this shitty turn of events, I don't know what to do.

Jeff is in a parking lot at Waimei Bay when I reach him. I am now a full-on sobbing wreck, burbling incoherently and basically ending his vacation. "Then this bitch told me I was a bad mother and then the price on the other place went up and oh my God oh my God."

"We'll figure it out," he says soothingly. "There's a plan for us. Our home is out there, and we will find it. It will happen."

He may be just saying what I want to hear, but I am so grateful anyway.

Two days later I am squiring the girls off to back-to-back kid birthday parties. Jeff, meanwhile, is back from his trip and doing the open houses at our two apartments. At the first, he meets up with Sanjay again, who scrutinizes him with disdain.

"After the way things ended last fall," he says, "I doubt the seller would be interested in an offer from you. We've had a lot of people here today and we're confident of receiving multiple offers." He then sidles up to an intimidated-looking young couple, brandishing his financial sheet.

Jeff walks around the apartment one last time. Another round with these clowns, and this time with even more bad feelings? He doubts he's interested either.

Jeff quietly walks over to the couple and whispers, "You should know this apartment has been available for a while. I really think you can get less than they're asking if you like it." Then he slips out the door.

At the other apartment he sees Oscar, the broker from the new, fancy agency. He recognizes him from an open house on Seaman Avenue last fall. A steady stream of prospective buyers troop in and out of the apartment. The rebranding must be working. As people come and go, Jeff stays, quietly looking out the windows, opening and closing doors.

When we meet on the couch that night, crashing in mutual tiredness, he is more sure than I've ever seen him since this, our long realty-based nightmare, commenced.

"How was Sanjay?" I ask.

He shakes his head with rueful amusement. "Mr. Pressure was doing his usual, 'We had a lot of people at the open house, and we think we'll get offers blah-blah-blah.'" he says.

"Maybe they will," I say, "because I didn't think that if we waited to bid on the other place they'd yank up the price, or that the crazy craigslist lady would go nutso on us, so what do I know about anything? Tell me what you think."

"I'm not drawn to Sanjay's apartment," he answers. "Seeing it again, I felt fine letting go of it. I don't want to live in a place because we feel like we don't have any other options. Shouldn't we want the home we move to?"

He doesn't wait for a reply. "I want the place on the park. I have a good feeling about it. I love the location. It would be like we were giving the girls a great big yard. It's kind of like Carroll Gardens—a slower pace, but still the city. That's where I see us."

I am simultaneously thrilled that he is saying with certainty—nay, near enthusiasm—that we could live anywhere else, and ready to claw my flesh off over the fact that this is the one the furthest out of reach.

"I've been thinking," I tell him. "Maybe that's a bad plan. We can't afford it at the new price. We need to get real here."

He's jet-lagged and exasperated. "You asked me to go, you asked what I thought. This is what I think, this is what I want. And I'm not clear if you even want the Sanjay place, or you're just tired of looking."

His words hit home. What's more, he has a plan.

"We don't acknowledge the price increase," he continues, "and we bid on the lower listing. We know how long it's been on the market, and how eager the owners must be to sell. We bid $350,000. What have we got to lose? Maybe we can be financially realistic *and* get the place we want."

I think this is the most idiotic thing he's said since he suggested the name Stanley if we had a boy. What I say is, "Great. Tomorrow you make the call. But if it doesn't work," I add, and I really don't think it will, "then I want to stop. We can't keep doing this. It's not happening."

"It's happening," he tells me as his arms enfold around my shoulders. "It's just not happening the way we thought."

"No," I say, pushing him away, waving the white flag over the ruins of the last few demoralizing years. Buying a home is like getting a job or finding a soul mate or conceiving a baby. It's a piece of cake. Except when it's impossible. "People want things and can't make it happen all the time. Wanting isn't enough. People want to have babies or to get married, or whatever, and it doesn't always work out. Life's not like that. I think we're not cut out to have a home."

Maybe trying to buy a home in a millionaire city on our middle-class budget was what we refer to in the online community as a "tinyass first-world problem." It's the one fate has handed us, though. We're living where our lives and destinies have sent us. We're just trying to pay our bills and give our kids an appropriate place to grow up. We have less than some and more than most. We are fortunate. I am wrecked.

The next day Jeff makes the call. "Tell the sellers we know the apartment was available for a different price last week. We don't want to insult them; we just want to make it explicit that we are bidding based on the old price."

He also sends over a financial statement, which, thanks to our two prior broken-down deals, was a snap to put together. The oddest thing about the strategy is the way it changes our personalities. Jeff, the guy who couldn't be less inclined to leave our apartment if he were soldered to it, blurts via email, "I have no idea what life's plan is, but I'm attaching much self-will and fear to getting the place."

I, usually all hand-wringing and nerves and weeping, view the enterprise with the pleasant detachment that one only gets from an exercise in futility. I'm going to ask Gina if we can paint the living room. I'm going to figure out how to put up a door between the girls' room and ours. I'm not going to look at school reports or mortgage rates anymore. I'm staying right here. Quitting is for pussies. I quit.

On Tuesday afternoon my phone rings. It's Oscar. "We conveyed your offer to the seller," he says, "and he's willing to come down to $390,000."

I find this intoxicatingly amusing. "It was $370,000 a week ago, so no thanks," I tell him.

Within an hour an email arrives, addressed to Jeff and me. It reads, "I feel confident that if you can come close to the price you originally saw the apartment at, we can do this deal."

Jeff and I exchange a flurry of communications, then we cavalierly reply. "We'd like to offer $360,000 as a middle point between the seller's original asking price of $369,000 and our offer of $350,000," the email we send back reads. "If this is acceptable, we're ready to move forward today."

It's a fortune. It's a steal.

By sundown we get another email. "Congratulations," it reads.

"We have a deal. They've accepted the offer. They're sending over the contract."

Dammit, playing hard to get does work. We have an apartment.

I can let myself feel this now—I am smitten with this little apartment with the blue kitchen and the white cabinets and the park. Maybe it's a case of wanting what you've got, of settling. I believe however it's something else. It doesn't matter that it wasn't a thunderbolt, love-at-first-sight experience at all. It was that when we had looked at dozens of apartments and houses over three years and four area codes, this was the one that would buy us the most bliss for our buck. I know in my bones, as soon as our offer is accepted, I don't want to live anywhere else on earth.

THE
RATE STUFF

"Do you know who you married?" I inquire into the phone.

Jeff considers his reply. "Is this a trap?"

"You married," I say, dodging the question, "the woman who got the last two six-packs at the Key Food."

We have had a stormy relationship, the Key Food and I. It's the darkest, most cramped, gruesomely dirty supermarket I have ever seen. It's where I've purchased oatmeal that expired a year prior and played "What's that smell?" in the meat aisle. It is, however, seductively convenient. For a family that's always a few short squares of Charmin away from disaster, that can't make a meal without running out halfway for more butter or broth, a nearby supermarket is a nonnegotiable. The Key is also cheap, which, given our lifestyle, is also nonnegotiable.

Now it's closing, to be replaced by yet another chain drugstore. Carroll Gardens is lately becoming infested with banks and pharmacies. You'd think with this many people flooding in, we'd need more places to buy fuzzy bread and tangy milk. Instead, we keep getting more grooming products and crisp twenties.

If the Key was dismal in its salad days, it's David Lynch territory now. Each day, the managers are marking the increasingly dubious remaining merchandise down lower, determined not to shut the doors until every last questionable item is rung up. The aisles are rapidly emptying and lights are burning out and not being replaced. All that's left to do is shop for off-brands in the dark. Today the final pair of six-packs on the shelf, a Costa Rican brand called Olé, went for $3 each. I feel smug out of all proportion.

My brain hasn't stopped whirring since our offer on the co-op was accepted. I've morphed into Buyerzilla, obsessing over every detail of the purchase, the move, the inhabiting. A few days ago we sent off the contract, along with the largest check, by far, either of us ever dared to write. Jeff had done the honors of signing it.

Now we have to secure the mortgage, pass the co-op board, and close over the next few weeks—transactions that all inspire a raft of form-filling anxiety. In the meantime, until the contract is signed, Oscar and his partner are going to keep holding open houses, which means that anyone who wanders in off the street willing to meet the asking price, or even slightly raises our paltry offer, can punt us out of the running and render all this work for naught. Hence, the edge-softening brews of Central America.

That night, Jeff and I sit down with a stack of forms that measures precisely six and a half inches—the mortgage application, the co-op board package, and materials from the mortgage broker. We

gather up our tax statements, 401k and IRA statements, and
statements, aware that several people will soon be scrutinizin
every ATM withdrawal, our every debit purchase at Marshall
figure out what we need to copy, file, and staple. We get vei
tion of our good tenantship and financial responsibility from
current and most recent prior landlord. We get letters of co
mation of our employment and salaries from our jobs. We o
three character references. We scratch in the details of our
and sign our names. We tuck things into neatly marked fol
We make a note of the contract clause stating that if we both
before closing, we will be refunded the down payment. So w
got that going for us, at least.

Jeff hates filling out forms. He seizes up at the sight of
and check boxes. "I'm so tired of high-pressure paperwork,
groans, eyeing the pile. "They don't even give us enough spac
write. I hate real estate and money."

"It'll all be over in a few weeks," I remind him. "Then
grow old and die in that apartment and never do this again."

I crack open an Olé. Is this craft brewing I taste? No. Pot
tially fatal bacteria? Possibly. Still, if I spend a better $6 this y
I'll eat my mortgage application. I take a generous swig. It's a li
flat, but it's still better than Coors.

"Why do you suppose I've never heard of the brand before?
muse aloud as I contemplate the label.

Jeff ventures wisely, "Because they stopped after twelve bottle

Over the next eleven nights we follow roughly the same proc
dure. The happy hiss of the last bottle opening coincides with t
end of our first mind-numbing round of paperwork.

Other, friendlier pieces of paper have been arriving lately als

It's a few days before Jeff's birthday. I flip through the mail and see a card from his cousin Sue.

Sue moved to the Lake Claire neighborhood of Atlanta in 1990, when her daughter was still a child and her income as a single parent was limited. "I always thought owning a home was unattainable for me, and I felt a real loss," she tells me later. Instead she found a pleasant neighborhood she could afford, "one with houses and yards." It was more than a dream come true; it was a dream she'd never even dared permit herself.

She's seen the city change dramatically over the last two decades. "Did you know it's one of the most sprawling cities in the country? It just sprawls and sprawls and sprawls," she says, her words trailing out like the city itself.

With no oceans or mountains to constrain it, Atlanta has in recent years pushed its boundaries to the limit. As far back as 1998, the Sierra Club named Atlanta it's number-one "sprawl-threatened" large city. L.A. got only a dishonorable mention. Untrammeled sprawl has translated into the obliteration of forest and farmland, air-quality problems, and a populace that's spending ever more time behind the wheel.

Lately, though, the population has begun to realize that a two-hour drive away does not a city's environs make. While commuter endurance has its limits, the creativity of developers does not. The sprawl has begun to boomerang back, this time extending vertically.

"There's been a lot of development in the city," observes Sue. "They'll take three houses and tear them down to put up a huge condo. The condos aren't horribly expensive, so a lot of people are

moving in." Still, she questions if the development is in proportion to the demand. "There seems to be overbuilding," she observes.

The effect of this rapid influx of residents—and their money—is obvious. "My neighborhood has been changing a lot," she says. "The city is changing a lot." And when new people come into a city, other people wind up marginalized. "Atlanta is so segregated now," Sue says sadly. "There are affluent African-American parts of the city, but they're subdivisions. So much is about race, so much is about class. The gentrification is out of control. I don't know where lower-middle-class people are going."

It's so expensive now, she says, she estimates she could fetch $350,000 for her house, her gracious house in her desirable neighborhood. This is what $350,000 means somewhere else. It means prosperity and acquisition. In New York it means almost nothing at all.

In the midst of our application hell on earth, I tour the local Inwood public schools. We've already read all the reports, but you don't get a sense of a place from data. I need to meet the teachers and see the classrooms and the kids.

My friend Ben's wife once asked him, as they were applying to every exorbitantly priced, top-tier preschool in Manhattan, what kind of track they were putting their son on. "Who cares," he'd replied, "as long as it's the best?" We don't define "best" the same way Ben does, but we do know that your geography can be your destiny.

The school our new home is zoned for, it turns out, is not the blackboard jungle the Net chatter I've been reading would lead one to believe. The hallways are quiet, the students soft-spoken.

It seems okay, blandly okay, but I'm tugged in the direction of another school instead, where the walls are ablaze in student art and the classrooms are cluttered with books and games. The parent coordinator, a large, earthy woman who keeps interrupting our conversation to greet kids by name as we walk together, tells me, "When children can learn from each other, it's a beautiful thing." Then I see a teacher leading a class through some hip-hop dance moves in the hall, and my *Fame*-loving heart is set.

The only problem is that they probably won't be able to admit my daughter. The kindergarten class is usually capped. As it happens, though, one child moved away a week ago, so there's a spot. It's a popular school, and if any family that already lives in the neighborhood wants to put its kid into the kindergarten now, that seat has to go to them. We can't transfer Lucy until we have a permanent address in the zone. The parent coordinator takes my information and tells me, "Call again when you move, or in the fall. You never know."

You never know. When we began moving forward on the sale, Roz had called us with what she said was the best mortgage rate around, 6 percent and change.

Oscar had suggested we talk to their mortgage guy about getting a better rate, and Jeff had blanched at the idea. He, ever loyal, couldn't imagine doing anything that smacked of betrayal. I, ever skeptical, smelled some kickback scheme. Still, it couldn't hurt to hear the guy out.

A day later Jeff had phoned me. "That mortgage broker Brian is cool!" He told Jeff about a program to get homebuyers and small businesses to settle into our neighborhood.

Because our property is in what's defined as a "moderate income" zone, we qualify for a thirty-year fixed rate of 4.6 percent and no prepayment penalties. It sounds like they're bribing people to move to my new part of town, but I'm not going to argue with it.

The Community Reinvestment Act was passed in 1977 to require banks and thrifts to offer lending opportunities throughout a broader spectrum of neighborhoods. It's supposed to be a way of making lenders accountable to their communities and reduce discriminatory lending practices.

The methods of assessment, however, have been steadily weakening of late. Combine the decline of "community banking" with the rise in independent institutions that offer easy loans and have low regulation, it's no wonder defaults are on the rise. I can find a no-money-down loan as fast as it takes to type the words in a search engine. It was only a fluke and a referral that brought us to this.

The rate Brian offered was better than good. I had called Roz and asked why she didn't tell us about it.

"Do you not trust me to do my job?" she had said. "I know about the other loan program; it's not possible with a no-doc mortgage. Does Brian know that Jeff had changed jobs in the last year? Brian is misleading you if he said he could do better." Her wounded rage blistered through the receiver.

"That's why I wanted to call and ask you about it," I had said, trying not to match her testiness. "We're going to be out of your lives in a few weeks. This mortgage will be for thirty years. We have to find what's best."

Ten minutes later, she had called back, and this time calm Roz was on the line, the one who seemed unaware of the existence of snarly, potentially fatal Roz. It seemed the bank had very, very recently changed some of its requirements, so we would in fact qualify. "You would have to pay 'points' up front," she said. Points are bankspeak for five grand for the privilege of getting a lower rate.

While this rubbed some of the sheen off the bargain, it was still a substantial deal. Roz could start sending the paperwork through immediately. "You have to do it," she said, like it was all her plan. "You'll be saving three hundred dollars every month. The five thousand is a blip to that."

It's a blip that will bleed us dry to cough up. Now we won't be able to put Lucy in camp this summer, which will make my workdays interesting.

I'd wager Roz had never heard of the bank program a half hour prior. It wasn't the hill I wanted to die on either. "Go ahead," I had emailed. "Send the forms."

A short time after, an envelope arrived. It was the paperwork for our loan approval. We had snagged, in our precarious economic climate, the rate Brian had quoted us. We also, I noted as the vein on my temple began to throb, had a thirty-day-lock-in to close. Thirty days to get the mortgage approval, meet with and be approved by the board, and have everything tied up. I wish I had more Olé.

Roz had told me not to worry too much. "If you miss the deadline, you simply reapply for the same rate. It happens."

Roz is the only blasé player in all of this now.

The imminence of the move is hitting Lucy. It's well past bedtime, and she is sitting in her top bunk, wailing. "I can't go," she cries, "I can't leave Brooklyn and my school and my friends and our home and all my toys." There's more, but it's muffled in sobs.

Jeff is wiping her tears. I climb up in the bed with her.

"The important thing is that we'll all be together," I tell her. "Besides, everything is coming with us, all your toys, all your books."

"Not everything," she snuffles in retort. She is pointing a finger accusingly at her closet door. "Not that."

She's got us on that one.

"I can't leave my door! I love that door!" she howls. "It's the first thing I see when I wake up, and I love it."

"We'll take a picture," Jeff says, "and we'll put it on the wall across from your bed."

"And this weekend, let's have a fun day in Inwood and enjoy the neighborhood without having to look at apartments," I add. "We can get pizza and go to the park. It'll be great!" I am overselling how much fun a daylong journey in the dead of winter will be, but it's working.

"Can we go to the Nature Center?" Lucy asks expectantly.

"It can be our first stop," Jeff says.

My daughters have lived their whole lives in this little zip code. It's the only world they know. My in-laws, who spent their professional lives in the peripatetic world of ministry, always say, "Don't worry about them. Children adjust so quickly."

Even if our kids fare better, what about us? How well will we adjust?

Chantal understands. I'm sitting in a café very late at night with her after we've fled an incredibly boring downtown party. Whenever I see Chantal, I think someone somewhere else must have been terribly shortchanged in life, because fate rarely pours such high-octane smarts into so va-va-voomy a vessel. She's a woman who has it all. Except when it comes to geography. Her husband's work and his children from a former marriage are upstate. Her creative career and spirit tie her to New York.

The conflict gnaws at her. It creates tension in her relationship. Just because you love a man, it doesn't mean you love where he takes you. But recently she and her mate have found their compromise spot. Last year they got out of their more conservative small city and moved to Beacon, New York.

Beacon is about an hour north of the city on the train. Chantal can come in easily for meetings or when she and I need to go to City Bakery for hot chocolate. Her husband can get to his job easily, and see his kids and have room for them in the house.

Beacon is still far enough from Manhattan and economically unprosperous enough that it hasn't become overpriced yet. Their house cost $300,000. Yet the town also has mountains, water, a diverse community, and Dia:Beacon, an outrageously gorgeous museum full of Richard Serras and Louise Bourgeoises in an old factory. Beacon is what Chantal and her husband could afford, it's what they both could live with, and as the seasons pass, it's a town they find themselves growing more and more attached to.

Tonight though, she's happy to be out in this small, heavenly spot in Soho, where striking up a conversation with the person crammed elbow-to-spoon next to you is practically unavoidable.

We glance over at two burly men in beards and leather vests. "Are those your bikes outside?" Chantal asks, and they beam proudly in the affirmative. She notices the delicate crème brulée they're cracking into. They strike us as more the rusty-nails-and-tree-trunks-for-breakfast types. "One more question," she says. "I have to know. Why crème brulee?"

The one on the left, with the eagle tattoo and the sunglasses, shrugs. "The soufflé takes too long."

It's astonishing, isn't it, in this hurried-up town, how much time you spend waiting? But some things are worth it. I hope to God this apartment is one of them.

This weekend we go for our fun day in Inwood, determined to convince the kids how wonderful it'll be. We go to the Nature Center and look out the telescopes at the geese. We walk by the river and I look into the woods. The trees are bare, and I can see straight into them. I think of Sarah Fox, murdered there.

This place is beautiful. It's not always benign.

People who grew up in the neighborhood can rattle off the names of the friends they've lost to bullets, kids they went to high school with who strayed into the wrong place at the wrong time. Nestled as it is between other historically high-crime areas of Harlem to the south and the Bronx to the north, the area has seen its share of rough years. It's also close enough to the George Washington Bridge to have once served as a convenient location for drug traffic flowing in and out from Jersey.

You can't live in New York without living near where something bad happened. I know this neighborhood is reasonably safe. Inwood and its next-door neighbor, Washington Heights, bear the distinction of being among the city's most improved areas for crime. According to statistics for the 34th Precinct, overall crime is down 85 percent since 1990. It must have been really something else here then, when there were 2,647 reported burglaries and 103 murders. In 2005 the neighborhood boasted a mere 286 burglaries and a slim 9 homicides.

Yet when we live here, I will lace up my sneakers and I will run in this park every morning, and I will never, ever go into those woods alone.

When we get off the train home, we run into our friend Bruno on Court Street. "What are you guys up to?" he says cheerfully.

"Just hanging out in Inwood," Jeff says. "We're moving there."

"Long Island?" he asks.

"Manhattan," I say.

Bruno looks at me blankly. "What subway line is that?"

"The A," I tell him as I watch for a trace of recognition. "We're already dead to you, aren't we?" I add, and he nods his head, only half-kiddingly, in assent.

Your neighborhood is your personality. It marks your tribe. Upper West Side. Lower East Side. Bed-Stuy. Astoria. Who would we have become if we were staying? Who does that make us now that we're going?

At Lucy's school a few days later, I'm walking out the door with Nina. Her son is currently in the other kindergarten class, though she vows he'll be in private school next year. Her family lives a stone's throw from us, in a duplex apartment they've rented for years. Nina is gym-toned, stylish, and impeccable. She makes a good living. We have nothing in common.

"I can't believe we won't be here for kindergarten graduation," I wistfully mention by way of idle chitchat, "but I guess we'll be moving before then."

"You're moving? You bought something?" she says, astonished and unguardedly appalled. *"You?* Where are you going? Are you leaving the city? Did you need a bigger place?" Her horror at her social inferiors engaging in something as potentially prosperous as homeownership is palpable.

"Actually, it's smaller," I admit, my self-esteem skyrocketing. "It's way uptown, but we were ready to buy and we like it a lot."

"Smaller?" she says. Relief floods across her expression and words rush out of her mouth. "That's why we're keeping our place. I mean, we could buy too; we have plenty of money saved up. Plen-ty. We could put a hundred thousand dollars down, no problem, but who wants to do that, right? That's insane. We could get a brownstone, but we don't even know if we want to stay in the city anyway. And who buys in this economy?"

I do believe I have just been privy to something that would have worked much, much better as an inner monologue.

Who buys in this economy, Nina? Everybody. One in three New Yorkers owns now, an all-time high. Ownership is up among whites, blacks, and Latinos. Forty percent of the city's homeowners are foreign-born. Ownership is rising rapidly in once-untouchable areas like the South Bronx, Harlem, and the Lower East Side. The statistics cut across race and even geography. The great obstacle is still class. It's not a simple case of more people buying. It's that more people at a higher income level are buying. And in lower-income areas where ownership is up, a remarkable spike in foreclosure is just around the corner.

At night I go out with Stephanie to see her friend's band perform at Arlene's on the Lower East Side. Ten years ago this street was barren. Now there are expensive restaurants and bars with winking names like "Tenement." Yesterday's urban blight is today's $15 cocktail.

Stephanie is a friend from college that I haven't seen in ages. She's a classic Upper West Sider: beautiful, athletic, and a successful manager in a high-tech firm. She goes to galleries and the ballet and reads everything and knows all about wine. She is also, coincidentally, just slightly ahead of me in the co-op buying process. She just had her board interview for her new apartment on West End Avenue. It's a modest one-bedroom that faces an airshaft. It cost half a million dollars.

"I am having such buyer's remorse," she confesses as we sip Red Stripe. "It was the weirdest interview. I got to the guy's apartment and nobody else was there yet. He didn't know what to do, and I didn't know what to do, so he gave me a tour of his apartment while I was too scared to say anything."

"What was the interview like?" I say. I picture a suit-wearing firing squad.

"Oh man," she says. "They were asking all these personal questions. I think it bothered them that I was single. They kept flipping through my paperwork, saying things like, 'Looks like you make good money.' How am I supposed to reply to that? At one point they asked if I thought I was being aggressive enough in my investments."

I am losing my appetite. "That sounds like a nightmare," I tell her.

We'd better get used to intrusive questions, though. Oscar's been looking over our financials. "Your debt to income ratio is good," he tells me when he calls one weekday morning, "but I'm concerned that you don't have enough liquidity to impress the board. After you get through the estimated closing costs, I doubt you'll have the full twelve months of payments on hand that boards usually require."

"What are you telling me?" I ask.

"With little liquid savings left after paying the closing costs, the board will reject you," he says flatly. "If you could get your hands on another $25,000, that would seal it."

Why didn't I think of that? Okay, then, I'll go grab those extra several thousand dollars we've had sitting in a box in back of the closet, for the sole purpose of dazzling the board with how much we have at our fingertips.

Is he fucking kidding?

I say something to this effect, possibly with less sarcasm and fewer expletives.

"Can your families give you a gift letter of fifteen to twenty thousand? It doesn't mean you can't eventually pay the money back, but the relative has to agree that there is no requirement that you have to return it." He presses on. "Can you borrow money out of your 401k? Or there's another tactic: you can agree to a higher price on the apartment but get the seller to pay the closing costs. You slightly increase your monthly payments by increasing your home-loan amount, but it preserves your capital after closing. It's called a 'seller's concession.' " Funny how it sounds like the concession would be ours.

"Twenty-five thousand dollars is a lot," I reply.

"Twelve months in reserve is a slam dunk. Six months is shakier," he continues. I say nothing.

"Okay," he replies to my dead air, "maybe ten thousand dollars would be enough."

When I tell Jeff about the call, he says, "He could be a little less alarmist in his wording, but whatever. It's just another inconvenience."

We call in our chips with Jeff's parents. They write a gift letter, and a check for $5,000. Jeff's parents are not rich people, but they do it to help us and we are grateful and uncomfortable about it.

I take out a $5,000 loan from my 401k. More paperwork. A week later, the money arrives, as does my paycheck, minus a percentage of the loan and its 8.25 percent interest. The money is at least going back into my retirement account, but I'm more than ticked I have to put on this charade in the first place. Jeff and I resentfully put the ten grand in our accounts, and count the minutes until we can put the funds back in their rightful coffers.

Then I call Oscar. "It's taken care of," I say. "Now what?"

NICKEL-
AND-DIMED

"Emergency drinks?" says Sharon. It's late on Sunday afternoon when the call comes. Sharon and I have an understanding. Neither of us has siblings, her parents are dead and mine barely speak to me. When we need each other, we are there unconditionally. Especially if there are nachos involved.

She hates her job. Her last few match.com dates have been duds. I've been too swept up in my own drama to get how fed up she really is. This woman needs a drink.

We're sitting at Lobo and calling for another bowl of chips and dangerously near the bottom of our second margaritas when she tells me. It flows out so casually, so devoid of any "I've got something to tell you" lead-up, that I don't grasp it.

"I've gone as far as I can here," she begins. "With the job, with everything. I did a lot of thinking when I was out in San Francisco last month. New York is kicking my ass. I'm moving back."

"Ah," I reply, nodding my head and sucking the puckery dregs of tequila from the bottom of my glass. "When?"

"Six weeks," she says.

"Good for you," I tell her.

Wait a minute.

Did my best friend forever just say she was moving to the other side of the country?

Of course she should go. Of course she'll be happier in San Francisco. I miss the city too. The weight of this, though, the loss of her, suddenly flattens me even more than the tequila. Two years ago, when she had surgery, Sharon told the doctors I was her sister so I could be in the recovery room with her. I did the same when I had my operation last fall. It wasn't a lie.

"Now you'll have an excuse to come out and visit," she tells me.

"I know," I reply, despondently dragging a chip through molten Velveeta. "I'm so happy for you." I don't look happy at all. That's because I'm miserable.

Later, Jeff tries to cheer me up. "Maybe the timing is good," he says. "You weren't going to be around the corner from each other anymore anyway."

"That's the point!" I snuffle back, weepy and half drunk. "It was hard enough that we were going to be in separate boroughs. I figured we'd still get together to look at crazy art and stuff."

Now I have two dates marked on the calendar. One is our proposed moving date. The other is hers. They're both approaching with alarming speed.

I still haven't made arrangements for Bea, so I take a day off to visit the local nursery schools. My first stop is a Protestant pre-school. I'm not opposed to parochial education, or even to sending my kids to an institution different from my religion if it's a good place. Heck, Lucy spent two years in a Hebrew school because we liked the teachers and the kids.

This school, in contrast, had set off my inner alarms before I'd even visited. My warning bells started ringing when the administrator asked the status of my daughter's toilet training. "We can't accept her if she's going to have accidents," she had said.

I have every confidence my two-year-old will one day be diaper-free, but Bea is nowhere near it yet. And I'm enough of a Freudian that the last thing I want to take on now is ramping up that particular pressure. On the other hand, if Bea decides to turn a potty-related corner in the near future and this happens to be an excellent place, why close ourselves off?

I am bustling toward the unassuming gray building at the end of an industrial-looking street, and I arrive as the tour is starting. No one's holding a latte or checking a BlackBerry. It's encouragingly normal. The parental makeup is a mix of working-class African-American, Latino, and white. While the classrooms are crowded, the kids seem happy and engaged.

We assemble in the auditorium. The principal, a rugged WASP staunchly in the Pa Ingalls mold, takes the podium. He begins, "I came here several years ago from the Midwest to do my ministry in the city. I have six beautiful children." Total salt-of-the-earth material. He talks about the community and the high faculty retention rate. Then it gets strange.

I begin to doubt the school might be the right fit for us when he launches into an observation regarding out-of-control teens these days, "with their sex parties." It's not the sort of thing I'm accustomed to at a preschool orientation. When he says "I heard something from Focus on the Family the other day . . . ," that's not working for me either. I'm a fan of Jesus, but I'm less into James Dobson.

Then a parent raises her hand and asks about the discipline policy. "We don't spank here," the reverend says. "Anymore."

"If a child is persistently misbehaving," he continues, "we will call you, and you can come in to administer the spanking." He's talking about toddlers. I am still busy picking my jaw off the floor when he throws in, "We have also had parents authorize me to do it, if that's what you prefer." I look at my watch. It's half past get the fuck out of here. I pick up my coat and walk out. I'm the only one.

As I reach the corner, I notice an auto repair shop, shiny hub-caps gleaming on the fence. I peer in and see a cat intently lapping at her bowl. Then I hear the unmistakable sound of crowing. It stops me in my tracks. There, pecking around the yard, is a rooster. He's got company too. At least half a dozen of the feathered crea-tures are strutting in the morning sunlight, contentedly basking in the automotive emissions.

I immediately pull out my cell phone.

"Once you get above 125th Street, it's all spanking and cock-fighting," I tell Sharon, "which is not as good as that might initially sound."

"Maybe the birds are for Santería," she says hopefully. But as I round the corner to a car-congested street, I discover that, in a burst of synergy unseen since chocolate first hooked up with peanut but-ter, the auto shop shares space with the live poultry market.

"Speaking of religion," Sharon adds, "I found a post on craigslist for a sublet in Noë Valley. It's a three-bedroom, except one of the bedrooms is a shrine to Buddha. I'd have to promise to help maintain it. How do you think Buddha is as a roommate?"

"Genial, likes offerings," I tell her.

"There was also an ad from a guy who lives near Caltrans and says he's not a nudist but is looking for a roommate who is," she continues.

"Didn't you think that at our age, we'd have different options?" I ask. "Remind me again why I'm spending $360,000."

"To get a bedroom door so you can get laid," she tells me, which is all the encouragement I need.

My next appointment fares much better. It's a family-run, dual-language day care up the street from our new apartment. The walls are covered with pictures and words in English and Spanish, and at my feet are several toy-wielding toddlers clamoring over their visitor. The rooms are airy and clean. There are books and a cheery space for napping. When I ask the teacher, "How do you handle corporal punishment?" she blanches.

"We don't do that here," she says. That's what I needed to hear.

I run off to two other appointments, but I'm already sure I want Bea in the school up the street. I call Jeff to tell him, "Good news! I think we're set."

Then I dash into a deli where men who speak Spanish make sandwiches for old Irish guys under the watchful eyes of the owner's Chinese good-luck statues. I ask them to put some ham on a roll, and a few minutes later I'm dining on the A train, hoping to get back in time for school pickup.

In Florida, meanwhile, Kate is finally unloading her house. She has been renting in Vermont for months while trying to sell the place in Naples. People are spooked by the hurricanes, and she knows she's going to have to drop her asking price. It has been less than a year since she bought her home in that gated community, which makes her an accidental flipper, one who harbors no illusions of getting rich off her real estate.

Kate's not a property shark. Kate's like me, a romantic with a practical bent. She sells for $650,000, which is $50,000 more than she paid, but doesn't make up much for all the money she sank into fixing it up. Then she's ready to buy.

"I started off looking at places at a too-high price range again," she later admits. Soon, however, armed with experience and her research on local property taxes, she sets her sights lower.

"I knew I wanted a quintessential Vermont farmhouse," she says. "I saw myself there, chopping wood." She is concerned that, as one who in the last two years alone has been married, had a child, divorced, bought and sold a home, and worked sporadically, she is in for tough scrutiny when she tries to obtain a mortgage.

None of that, it turns out, matters much. She finds an 1831 farmhouse for $300,000 and pays half up front in cash. "You get a lot more for your money here," she says breezily, "but it's a tiny little house, and it's definitely got problems because it's old." It's a home, though, and hers and her son's. All that's missing is a white picket fence. So she puts one in.

On a March afternoon as our daughters are running wild in a chilly playground, Margot and I are talking about the imminent move. "You know, my husband's coworker and his family are up there. They're great," she says. "They have two daughters too." She opens up her cell phone and produces a number.

John used to live in Brooklyn too. His younger brother trailblazed Inwood; John and his wife followed two years ago. When I call him, I pour out a stream-of-consciousness version of our odyssey, then I launch into the interrogation. "Do you like the neighborhood? Do you feel safe? Do you think the schools are okay?"

John is open about street noise, subway service, the vicissitudes of raising two little girls in the area. "Okay, in December a guy did get mugged for his Christmas presents on our street, but that's unusual," he says, adding, "Where's your apartment?"

I tell him.

"That's our street," he says. "What building?"

As it happens, we are moving down the hall from his family. He's on the co-op board. Things are looking up.

The co-op board is, along with the preschool admissions officer, the scariest nonautomatic-weapon-toting entity in New York City. Its ways are mysterious, secretive, possibly arbitrary and vindictive. It has instilled a heaping dose of the fear of God in me. It's a fear that doesn't come cheap either.

"There's some serious bilking going on in the co-op racket," Jeff notes one evening as we slog through the litany of what we're to pay up.

There are fees for running credit checks. Penalties if we don't close in one person's offices, fees if we do close in someone else's. A $250 lien search fee. A corporate counsel fee. A $100 "application-processing fee."

When I called Oscar a few days ago to inquire why the board

had tacked a $75 "copying fee" onto the application, he fired off a terse email, "Best not to question them." I called him immediately.

"What does that even mean?" I said.

"People asking questions raises the hairs on the backs of the board's necks," he replied irritably. "If you don't pay it, they're going to think seventy-five dollars is a big deal for you, and then they're going to wonder about your money. Do you want to lose this apartment over that minor a thing?" He added darkly, "It's up to you." Oscar was also concerned that my husband and I have different last names. "We may need additional letters stating you share money," he'd said.

Is it all a test? Anything less than an unquestioning opening of our wallets and a tidy commingling of our nomenclature is seen as potential insubordination? I think of all the forms we've received addressed to both of us but with only Jeff's last name, and I could blow another gasket. But I remember I have a friend on the board, or at least a friend of a friend. Oscar's scare tactics have lost a portion of their power. We keep our mouths shut about the fee and figure if the board needs proof of our relationship, we'll submit the kids.

I'm already stressed out enough. Then Roz calls me. "You should know," she starts, gently aiming her informational rocket launcher, "that the interest rate on your mortgage has risen. It's at six now, and it's probably going to keep going up. So, I'd advise you to push the closing before the lock-in period expires." The deadline is April 3. We have three weeks.

Interest rates have been rising lately. They haven't been this high in years. It's bad enough for new homebuyers like us, but woe unto those with ARMs. About $330 billion worth of mortgages will reset this year. By the end of 2007, that figure will edge toward the trillion-dollar mark.

For us, those extra interest points could amount to around $300 extra per month. Every month for thirty years or until we sell the apartment or drop dead from the stress, whichever comes first. We haven't had our board meeting, we still don't have a vast number of links on the chain of paperwork we need. Roz is asking the impossible.

"You told me not to worry," I sputter. "Did you plan this all along? Did we only get this rate because we couldn't possibly meet the terms?"

She says, "This almost never happens. See what you can do."

"If we can't make it happen, we have to pay the new rate? Is this a bait and switch? Was this what you meant to have happen, to get us to pay more?"

"I'm doing everything for you," she replies, through what sound like gritted teeth, "and I'm hardly making any money off this. It's still not over. Just push the closing."

I call Kenneth, Oscar's partner, in a panic, and he immediately sends an email to the building's business office. "There has been an inquiry into pushing the closing," it begins. "Can you please check with the board when the possibility of an interview would be feasible? The reason is a change in the financing past the month of April."

We soon receive a terse reply from the property's corporate representative, stating, "It is premature to discuss an interview time. Additionally, the approval is not necessarily a foregone conclusion." She further informs us that the board usually takes a week or two after receiving the board package to schedule an interview.

Now I'm mad.

"If we go down in flames," I tell Jeff, "I am taking everybody with me."

"Remember to pay the hundred dollar down-in-flames fee," he replies.

When we have completed the board package, Jeff and I meet up at the realtor's Upper West Side offices to review it with Kenneth. If there were a movie of our story, Kenneth would play himself. Kenneth has perfect white teeth. He teaches swimming to kids in his spare time. After Katrina, Kenneth went down to the Gulf for a week with a humanitarian organization to aid in the rescue efforts. He's a Buddhist. I'm not positive about this, but his only flaw may be a slight allergy to Kryptonite.

The bleak Lenten sky and steady drone of a jackhammer outside the offices provide a suitable accompaniment to the atmosphere. Kenneth painstakingly reviews every detail of our submission, looking for a hint of anything that throws a wrench into the process. It's a Starr Report–sized pile topped with the maraschino of a personal letter of supplication. The brokers suggested we add it, a direct plea to the board to entrust us with the apartment.

"Dear Members of the Board," I had written,

Everyone says that buying a home is an investment. For us, that investment goes far deeper than the financial aspect. It means the investment of our hearts, in a place we can envision our children growing and thriving. It's an investment we have not taken lightly, scouring a wide variety of neighborhoods and dozens and dozens of properties over the course of three long years. We believe that this community, and this property, are what we have been looking for all this time. If you agree, we will know for certain that our patience has been worth the wait, and will do all we can to uphold the high standards of your cooperative, both as shareholders and as neighbors.

I meant every word in it, but I've laid it on thick as birthday cake frosting.

Kenneth sits quietly as we drink the coffees he's brought us and try not to fidget from all the caffeine and adrenaline. "This is good," he says finally. "This is all good."

We sigh in relieved harmony. It seems safe to ask now. "Why do you do this?" Jeff says to Kenneth. "Dealing with all this paper-work? All these crazy people running around all the time, yelling at you, in the worst shape of their lives?"

"I used to be in wealth management," he explains. "I didn't like it. But this? This works for me." It fits in better with his Buddhist principles. "I love the people contact," he says. "I like the challenge of being compassionate. And I get to make people's dreams come true." There is not a note of hucksterism in his words. We are in the throes of a nightmare. He sees the reverie that got us here.

He runs off several copies of our package and prepares to send it to the board. "We should hear back in a few days to schedule the board interview," he says. "I'll call you then."

Kenneth's motivation does much for Jeff's perspective. "If I had been offered a multiple choice to pick the real estate broker I would like," he says as we step out into the jackhammering, "I'd have checked 'compassionate Buddhist.'"

While we are going somewhere new, Cynthia has gone home.

One month after Katrina, she returned to New Orleans, but New Orleans had not nearly begun to return to itself. Cynthia lives on the edge of the Garden District, in Central City, an area that sustained minimal flood damage but suffered its own emotional ravages. When I talk to her, later, the familiar sweetness in her voice is still there, but with a new weariness as well.

"There's so much heartbreak on a constant level, it's exhausting," she says of the excruciating rebuilding process. "The tedium of what's happening here is a slow death in some ways. It's like chopping off a dog's tail an inch at a time so it'll hurt less."

Now, to make it worse, "the housing market's volatile, and the rental market is supertight," she explains. "They talk about the footprint being smaller." This is what you get when most of a city's housing is destroyed. "I have a real steal of an apartment by new criteria. The middle class is getting squeezed out here. There is an incredible number of contractors, and a migrant worker population living twelve to an apartment."

Yet all that frustration and pain are what keep her rooted. "I think if Katrina hadn't happened," she continues, "other factors might have led me to leave. I don't own my home; there aren't tons of opportunities. This is an amazing place, but the chance I was going to be here the rest of my life was slim."

But, she says, "I understand the enormity of what's been lost, and there's a certain gratitude for that. Being able to grasp that is a gift. A full fifty percent of my social group left. Others bought *more* property, bought *two* houses, dug in, had babies. I don't know that many fence sitters." She stays, she explains, because "there are moments when history swells up and swallows you, and where you happen to be standing in that moment is who you are. You can't sweep away the shreds of the fabric of your life. Place is identity," she says, her soft southern accent growing steely. "It's not even a part of it. It's all of it." And now, by a twist of fate and the wind, this is hers.

When you see something big and awful hurt your home, kill your neighbors, savage your community with unfathomable grief, it gets inside you. It lashes you to a spot. Even if you leave, part of you belongs to it forever.

When I talk to Kenneth after he's sent in our package, he advises, "Call your friend on the board. Make him aware of what needs to happen. These people understand what it means to have points change on a mortgage rate. They understand you're not rich, but don't give them the impression if the rate were to change you would struggle. Just use your finesse."

I call John at his work and attempt to use my finesse. "We're almost at the end of our lock-in period and the mortgage rate has gone up, so we need that board meeting, and we need that approval, or we are massively fucked, so can you please, please help us?" I plead.

Then I put down the phone and think, well, who wouldn't want the chance to live down the hall from all this?

Apparently begging works, because the next day, Thursday, we receive the directive from Kenneth. "You're to appear before the board Saturday morning," he emails. It is, poetically, April Fool's Day. We then get a call from Roz. She's got a one-week extension for the rate.

Jeff and I get up early and attire ourselves in dark-hued clothes that convey that we are stable people with good financials, no bad habits, and quiet children. My skirt has never had so much to say.

Meanwhile, all the fears I've ever had about not being good enough, about being too poor and too trashy, are ripping through my psyche. These people are going to judge us. They're going to see right through us and turn us down.

We arrive a few minutes early for our board interview and take a spirit-shattering walk around the park. Jeff takes a piece of paper out of his pocket, and we run down the list of advice Kenneth sent us, his golden rules for impressing a co-op board:

- Please dress nicely.
- Be about ten minutes early.
- Thank the board for taking their time out to meet with you. This is rather serious.
- SAY NOTHING unless directly asked a question. If they ask, "Do you have questions?" the answer is, "No, everything explained to us seems very clear." However,
- If you are asked questions, answer the questions! Please be short, polite, and direct.
- Try, try, try, to just be upbeat and yourselves!

On the bottom of the page, there is a photo of Kenneth, smiling, and the words "We believe in you."

I'm concentrating mightily on being myself, minus the oversharing and nervous talking. Given Jeff's innate WASP reserve, the plan is to let him be the spokesperson of the couple.

"If we lost it, I wouldn't be devastated," Jeff says, "but it would suck to do this all again."

Then we go sit in a book-lined apartment with three staid, smart-looking men. There is the perfunctory small-talk acknowledgment of John's and our mutual friends. No one offers so much as a glass of water, and I'm pretty sure even war criminals get a glass of water. The men are all clutching our opus of a board package, which includes the particulars of every dime we possess, the numbers on our paychecks, every bank transaction we've made over the last three months. Were I sitting here in my underwear, I could not feel more exposed and invaded. I'm beginning to understand why the procedure is sometimes referred to as a co-opscopy.

James Number One, the board president, opens the proceedings. "Sounds like you have a good situation in Brooklyn. Why do you want to live here?" he asks. I point out the window, toward the park. "Well there's that," I say, immediately forgetting that I was going to be silent and not ruin it for us today.

"Your financials seem to be in order," says James Number Two, the board vice president, "Do you have any questions for us?" We shake our heads in the negative. Then I can't help saying, "We love this place. We want to live here. We've been looking for three years, and this is the one."

It's not the best half hour of my life, but it's not a scene from *The Deer Hunter*. Mostly, we exchange pleasantries about where to eat in the neighborhood. The men, I later learn, consider this mostly a formality. We have been primed for an inquisition. As we leave, John shakes both our hands warmly and smiles. "I'm looking forward to being neighbors," he says.

As the green of the park melts into the grit of Broadway, I wonder when, if ever, the chain bookstores arrive, and the grimy old bars are replaced by self-consciously grimy new bars. And I wonder how I feel about that, how it will feel to watch this neighborhood evolve. My friend Antonio, a real estate broker specializing in Uptown—way Uptown—tells me later, "There's a prestige to living in Manhattan. I think eventually everyone will know about every nook and cranny of it. And this neighborhood is bucolic but still not bridge-and-tunnel. It has a Park Slope, West Village vibe. It's attracting a lot of, for lack of a better word, hippies. Environmentalists. Because the nature doesn't exist anywhere else. The old owners aren't being pushed out; they're cashing out." Sounds familiar.

The next day, Kenneth calls. We've been approved by the board.

INTO THE
WOODS

I call Roz first thing Monday morning to give her the good news about the board. "That's wonderful," she says, relieved. "Just as soon as I get the approval letter, I'll get the Aztech forms moving."

The what?

When I ask Roz what the Aztech forms are, she replies, "It's the same as the recognition agreement," like that clears it all up. It was the same answer our lawyer and realtor offered as well.

"This is the part where a guy in a feathered headdress rips out our hearts, isn't it?" Jeff says when I relay the message later. I tell him there's also a $100 blood ritual fee.

What I later manage to glean is that the Aztech is a written acknowledgment by the co-op of the lender's commitment. Yes, it says, we are truly a co-op and you are a lender and these people are purchasers, in phrases like "appurtenant thereto." I prefer to think of it as one more useless form we have to pay for. The lender or lender's attorney generates it, and then requires the purchaser and cooperative's corporation to sign it.

Soon the signed agreement letter from the board arrives at Roz's office. There is however a typo on it. Our building's managing agent has us down as approved to move to the wrong address. "Can't we scratch that out?" I ask Roz naively. *Au contraire.*

We lose two days as it's redone and resubmitted to Roz. Then it has to go through the offices of a panoply of bankers, lawyers, and administrators, until it quickly drops off the radar. Meanwhile, the deadline to close on the apartment to keep our mortgage rate is bearing down on us with stomach-churning inevitability.

I spend the week on a labyrinthine quest to track paperwork whose nature and purpose I don't fully comprehend through the offices of a half dozen parties I don't know. Somewhere in the tristate area, someone is holding on to my mortgage agreement. Someone who doesn't see this as the life-or-death deal Jeff and I do.

"Where is the paperwork right now?" I bleat into the phone at Roz. "What do we have to do? It's like everybody's dragging their feet and nobody cares."

"It's going as fast as it can," she says with the detachment of one whose monthly house payments aren't riding on this.

"Can I pick them up in person? Why do they have to be sent to you? Can't they be messengered to me?" I beg.

"This is the procedure," she insists. "The papers are supposed to come in by noon tomorrow via FedEx. I have to sign them and then they can go to you both to sign as well. Then they go to the board's lawyer, and he has to review them before he signs them. *Then* you can schedule the closing."

Insert your Kafkaesque, Orwellian nightmare metaphor cliché here.

"Tell me what we need to do to make it happen and I'll handle it," I say. "I'll be there tomorrow at twelve."

On Friday it rains. I get off the subway in Midtown with exactly fifteen minutes to walk over to Roz's office before noon. I march through the streets precariously balancing my umbrella and speed-dialing her office.

"They're here," she says.

I'm soaked and panting when I get there. I have never met Roz, but when I see her charging through the cubicles, I recognize her at once. She looks exactly like her phone persona—hair a little too brassy, lipstick a little too dark, and an air that says she doesn't give a damn either.

"Good luck," she tells me, and I sprint out into the street again.

"Meet me on the Spring Street subway platform in twenty minutes," I bark into the cell phone at Jeff. When I get off the train, he's waiting on a bench.

Jeff looks at the agreements for the place to sign, barely paying attention to the words. "I am way burned out on paperwork," he says. "I'm tired of wasting time trying to prove we're okay. What matters doesn't go on forms. Everybody's so freaked out."

"Including us," I answer.

There by the turnstiles we sign the papers together, and I wait for the next available train.

"Good luck," he says as the doors close between us.

I get off again downtown, near the office of the co-op's lawyer. I whip out my phone yet again, punching numbers like they're the faces of everybody who's slowed us down through this whole debacle.

Then I put on the voice, the silky cool one I used through every receptionist gig I ever had. There's very little *fatale* in my *femme*, but it doesn't stop me from the most brazen attempt at persuasion of my non-drunk-and-single lifetime.

"Hello," I drawl to the admin assistant, "can you tell Marty it's the buyer for the unit in Inwood? I'm in the neighborhood, and have the papers so I'm coming up in five minutes." I polish off my coffee, pop an Altoid, and go.

These are not the offices of the city's most powerful firm. They are instead as threadbare and seedy as the set of a low-budget porn movie. The rug is a well-trod tan, the furniture is a hodgepodge of factory remainders, and the reception hub may have once done duty on the Starship *Enterprise*. I can handle these bastards. "Mary Elizabeth," I purr to the front-desk person. "Tell him I'm here."

A beleaguered-looking fiftyish man with a substantial paunch over his belt comes out. I am still simultaneously smiling a toothy beauty-contestant smile, flipping my hair, and extending the palm I have wiped free of perspiration when Marty says, "I don't want to burst your bubble." He looks like my bubble is the last thing he gives a hoot about.

"Great!" I reply. "So if you'll sign these, I'll call my lawyer to set up the closing." I thrust the papers under his nose, and he takes them.

"No, I have to review them." he answers decisively, as if they aren't boilerplate. "What's your deadline again? Because I wouldn't be optimistic you're going to make it."

I hate this man like I haven't hated anybody since that bitchy realtor. My husband and I have jumped through every hoop, danced every dance, kissed every ass. Our last-ditch deadline is Monday, and we can make it. He's the one thing standing between it and us.

"Okaaaaay," I say in a tone that shaves off several IQ points. "Thanks!" I want to throttle him.

I call Kenneth and ask him to put in a beseeching call to Marty as well. What he says when he calls back isn't cause for cheer.

"What did he tell you?" I ask, picking at a little bit of cuticle till it bleeds.

"I'll put it this way," says my chipper, altruistic, Buddhist broker, "I am so sorry his mother didn't love him."

The lawyer had told him that we were nowhere near scheduling a meeting, and that we should forget it right now.

"We're not letting it go," I tell Kenneth.

"If you pull this off," he says, "it'll be one for the books."

A few hours later our family is sitting together at the table, distractedly trying to eat our pasta, when our lawyer Sean calls. Marty has the signed papers.

I'm sure my charm had nothing to do with it. He may just be the type of guy who likes feeling power, who enjoys sporting with people's emotions. And who, on this day, gave him more opportunity for both than I?

Meeting our deadline is still a massive long shot. But we might in fact be dealing with people who will help us make it happen.

"I'm still trying to push for the closing," Sean says. "I'll call you the minute I can schedule it."

Over the weekend, I am peddling castoffs at another stoop sale, this time our own. If Gina's apartment felt too crowded, how will we ever manage in the new, smaller place? Gone is the butcher-block table from our office room. Gone are the toy chest, several framed posters, boxes of books, a globe, most of the last of my vinyl collection, the garment rack, and a bunch of clothes with it. As we watch our possessions disperse into the hands and homes of strangers, Jeff holds an envelope full of cash and looks bereft.

"I feel bummed out," says Jeff, as a goateed guy in a frayed T-shirt rolls our microwave cart toward Court Street. "It's hard to accept that we're going to have less space. Considerably less space."

"At least we'll have doors and halls," I remind him, "which will be a nice change from the nowhere-to-hide setup we have now."

I also feel just a little virtuous about simplifying. We're not especially green. But our constraints will keep our consumption in check. We will occupy a space that, by dint of its 900 square feet, is relatively heat-and energy-efficient. We will not succumb to the temptations to wanton consumerism, not in a home where every incoming item will have to be scrutinized.

On Monday, I jolt awake before the sun is even up, eager for 9 A.M., the time to start making calls. I am jittery before I even have my first cup of coffee. This is it. Our final deadline day.

Unless we are sitting in a lawyer's office sometime today and signing papers, we will have missed our thirty-day lock-in period, our mortgage rate will go up two points, and we will be screwed to the tune of $300.00 extra every month.

We're walking out the door to take the girls to school, and Jeff isn't looking so good. He's weary. Maybe he's coming down with something. His face is flushed; his wheeze suggests his asthma is kicking in.

"I'm okay," he says, "I just need to get more rest." We kiss at the corner, and I apprehensively watch him march toward the train.

At nine o'clock I begin dialing. "Can we get another extension?" I ask Roz.

"There's nothing more I can do," she tells me. "The banks won't budge if the date passes without a closing."

Marty's office tells me to leave a message. Our lawyer Sean says, "I'll call you back; I'm waiting to hear back from the bank's rep."

Then Kenneth calls. "You can't do the closing without a walk-through," he says. "You and Jeff need to get up to the apartment and verify that it's in good condition, and you accept it as is, before we can make another step forward." I call Jeff, and we both drop everything and race uptown.

I'm the first one to arrive. I use the time to talk myself down from the ledge of panic. I sit outside the playground, watching moms and babysitters pushing toddlers on swings; couples are walking hand in hand by the water. That will be us soon. That's what we're doing this for.

Jeff comes next, and he looks unambiguously sick now. His face is a mask of perspiration, his breathing is off. "This wasn't a good day to have to take off time," he says in a soft, shallow tone. "I have a lot to do." He checks his watch.

A few minutes later, Kenneth arrives, brandishing the keys,

and leads us upstairs. It's the prettiest time of the day in the apartment, with slivers of sun coming in through the uncurtained windows.

We walk into the square of space that will be the dining foyer. To call it a room would be far too grandiose. Still, it's a separate area for our meals, something we have never, in either of our adult lives, had.

"Let's just stand right here a bit," I tell Jeff. "We won't be able to do it again once we put the table in."

He flinches away, unnerved that our beloved table will be in this spot, this portal to a hell dimension. He begins pacing the apartment, flicking every light switch.

"I guess it's okay," he says. "How can we tell the outlets all work? I should have brought something to plug in. Why didn't I think of that?"

"Are you okay?" I ask, and don't mention what I'm thinking, which is that I am really, really scared he's going to have a heart attack. Sweaty and shaky aren't the hallmarks of rosy health.

"I'm fine," he says. He turns to Kenneth and says, "It's fine."

We ride together on the subway until his stop and say we'll check in later. I can't even remember anymore who we still need to call, or what we're supposed to do about the closing.

He's changed his mind, hasn't he? He said he was ready; he said he wanted to be open. Now it's happening, though, and he feels trapped.

"We don't have to do this," I say.

"I'm fine," he replies. He is so clearly not.

An hour later I'm walking with Bea to pick up Lucy. My phone rings and it's Sean. The bank guy couldn't do the closing today, so it's definitely off. Maybe tomorrow. Passover begins on Wednesday evening and people are taking days off. If the closing doesn't happen soon, it's not happening until at least next week.

"Do we get an extension on the rate then? They can't refuse to meet with us and then not give us the rate. Isn't that illegal or something?" I demand, although I have zero idea if this is true.

"I'm on it," says Sean, and there's just a little pleasure in his voice at the prospect of playing hardball with the bank. "Don't worry. I'll tell you as soon as I hear anything."

I'm in the schoolyard with the girls. Lucy and her classmates are running around in a postdismissal dervish, and Bea is stumbling around chasing them. My phone rings and my stomach clenches reflexively.

"I have some bad news," says Jeff.

Oh fuck. He's heard from Sean. Or Roz. We blew it. We lost the rate. We're doomed.

"They're making some budget cuts at the publishing house," he continues. "So after the quarter, they won't be needing me anymore. I'm out of work."

There is an eerie silence on the phone line. We'd been so wrapped up in the homebuying, we'd assumed nothing else us could touch us at the same time. We forgot that life could offer any other shocks.

"I'm so sorry," I say weakly. He loved that job. He was good at it. And my change-resistant mate was trying to deal with enough upheaval already, thanks.

"We'll figure this out," I say, repeating my cheerleading speech from the last time this happened. "We can both pick up more work. It'll be all right."

They've been generous with their notice. Jeff still has six weeks left before the next financial quarter. The company might even need him for a week or two in a few months. Furthermore, because we've been through this before so recently, our insurance is with me, and Jeff doesn't have a company 401k to roll over anymore. At least we have less paperwork this time.

"What are we going to do?" he says. "Should we cancel the closing?"

At lunchtime I was telling him we could back out and thought I meant it. Now all that would entail leaves me overwhelmed. We're in sickeningly deep. We've liquidated assets. We've written checks. The landlady is showing our apartment to defectors from Gramercy and Tribeca who can pay her a lot more rent. Should things get very dark over the next few months, the nest egg is already gone. There's no way to back out without losing most of the money. We're in the financial quagmire of our lives.

I'm holding Bea's hand as she wobbles up the ladder of the slide. "You might have another job in a week," I tell him. "You'll freelance. We will make the work thing happen. But if we lose the apartment, we've got nothing but starting from nothing again. I say we keep moving forward."

I'm glad he can't see my face right now. I'm glad I can't see his. If we could, somebody might blink.

"Yeah," he says, "I know. Think—if this had happened a few weeks ago we couldn't have gotten the mortgage or the board approval. I guess it's meant to be."

They say that you can have a good relationship, a good career, and a good place to live—but you can't have all three at once. I say fate has quite the ironic sense of timing.

We are now not merely buying a home. We are signing up for a mountain of debt while our income has, in an instant, been cut in half. A sea of laughing, yelling children swirls around me. I shut my eyes tightly for a second and inhale deeply. I'm not going to panic. Not going to cry. Not this week anyway. Too much to figure out now.

The trill of my ringtone jars me out of my thoughts. This time it's Sean. "The closing is on Thursday," he says.

"We'll be there," I answer. "Is the bank going to give us our rate?"

"I don't know," he replies. "I guess we'll find out."

When Jeff comes home that night, I put my arms around him and tell him, "It'll be all right. We'll get through this."

"I need to be alone for a few minutes to pull myself together," he says, and because there's nowhere else to do it, he goes into the bathroom and shuts the door.

It's drizzly and chilly as we hustle off to Marty's financial district office three days later. School spring vacations have already begun, so the in-laws come to babysit. They get stuck in traffic on the way, so by the time they arrive, they can barely take their coats off before we fly toward the subway.

There are papers yet to sign, a lot of them, which we haven't even seen. Everything is so ephemeral right now we honestly don't know what awaits us. "What'll we do if the bank gives us a different mortgage rate?" I ask Jeff, for the nine thousandth time. We haven't talked much about a real strategy since we agreed to proceed with the closing. "Would we leave dramatically, with our down payment and our extra five thousand dollars we paid in points and the lawyer fees and broker fees all up in smoke?"

"I don't know," he answers. "I don't care."

"They were the ones who delayed the closing, so they're the ones who should be held to the original rate," I continue, my righteous indignation meter set to maximum. In reality, it has come to my attention that banks aren't always fair.

If the rate has changed, we simply may not be able to pay it every month. It happens all the time. Another apartment downstairs in our new building recently went into foreclosure. What if everything we believed is wrong? What if buying a home, instead of strengthening our personal economy, is the thing that destroys us?

I jab at an elevator button and soon I'm guiding us back to Marty's shabby offices. The receptionist looks up from his crossword and buzzes an intercom. "They're here," he yawns, then returns to his puzzle.

A minute later Marty appears. He eschews hellos, greeting us gruffly instead with "Were you really in that big a hurry?"

For the first time in days Jeff laughs.

Jeff and I sit down at a very long table, and as the minutes tick by, the seats fill. Our lawyer Sean sits next to me. The representative from the bank, who looks all of eighteen and appears even whiter with fear than we are, positions himself at the head. The co-op's lawyer, Marty, takes the other end. The seller and his lawyer sit across from us. Our realtor Kenneth is next to them. I am the lone female in a roomful of suits.

The bank rep hands us a sheaf of papers. Our eyes hurtle through the pages, searching until we find it. There it is. The number. We've got our 4.6 percent rate. We're buying an apartment today.

Jennifer has told me that when she and Vincent closed on their house, they carefully read over every paper they were handed, asking questions and pausing to hammer out details. I'd assumed we'd do the same, envisioning every possible scenario wherein it would all explode in our faces. Instead, I decide this will not be a day for confrontations, or mix-ups, or disasters. It is a day to chomp through and move on to the next thing. It might even be a day to celebrate.

I look at the stack of papers and Sean one last time, "Everything check out?" When he nods in assent, I start signing and don't stop until the whole pile has moved from my immediate right to my immediate left, where Jeff sits scribbling his name next to mine. From time to time, he shakes his right hand out, like he's trying to purge the pain from his wrists. For over an hour, I scrawl my signature with escalating illegibility while we all make chitchat about music and weekend pursuits. Papers are shuffled, certificates handed over. I glance briefly at our proprietary lease. It's a blurry, several-generations-down photocopy for a 78-year term.

In real estate transactions it's customary to keep the seller and buyer as far apart as possible for as long as possible. Like an arranged marriage, it's a deal conducted entirely, until the last minute, through intermediaries. But unlike a wedding, this is where paths cross, not converge. It's called a closing for a reason. It falls far short of the pomp of matrimony but seems far more binding. The seller's and my eyes barely meet the whole time, as if we might break some protocol if they did.

Then he hands me a red folder that his wife put together. "It's the instructions and warranties on all the appliances that came with the apartment," he says. "There's one more thing—we have a stack of envelopes embossed with the address, left over from before the move. You can use them for your change-of-address letters," he tells me shyly.

A series of letters and numbers is shining in gilt script. That's where I live now. "Thank you," I reply.

I glance up and study the seller's face for the first time. This dark-haired fellow of about my age, this father of two, is the man who took care of our home until it was our turn, the one we finally said yes to, who said yes back to us.

I know very little about him and his family. I don't know where he went, or what made his family want to leave the same place we were so eager to obtain. As it happens, his wife Dawn and their children still have deep ties to the neighborhood and her friends in it. Soon, I will run into her at the playground and my building's hallways. She and her offspring will sit with me and mine in their own former living room.

So when I ask her later why she moved, she tells me.

"We were out of room," she says. "We have two kids of the opposite sex, which meant sharing a room would be complicated. We had a garage on Tenth Avenue for $300 a month, which is hatefully inconvenient. When I parked our car on the street, our headlights were stolen twice. And I wasn't impressed with the local schools. When we looked down the road, we couldn't figure out how to make it happen. There's a real evaporation of kids who have English as a first language. I wanted reading, writing, and arithmetic. I wanted a school where my child and children like him could go."

While we were searching, so were they. They looked for over

a year, from New Jersey to Westchester to Long Island. She had a colleague in Pelham who offered to show her around.

"It's out of a storybook," she says. "Everything is walking distance and there are four elementary schools. I told my husband, 'It's twenty-seven minutes from Grand Central. You'll be at work sooner than you are now.'"

In 2005, houses there were starting at around $450,000. They found a Tudor they liked offered by a couple who were divorcing and eager to sell. In life's cyclical fashion, the wife was miserable in the suburbs and anxious to return to the city. Dawn and her husband offered asking and got it. Her parents, who previously had nowhere to stay when they visited, bought a co-op in the same town.

She had lived in our apartment for four years. They had friends downtown in Soho who griped about visiting them in Inwood, saying, "That's what you get for not living in the city."

"I'd tell them, 'We do live in the city,'" she says. They're the same people who've never visited her yet. "Plenty of people can bring their kids to the burbs, just to see what a house looks like," she counters. "But other people get so self-righteous about whatever they're doing."

I think of all the people along the way, the family members, the ex-neighbors, the brokers, who've given us crap for choosing to stay in the city. I think of the crap this woman's dealt with for leaving. We all make our choices. We get married or we don't, we have babies or we don't, we stay at home or we go back to work. And it strikes me as extraordinarily liberating to know that whatever we do, someone will be there waiting to bust our chops for it.

Newton's third law dictates that for every action there is an equal and opposite reaction. Far be it from me to dispute Newton or the law, I just think some people carry it too far. They take any lifestyle that differs from their own as a declaration of war. Do they need everybody to make the same choices they did to validate them? I think most of us just do what we do because we want to be happy, and that's a goal I'd rarely begrudge anybody else. All both of the families moving paper around this table today want is a place in the world that makes us happy.

When the last form has made its way around the table, Kenneth, who has been uncharacteristically quiet this whole time, takes his moment. He stands up and walks around the table to my spot. "On behalf of all of us," he says dramatically as he presses a set of keys into my hands, "congratulations on your new home."

I never dreamed I could work so hard for something that tucks into my pocket. I look down at these little bits of metal on a ring, and throw my arms around Kenneth and hug him tearily like a child. Then I look around, abashed, and ask, "Was that too much?"

By the time we leave the office, the clouds have broken and the temperature has gone up a good ten degrees. "Do we have time to walk over the Bridge?" Jeff asks.

"I think it's a necessity," I reply. We are carrying an alarming amount of paperwork, a celebratory bottle of merlot from Kenneth, and our coats. We are walking toward the place we're leaving.

"Thirty-year mortgage," Jeff says. "Damn."

The view from the Bridge on the way in to Manhattan is a showstopper. There's an awful lot to be said for the other direction too, though. Our first year in Brooklyn, Jeff and I would meet once a week at his office and walk home together, the route growing colder and more arduous as the baby inside me grew. A few years later, on the night of the blackout, Jeff trod gingerly over it, feeling it sway under the weight of so many other stranded commuters. For every time we've ever stood in awe of the vista from it, what we've loved most about the Bridge was the way it always brought us home.

Jeff looks at the low skyline of our borough sadly. "To have to leave Brooklyn feels like a failure to me," he says. "I feel like I failed myself and us because we can't afford to live here."

"This isn't a failure," I tell him. "We did it." But it doesn't feel like winning the Super Bowl either.

When we get home, Lucy bounds to the door to greet us, but Bea is sitting quietly on the couch. "She's been like that a while," says my mother-in-law. "She missed you."

Jeff scoops her up into his arms. "Did my baby miss me?" he says gently, snuggling into her. She's warm and flushed. "Is she too hot in her shirt?"

Bea looks at her father thoughtfully and then replies by vomiting all over him. It's our first day as homeowners. It looks a lot like most other days.

WHERE THE
HEART IS

Two days after the closing, Sharon and I meet up in the city. She has been having a whirlwind last day trying to squeeze in all the touristy things she never got around to in her five years here. She lasted half an hour on the sightseeing bus before jumping ship.

Now we sit in a bar in Union Square doing what we usually do, which is eat fried food, drink beer, and discuss this week's issue of the *Star*. Until the inescapable moment arrives.

I stand out on a crowded street corner with her, glumly puffing my second cigarette in ten years. The other one was on September 12, 2001. It's just as disappointingly gross as last time.

"I've always felt like my mother is watching over me," she says. "I think she must have sent you to me."

"I think she sent us to each other," I tell her.

Then she's gone.

I walk over to Tompkins Square Park and circle it for two hours straight, spinning myself into butter in a thicket of downtown humanity, until I'm too exhausted to be grief-stricken anymore.

Now the real work starts. We can't afford to pay rent and a mortgage, especially not in our newly extra precarious financial situation, so Jeff and I have two weeks to pull together the move. What have he and I been talking about these days? Details, mostly. What to cancel, what to transfer, what to keep, what to throw out, where that towel or that pot went. There's almost no time to angst over all the tumult, let alone talk about it. It's temporary, but ill timed and lonely.

Friends offer to drive us to Staples for bubble wrap and packing tape. Evenings are spent in a steadily increasing frenzy of diminishing perfectionism. Box by box, our home disappears from the shelves and walls. Jeff and I do reasonably well until somewhere around 2 A.M. one bleary-eyed night, when, too tired to muster up a real argument, we degenerate into a series of exasperated glares over packing prowess.

I tell the people at the nice day care up the street from our new apartment that we won't be enrolling Bea after all. At least until Jeff finds a job and we can afford it, I'll have her at home with me, cobbling my workday around her schedule.

Then I call up the public school where I'd had the great tour, hoping against all laws of logic that the single spot in the kindergarten class is still open. If it's not we can suck it up at the other district school for a few weeks, and try a transfer again in the fall. I figure Lucy's stressed out already, what are a few more abrupt life changes?

But the parent coordinator has miraculous news. That one coveted place in the grade is still waiting for us. Until we are officially residing in the neighborhood, however, anybody else with the right address can still claim that place in the class. "Come in next week anyway to fill out the forms," she says, "and we'll cross our fingers."

While I've been buzzing over every detail, trying to tamp down anxiety with activity, Jeff has spent the last few days in a semicatatonic state of shock. "You're a woman of action," he says. "I'm a guy who needs some freak-out time." He sits silently at the dinner table with us, a million miles away. He stares, dumbfounded, at piles of books, looking like he has no idea how they'll ever get into those boxes. He is changing his home and his neighborhood. He is losing his job. He is totally depressed.

We turn up the white-noise machine and whisper in bed.

"Why did you lie to me?" I ask him flatly. "Why did you say you were ready for all this?"

"Some days I think I am," he replies. "But I still have a different picture in my head of what our home would look like. Someplace bigger, in a nicer area. It'd be different if we were moving into a dream house. Maybe I'm not a dream-house guy. I'm sorry."

So am I.

I talk to some movers and get quotes for how much it'll cost to haul our belongings to Jeff's not dream house.

I often wonder what kind of alternate reality we might have had if we hadn't moved around so much and had been able to buy earlier. How different would the housing bubble have looked?

As struggling renters, all we could see was untrammeled housing hyperactivity, and it scared us and it made us envious at the same time. Now we're becoming owners, but it's too bad a time to feel good about it, to believe in the value of the investment. Maybe someday.

First, we need to mark our new territory.

The following Saturday Jeff's parents once again mind the girls while we throw several gallons of paint and a ladder into the backseat of their car. Other people can pay movers to pack their boxes, painters to paint their apartments. Fortunately, we're both control freaks, so enforced thriftiness works to our advantage.

Jeff parks the car. We unload, and enter our home for the first time as its owners. If we weren't so rushed and Jeff weren't so depressed and I didn't have to jiggle the key for five minutes to get the door to unlock, the occasion might feel somewhat momentous.

We won't have time to do the whole place, so we hurriedly lay down drop cloths, cover up moldings with painter's tape, and set out transforming what we can of the space. The girls' tiny room is bathed in pale lilac; our bedroom goes a shade of blue we picked largely for the name—Serenity. With every sweep of the roller the place becomes more our own.

We are racing the clock to get back by dinnertime, waving big streaks of color across the walls at a kamikaze pace. As we paint, though, a more pressing realization passes between us. It's the first time we've been truly alone, and in a fairly low-stakes environment to boot, in months. We're in our grubbiest clothes, flecks of Benjamin Moore in our hair. We fall to the floor and have the most intense sex we've had in ages.

Later we sit on the single step that separates the dining area from the living room, eating sandwiches and potato chips.

"When do you guess we'll be alone again like this?" I ask him.

"Don't start," he says, and he shuts me up with a kiss.

Two days later it's our wedding anniversary. We can barely come up for air to acknowledge it, let alone celebrate.

"It's your anniversary and you're not doing anything? Oh for God's sake, I'll take the kids for a few hours," says Elinor that afternoon as we pick up our kids from school.

So Jeff and I go to the Cubana Café because it's cheap and close, and hold hands over the pork. Not too many doors away, Johnnie's Bootery, where I bought the girls their first pairs of shoes, has now become a comic-book store. "Remember our first day in Brooklyn?" I say, "We ate right up the street at Zaytoons. And now this is our last date here."

Jeff's been having the worst couple of weeks ever. But he's a guy who badly needs to believe in an optimistic destiny. "We'll have lots more dates," Jeff tells me. "New adventures."

First, though, more goodbyes.

My comrades of parenting boot camp—Margot, Geri, and Jennifer—give me a sendoff night at an Italian restaurant. We sit drinking two-for-one happy-hour beers and noshing on five different kinds of cured meat and remembering the fevers and the play dates and the mornings after the nights with no sleep and the trays of food when the second babies came. That they will be hanging out together on the same playgrounds next week and I will not seems impossible.

Lucy's kindergarten classmates make her a special card, signed by each child, that reads, "Good luck and happiness in your new home. We hope you enjoy your new school. We love you and we will miss you."

Bea has her last day in nursery school, and as we get ready to clunk the stroller out the door one last time, the head teacher is choking back sobs.

We throw a big farewell pizza party in Carroll Park, paid for with the proceeds of the stoop sale. We tell everybody we know to show up, and they all pretty much do. Some of these people, we know, will be in our lives forever, and some we'll never see again. That's what happens when somebody moves.

I stand up on a picnic table and attempt to say a few heartfelt words of thanks and farewell; a gesture that's undercut when Elinor interrupts to say, "I think your fly is down."

I look out at everyone gathered, and I don't just see the faces of those present. I see Jill and Carmen and Debbie and Chantal and Kate and Cynthia and Aaron and Quinn and Sharon and Jane and Barry. I see the people I sat next to one day at school or at work, who became, by the randomness of those events, indispensable in my heart. Life has scattered all of us to different places, and I doubt it's done with any of us yet. For a time, though, we had the blessing of proximity. We weren't just friends; we were neighbors.

There's more of the bottomless slog of packing and planning ahead when we get home tonight, so I savor the day, hanging out with people I love. I'm even surprisingly relaxed and happy. Then, when most of the families have taken our change-of-address cards and wished us well and drifted off, I spot Lucy and Harry playing together by the swings.

I remember meeting Jennifer in this park. She was sitting on that bench, right over there, with a seven-month-old baby on her lap. The kids look so big all of a sudden. I look over at Jennifer. There are tears flowing down my face.

Christ, imagine if we were going somewhere far away, like Jersey.

On our last day Jeff and I take turns with the kids in the park while the other stays in packing and cleaning. In the distance, we watch plumes of smoke from a distant fire in Greenpoint cloud the city.

Together we hoist the air conditioner out of the bedroom window. That's when we hear an insistent cooing coming from underneath. There, on the windowsill, is a chubby pigeon looking embarrassingly exposed in her nest.

"Where will she go now? Will she be okay?" the girls chime in unison.

Jeff peers out the window. "The symbolism here is *ridiculous*."

At around four, the cell phone rings, and it's Jennifer. "We're bringing over some food," she says.

I demur. "We're all set," I say. "We don't need anything." She is persistent.

"We're coming over and we're bringing food," she insists. "Now when should we get there?"

Two hours later she and Vincent are at our door with several shopping bags full of barbecue and beer. They've even left their kids with a babysitter so they can give us any help we need. I am famished, and tear into the ribs like something out of Animal Planet.

"I guess we needed that," I say.

Early Monday we wake up with no help from any alarm. Almost 40 million Americans will move in 2006. Today we are four of them. In addition to being our last day in our apartment, it's Lucy's first day at her school. It will take over an hour to get there, so there's no time for lingering last looks. There are still boxes unpacked, clothes to be organized, lunch to be made, and paperwork to be filled out.

Bea is running around trying to climb on any cardboard tower she can claw her way on to. Lucy and I are so busy dressing and gulping down breakfast we hardly have time to register it's the last time we'll be doing it here. The apartment doesn't look much like our apartment anymore. I don't know if this makes it easier or harder to go.

We throw on our jackets and head down the staircase. Gina fixed it two years ago, but the steps are still unpainted. Then a moment before we whizz out the door, I catch a glimpse of Lucy and me in the big, antique hall mirror and stop.

"What are you doing?" asks Lucy.

"Just looking," I say, and hear my voice crack. "It's hard to leave it behind."

"If you love something, then it's always in your heart, Mom," she says, like I'm an idiot for not knowing the wisdom she picked up from the Berenstain Bears.

We walk out in the early-morning sunshine, down the brown steps, past the Saint Anthony. I glance up into the window. Jeff is holding Bea and waving goodbye. He's wearing the same look he usually reserves for the last reel of *Brian's Song*.

Lucy and I stand on the A train all the way to 125th Street. We have eighty blocks to go after that. The coffee I had at six is completely worn off by the time we get off the subway.

As we arrive at the schoolyard, my eyes search for a friendly face. I've been emailing lately with a parent from a Yahoo! discussion group whose child is in the same grade here. She's answered my questions about the teachers and her experiences with the school, reaching out to this total stranger simply because she asked for help. I'd emailed her, "Our first day is Monday. I'll be the confused person in the flowered coat."

A long-haired woman in big shades takes one look at the harried, undercaffeinated woman and six-year-old, and smiles broadly. "I'm Shannon, and these are my daughters," she says, gesturing toward a pair of differently sized Botticelli angels. Her girls are, conveniently, the same age as mine.

"I have to run," she says, "but let's meet up at the playground later. Are you going to the school fair this weekend? Have you heard about the school fair? Are you going to join the CSA?" As she darts after her younger offspring, I can tell immediately that we have been taken under someone's wing and that we picked the right wing to be under.

Lucy's teacher immediately recruits a posse of the class alpha girls to show her around. Delegation. Smart. Lucy seems uncharacteristically reserved, and I realize her discomfort is directed at her nervous-looking mother. "Have a good day," I say, and kiss her as casually as I can muster. And then I silently say, "Please, God, let her be okay."

I go to the C-Town and arm myself with the immediate necessities—milk, juice, toilet paper, and an industrial supply of garbage bags. I think the C in C-Town stands for, "Check the ingredients." In the meat department, I spy a handwritten sign that reads, BRAIN? HEARTS? KIDNEYS, TOUNGES? IF THAT'S WHAT YOUR INTO, WE GOT IT!

At the checkout, I run into Clare and her sons.

"It's our moving day," I tell her.

"Ours too!" she replies, beaming.

Crap. The one family we know is leaving.

"We're moving a block away," she quickly adds. "We bought a place."

It's Crazy Craigslist's apartment.

She says when they looked at it in January, the broker, Karen, told them the asking price was firm, as they'd recently learned from another bidder's experience. She says she only met the seller once, at the closing, and the woman seemed to have a slight case of kooky. Not that it's a diagnosis, but I will note here that Clare's a shrink.

I lug my shopping bags to a bench outside the park and check in with Jeff on the progress of the movers. "They're here now," he says to the background tune of men grunting. "It's chaotic. Bea, no! Get out of that!" I let him go.

I then walk inside the biggest building I have ever inhabited, to spend the next few hours unpacking supplies, wiping down surfaces, and breathing in the empty silence one last time.

I think of my ex-roommate Jill and her wife Michele, who weathered the hurricanes Wilma and Rita last fall. I think of the luxury condos that were shells when I visited her a year ago and remain so.

"They overbuilt," Jill explains later. "They started and they're just not finishing. They're just empty hulls. It's not so much the hurricanes; it's that Miami is built on greed and money. There was no regulation about how many condos went up and what historic things went down or what environment was wasted. Miami is one of the worst for preservation," she says.

The past isn't the only thing that's been decimated. "If you try to go to the beach, there's one public place to park," she says. "They've taken the beach away from the public. Now there are just these empty condos."

When I pick up Lucy a few hours later, she's giggling with a curly-haired girl. "Hi, Mom," she says carelessly. "Trinity and I were just playing." One day down, I think, and this one was good.

I take her hand and we walk together. As she tiptoes like a tightrope walker along the walls that frame the park, Lucy unspools the chronicle of her day for me: where she sat, who she ate lunch with. Already she's carving out her weekday routine.

We're turning down to our street when the truck pulls up. "Follow me," I say, and I lead the movers inside. As the men deposit the contents of our lives within a new set of walls, Lucy methodically walks through each room, looking out every window.

Most of the day, her bedroom is dark, but at this magic hour, the one Lucy's come home to, the sun passes at the right spot and floods the chamber in sunlight. Clearly, the architects were ancient druids. Lucy twirls around the lilac room, bathed in afternoon gold. "It's pretty," she says. She notices the book I've left for her in the corner, and plunks down on the floor to read.

A half hour later Jeff and Bea show up, and we spend the rest of the afternoon amusing the girls and pointing where boxes and furniture should go. Then the men leave and Jeff's parents arrive, bearing a pan of lasagna, which we gratefully inhale. It's the first time they've seen the apartment, and the neighborhood.

"This is lovely!" my mother-in-law exclaims diplomatically, shimmying past a cardboard obstacle course and several garbage bags toward the kitchen.

After dinner, my father-in-law and I walk to the corner store to get ice-cream sandwiches for everybody. We take a circuitous route, winding through the park and by water. Out on the peninsula, chalked onto the ground, someone has written THIS PARK IS A BLESSING.

"This area is so beautiful," he says. "I think this is the nicest place you've ever lived. And I think you made a smart investment." My mother doesn't even know we've moved. I'll tell her when I call for Mother's Day next week, assuming she answers the phone.

That night, we plop our mattresses on the floor, life rafts mooring us toward our new life. The girls sprawl side by side in their room, their arms and legs outstretched in surrender to sleep. Jeff and I meanwhile curl tightly, restlessly together.

Sometime around 2 A.M., Bea wakes up, crying. "I want to go home!" she sobs. She runs to the door and rattles the knob furiously. "I want to go home!"

"This is home," Jeff and I both say sleepily, not quite convincingly. We tuck her back in bed, smooth her hair. She falls easily asleep a minute later. We are wide awake.

At the week wears on, areas of wall and floor begin to emerge from the rubble of cardboard. I put less conscious thought and more muscle memory into turning on the light switches and taking out the plates.

A few nights later I turn in early, collapsing on our freshly assembled bed. In the morning my nostrils awaken first, roused by a faint turpentine aroma. I follow them into the living room, which Jeff has painted overnight.

"I wanted to do something special for you," he says. There are dark shadows under his eyes. The boxes that had been piled haphazardly around the floor are stacked in the entryway. I inspect the walls, awash in a warm, friendly shade of yellow. "It's perfect," I tell him, and it really is.

I peek in on the girls in their room. There's a moment of panic when I realize Lucy's bunk is empty. Then I look down and see her, entwined in the lower berth with her sister, two baby dolls, three Teletubbies, Elephant, Tiger, and Bunny Rabbit. They all look very comfortable.

In time, we'll meet other people who found a way to be comfortable here as well. Other exiles from Brooklyn and the Upper West Side. The gay couple who moved from the Midwest, who chose the neighborhood sight unseen after studying a map of Manhattan. "It was near the green and the blue, so we figured it would be good," Corey says. The Hell's Kitchen bartender and her boyfriend who assumed, rightly, that anything on the last stop of the subway would fit their budget. The Irish girls who grew up here, with stories of high school friends who were casualties of the neighborhood's high crime years. Our community.

On Sunday we go to the corner store to get the paper, and spread a blanket on the cool grass in the park to graze on bagels and the "Week in Review." How many Sundays over the past three years have we spent dragging ourselves to how many places, all so we could one day unpack ourselves here? I instinctively reach for the real estate section before realizing I can read it purely as a spectator now. Or not read it at all. I do anyway.

We may be out of the hunt, but the story is becoming more dramatic.

There are clouds gathering in the housing market. In 2006, the rumblings of a subprime meltdown are beginning. Foreclosures are spiking ominously. Later, when I talk to Frank E. Nothaft, the chief economist for Freddie Mac, he tells me, "In 2001 subprime mortgages comprised five percent of the single-family market. By 2006 it was twenty percent. It quadrupled in five years." That kind of thing doesn't happen by accident. It's pushed along by what Nothaft terms "a deterioration of underwriting standards." Simultaneously, home sales have not kept pace. "Everything would be hunky-dory if home values went up twenty percent a year," Nothaft continues. "If you got in trouble you could sell, pull out your equity or refinance. It looks great if it's a sure bet, if you're guaranteed value is going to go up."

Then he says five words I wish I could write across the sky, emblazon in the mind of anyone anywhere who ever tries to buy a home.

"There is no guaranteed bet," he says. A year after our conversation, Freddie Mac will be taken over by the government as part of the largest bailout in American history. No guaranteed bet indeed.

It wasn't just a case of too-casual regulation, though. Lenders, after all, must have had some standards for determining who obtained all those dodgy subprime loans. Some banks, for example, have branched lending arms, creating different divisions for different kinds of borrowers. An institution can funnel clientele to the types of lenders for which they deem they're more fit.

As with all things, the cards are not evenly stacked. A recent federal mortgage-lending study revealed that African Americans were 3.8 times likelier to receive a higher-cost loan than white borrowers. Latinos fare better—they were only 3.6 times more likely overall. In Chicago, African-American borrowers were 14 times likelier to be given a higher-cost home-purchase loan from Wells Fargo than their white counterparts (35.3 percent vs. 2.5 percent). Again and again, across the country, people with darker skin are steered to shittier options.

The other dangerous aspect of all this has been the subprime industry's apparent reluctance to guide potential buyers who may in fact qualify for lower-interest loans toward them. A few blotches on a credit report are not an automatic sentencing to higher interest. But why would it be in the industry's interest to disclose that?

Like the termites in that house in Kensington, though, you can only eat away at the foundation for so long before things start to collapse. Buyers are defaulting on their loans. Houses are going into foreclosure. It's a crisis that will radiate to some of the nation's biggest lenders. By 2007 many lenders will file for bankruptcy protection and stop originating subprime loans, and several others will go out of business entirely. Or, as my banker friend Kevin puts it, "It's like the industry is the Peanuts gang. They've been playing with Pigpen for so long, suddenly they're realizing everyone is dirty." The crisis will radiate out to affect other types of loans, as no-doc mortgages like ours become harder to obtain. Timing is everything. We were fortunate to get the loan we did when we could.

On our first Sunday afternoon as Inwoodites, we gather up the family and take the train back to Brooklyn, to Jane and Barry's going-away party. Tomorrow, they're moving to Chicago.

We get off the train at our old stop. We spend the afternoon nibbling doughnuts, chasing toddlers, and saying more goodbyes. "I guess it's your turn now," I tell Barry.

He's holding his baby and he's smiling. "Last one out of the borough," he whispers as he bends toward my ear, "don't forget to turn out the lights."

When we leave, we walk down Court Street. It's exactly as we've done for years, but somehow it looks, it feels, subtly different. It's like when you leave school. Once you walk out the door, the place is no longer yours. You don't love it any less. You just don't belong to it anymore.

"Should we head back to Manhattan?" I ask Jeff.

"Absolutely," he replies. "I hear it's the new Brooklyn."

I wonder who will be the next to go, and where. Our friends Malcolm and Amy are making noises about moving the family out to Long Island. "People who grow up in the city," Malcolm says, "have issues."

He may have a point, although I'm rather a fan of issues, and baggage. Besides, I don't know anybody who's ever said, "I grew up in New York, and I couldn't wait to run away to somewhere interesting." Who knows, though? Maybe my kids will. Kids have to resent their parents for something. I wouldn't blame them for hating us for raising them in a cramped apartment on the edge of a noisy park, where they'll daily have to temper their youthful boisterousness with their parents' pleadings not to disturb the neighbors.

I've thought about this a lot over the last few years. I've thought about it inside every home we looked at. I've thought of it every time I've agonized over where to put a toy and wondered what would have to go out to make room for it. I've thought about it as I've obsessively pored over public school rankings or laid awake thinking about terror warnings and crime statistics. I've thought about what we'll do if the girls one day tell us we've failed them. At least for that last one I have a plan.

We'll take them to the Brooklyn Bridge, to walk them over it again as we have so many times already in their lives. We'll tell them that we're sorry that we couldn't give them a backyard to play in, or a bedroom bigger than a death-row inmate's cell, or even stairs to descend from on Christmas morning or prom night. We'll say it must have been hard not to have space to get away from each other when you needed to, to not have cookouts, or a porch, or fireflies. We'll explain that we couldn't do it because we lacked the income and, frankly, the imagination, to live anywhere else.

We'll say we gave you what we could. We gave you Park Slope and Chelsea, Times Square and Wollman Rink. We gave you the cherry blossoms at the Brooklyn Botanic Garden, and the tree at Rockefeller Center, and the carousel at the Bronx Zoo. We gave you edamame and plantains and egg creams. We gave you Arabs and Jews. We gave you the Statue of Liberty and the *Demoiselles d'Avignon*. We gave you the Cyclone and the Mets. We gave you Bendel's and the Bleach House. We gave you everything we wanted for you and needed for ourselves. We gave you New York City. We hope it was enough.

We're all drowsy when we surface at the other end of the subway line an hour later. We stroll through the late-afternoon bustle of Broadway, watching the buses swoosh past. Jeff asks, "What do you guys want for dinner?" and the girls perk up enough to demand pasta.

"Do we have everything we need?" I say. "Do we need to stop at the C-Town?"

"We're set," Jeff answers. Our cupboards are full.

Then we turn—and this still staggers me—toward the woods, to a place our family is putting down its own roots.

"Do you ever wish we'd just bitten the bullet and bought one of those little co-ops in Carroll Gardens three years ago?" I ask him.

"No," he replies. "What good does that kind of thinking do? Everything that happened got us here, so I have to believe that here is where we're supposed to be."

Owning real estate won't magically change our lives. It may be smarter in the long run to be paying off our mortgage instead of Gina's, but it hasn't made anything easy or secure. It didn't stop Jeff from losing his job; it doesn't make the future any less difficult and scary. Getting here was hard. Being here will be hard too. Life doesn't tie itself up in tidy bows; it doesn't offer neat happy endings. It gives you complications and setbacks, obstacles and flaws. It says, okay, hotshot, find the joy in *that*. And if you're lucky, you do.

We walk lazily together through the late-day shade. A few blocks from the A train, baby ducks are gliding on sparkling water. Our family will have picnics in this park. My children will ride their bikes here. We will make friends, and we'll gather here in this place together.

"This summer, we should explore around Riverdale a little," Jeff says. "Who knows? Maybe in a few years we could decide we want a bigger space and check it out."

"Are you being . . . open-minded?" I ask, skeptical. "Who put you up to this?"

He doesn't answer. He just looks toward the sliver of Manhattan we now possess and smiles.

We cross onto our street and walk toward a big building that holds a small apartment. We go through its front door and step into the lobby. The super is coming out of the laundry room. "Hi, Raoul," we chime in unison as he nods in greeting.

We pile into the elevator, and when it stops, we get out and make our way to a door where the key in my pocket fits. On the other side are unopened boxes, unassembled pieces of furniture, and unlimited possibilities. I slide the key into the lock, turn it till it clicks, and push. And we're home.

EPILOGUE

Then it all hit the fan.

The year I moved, 2006, condos were still rising in previously desolate areas with the expectation that buyers would arrive to fill them. Properties were still escalating in value in the course of mere weeks. But homes weren't moving at quite the breathless pace they had previously, and the economy was sliding headlong into the recession zone. That summer, in a *Barron's* story called "The No-Money-Down Disaster," writer Lon Witter astutely observed that the industry had been in the throes of a "lending bubble" and warned of an impending housing crash. Back then, there were $600 billion worth of subprime mortgages out there, accounting for one-fifth of the U.S. loan market. By 2007, the value of sub-prime mortgages in this country had risen $1.3 trillion.

Today, one in ten homes in America is delinquent in mortgage payments or in foreclosure. The numbers are even worse for homes with subprime mortgages: roughly a quarter of them are now delinquent. As I write this, the Treasury Department is whipping up a $40 billion rescue package to help people who are behind on their mortgages avoid losing their homes, and the Fed has cut the federal funds rate to an infinitesimal 1 percent.

On October 3, 2008, the Senate passed the Emergency Economic Stabilization Act of 2008. The Act, which began its life as a pithy little three-page document (but ultimately wound up 107 explanatory pages longer), gave the U.S. Treasury the green light to spend somewhere in the neighborhood of $700 billion to tidy up the economy. That same October, the Dow Jones clocked in its worst month in twenty-one years. It is likely to go down as one of the bleakest periods ever in stock market history. The United States now has a Troubled Assets Relief Program and an Office of Financial Stability, headed by a thirty-five-year-old whose high school yearbook entry features quotes from George H. W. Bush and the Canadian supergroup Rush. My kids' college funds and my 401k currently look like road kill. Of course, it could get better. Or we can all just go to bartending school.

I watch it all unfold, feeling like I have in the past when I've cut myself badly or been in an accident and think, *gosh that's sure a lot of blood; I'll probably have to go the emergency room or something* before the actual horror kicks in.

So it goes. The world has changed dramatically since the peak of the bubble, and so have the lives of people affected by it. Books have endings. Real life doesn't. It just has new chapters.

• • •

Carmen, who built the 4,000 square foot home in Maryland where she thought she and her husband would raise their three children, divorced in late 2006. After her marriage ended, she hoped to buy a new house, one with a smaller monthly overhead and no memories to haunt her. She put her place on the market in early 2007 but ran into obstacles immediately.

"I had no offers," she says. "None. Overnight the housing market just crashed."

She's a single mom carrying a big bundle of expenses. She recently left her comfortable government job for a higher paying one in a volatile industry, and took the house off the market and refinanced the mortgage.

"The property's depreciated a ridiculous amount," she says. "When we bought for $546,000 in 2005, I could have turned around and sold the property for $750,000." Considering it again in the summer of 2008, she says, "Now I'd be lucky to get $535,000."

She keeps her fingers crossed. She keeps her sense of perspective. "All that matters is that the kids are healthy and you're healthy and happy," she tells me. "It doesn't matter where I live."

Jill and Michele sometimes talk about leaving Miami and moving back to Philly but are staying put for now because this is where their careers and their friends are. Apartments in Jill's building, meanwhile, are going on the market for double what she and Michele paid in 2003. But Jill says nobody's buying them. Miami currently has one of the highest foreclosure rates in the nation.

When she moved back to San Francisco, Sharon rented a loft in an up-and-coming industrial neighborhood and took a job at a corporation that sells upscale home furnishings. For a while there, I had a nice discount on drawer pulls.

Shannon, the first friend I found in Inwood, became a home-buyer in the summer of 2007. The apartment is directly above one of the first ones we looked at in the neighborhood, across the street from Paul and Clare's place. The view of the park is killer.

Clare accepted a job offer in London, and her family moved in July of 2008. She and Paul put their apartment back on the market, stove and all, and then took it off again as the market slowed down. They instead eventually rented it, to a young family who moved to the city from Georgia for the husband's work. He started at Lehman Brothers on the morning the company filed for bankruptcy.

Andrew and Patricia left the city in 2006 for a sweet rental house in Los Angeles. They're now expecting their second child and hoping to buy a home. A broker friend in the neighborhood tells them he doesn't lack for financially desirable potential homeowners—it's the stability of some of the local banks that concerns him.

Quinn's husband got a new job opportunity in Chicago, and in the summer of 2008, she and her family moved to Illinois.

"Our neighborhood in Harrisburg flattened out," she tells me. They had serendipity on their side—a neighbor wanted to buy their house before they even put it on the market. They didn't make much of a profit on the property, only about ten grand, but it was good enough.

Like many Americans who have to relocate to a new town, they conducted most of the hunt long distance. "We're research junkies," Quinn says. "We read up and went to every Web site, and we talked to realtors."

"Quinn's husband, meanwhile, went out to Illinois and looked at twenty properties in a single reconnaissance weekend. He came back with an accepted offer on a house in a diverse neighborhood in the southern section of Evanston, a neighborhood Quinn had never visited and a house that she had only seen online.

"We bought a great place in Harrisburg for $170,000," she says. "Our cutoff this time was $300,000, and for our money there were a lot of dumps. I had to adjust my expectations. But my husband says we're getting a really great house; it just needs a little love in some places. We got a yard and a good school." They got a decent mortgage with a company that will automatically refinance for them when interest rates go down. "For our money, we can't get the house of our dreams yet," she says, adding, "but at some point we'll get to the place where we can." Because we all still dream, don't we?

Aaron, who said he didn't have to live in San Francisco to be happy, sold his house in St. Louis and moved with his family back to San Francisco.

"Without completely disavowing my earlier claims, I'd started to get a little bored there," he explains. "More than that, I started to think about where I wanted my kids to grow up. I wanted them growing up in a vital, progressive, diverse place with a lot of energy. Or at least some of that. St. Louis was easy to live in, nice, you could always park. But you wouldn't call it progressive, or energetic, or vital. Somewhat diverse, but the diversity is mostly black-white, and the segregation is stark. Most of all, there's a sort of satisfaction with the status quo. People grow up, buy a house down the street from their parents. A big life adventure is to go to Mizzou for four years. There isn't hostility to new ideas—it's a staunchly Democratic town, so it's not conservative—but they aren't exactly welcomed either. You still hear pretty casual homophobia in polite conversation, and racism in not-that-far from polite conversation. My kids wouldn't hear that at home, but I didn't want them swimming in that ocean every time they walked out the door. I also wanted them to be big-city kids, kids who could go to New York for the first time and not feel overwhelmed by it. Then my parents chimed in with an offer to help us buy a house—by advancing us an inheritance, basically—if we'd move their grandkids west instead of east. We decided to do it."

He and his wife moved in the summer of 2007 and rented an apartment in the Mission for almost a year. They settled in the Excelsior District of San Francisco, another burgeoning neighborhood in the southern part of town. He tells me, "It's traditionally Italian and working class—right down the street is the Italian-American Social Club. The Italian immigrant community has mostly moved on or died out, leaving an ethnic mix that's similar to the Mission District, mostly Latino and Asian. It's very much like the pre-hipster Mission of twenty years or so ago. Just a lot of regular working folks, families, with non-chic restaurants and businesses, including a few old-school holdovers, like a fab Italian deli and a bakery." He's been a modest beneficiary of the cataclysmic economic times. "Over the course of the year we were looking at houses online before we moved, and the six months we were looking after we moved and got our sea legs, house prices did come down noticeably, but not nearly at the rate we've heard and read about elsewhere. I'd say it was about a 6 to 10 percent drop over the two years, in the price range and areas were searching in." They've done all right. They're settled and happy, for now.

Cynthia, who said she couldn't imagine leaving New Orleans after Katrina, said yes to a job opportunity in New York City and moved in January of 2008.

"I was just tired, and my sense of fatigue was starting to affect things," she admits. "There were so many young people moving to town to be part of the recovery and were seeing things so hopefully. I realized how negative I'd become, both about myself and the city. I wasn't seeing the possibilities anymore."

But she knows what it means to miss New Orleans. "I still feel that sense of loss that I don't get to be there," she says. "A lot of people who'd left are going back. That makes me think in the back of my mind: maybe I could go back too. The word 'community' is so grounded in geography. Your geography is the people who are around you. I can't imagine I'll ever know anybody better than I will the people I was around during Katrina, and I can't imagine anybody will ever get to know me better than I was then. I don't think that anything has ever contributed to my character as much as living in that city." She now resides in Brooklyn, not too far from where I used to reside.

Enrique's still in Brooklyn, too, though he's moved recently. Enrique's great deal in Williamsburg came to an end when his landlord decided that rather than lay out the money to upgrade the building, he'd just turn it into something more profitable. José, his wife, Martine, and their dog, Chula, had to leave. A few months later, they found another place in Williamsburg via craigslist.

"The landlord of the old place was very cool about us taking our time and getting out," he says, "but as soon as we were out, they tore everything down and turned it into commerical space."

Though they had paid through their final month, the landlords got a little eager when they realized Enrique and his wife had already taken up residence in their new space. "I came into the apartment before then, and the stove—which we owned—and the shower were out."

Other residents fared even worse. "They took out the stoves, they blocked up the showers to prevent people from living there," Enrique says. "There are still a couple of people living there as holdouts, but we washed our hands of it."

They now pay $1,000 a month more for an apartment half the size of their old one. But they do have a nice deck.

I was there for a party recently and ran into a friend who still lived in Carroll Gardens. We talked about the neighborhood, the one we remembered and the one it had become. Two days later, her landlord called to say he was raising her rent by $500 a month.

She and her husband are now moving to California.

And us?

The months after we bought our apartment were fraught with every kind of stress imaginable. I learned that as we stewed in our newer, smaller quarters that first summer, the sound of radios and car alarms blaring outside. Jeff hustled for freelance assignments, I continued to work from home, and we couldn't afford childcare or camp, so the girls were underfoot the whole time.

Armed with our MacGyver-level ingenuity, we managed to cobble together an alternating system of working and minding the kids and only sometimes completely freaking out. I consider the fact that we all didn't eat each other a huge triumph. My daughters watched a hell of a lot of television that summer, and anyone who wants to judge me for that can kiss my marginally employed ass.

By the fall, Jeff had found another job—ironically, at his former company. The pay was less than he'd been earning before, and our mortgage and maintenance were roughly double what we'd been paying in Brooklyn.

It was a scary, scary place to be. I developed insomnia and got migraines so bad and so often I acquired a neurologist, eventually finding myself, one bitter winter morning, going for a ride inside an MRI tube. Good thing we still had health insurance.

Through it all we managed to keep our headachy heads somehow above water. We didn't, like a lot of Americans, go into foreclosure. Our credit wasn't destroyed. Make no mistake, we went through hell. Our personal and financial lives are not the same now and they never will be again. We got off easier than an awful lot of people.

More than $2.28 trillion worth of adjustable rate mortgages originated between 2004 and 2006. When these mortgages began resetting, not everyone was able keep up with the new rates. During the second financial quarter of 2008, one in every 171 households in America received a foreclosure filing. In Las Vegas, it was one in every thirty-five. In Stockton, California, it was one in every twenty-five. Between 2007 and the same period in 2008, foreclosure actions rose in forty-eight states and ninety-five of the top one hundred metropolitan areas. The American dream is being repossessed.

I wish I could tell the people who did lose their homes in this whole mess that it's going to be all right. I wish I could give us back our hope. I never thought that a home could fix anybody's life, but I sure as hell don't know anybody who bought one thinking it would ruin it.

In the first quarter of 2008, the country's largest mortgage lender, Countrywide, claimed $893 million in losses. It was acquired by Bank of America that July, and B of A promptly announced it was slashing 7,500 jobs in the merger. Countrywide's CEO, Angelo Mozilo, departed the company in July 2008. He is currently under SEC investigation regarding his stock sales.

Freddie Mac and Fannie Mae, which held about $5 trillion worth of the nation's mortgage debt, have been assimilated into the borg and bailed out by the government. After the bailout, both of their CEOs stepped down. What a difference a year makes. In 2007, Angelo Mozilo received a $1.9 million salary, $20 million in stock and option awards and $176,513 in other compensation. That year, Fannie Mae's CEO Daniel Mudd earned $11.6 million in salary, stock, and other bonuses, while Freddie Mac's CEO Richard Syron netted $18.3.

One of the great scapegoats in the whole fiasco has been the Community Reinvestment Act, the very program that helped my family—and thousands of others over the past thirty-plus years—get a mortgage at a decent interest in a developing neighborhood. Commerce Bank founder Vernon Hill, for example, stated to *The*

Philadelphia Inquirer reporter Joseph N. DiStefano, "the feds went on this jihad—I don't have any problem with using the word jihad—they said we should lend in these low-income areas regardless of whether the credit supported the loans."

Considering the way the government has been chipping away at the CRA since the Reagan era, considering the fact that the Act applies to banks and not the numerous mortgage firms that sprang up in the bubble's frenzy, and considering the lending industry's less-than-noble track record of pushing higher interest rates to minorities, it's no wonder the sound you hear coming from my little uptown enclave is that of mirthless, derisive laughter.

We are all accountable for the wisdom or lack thereof in our choices. At the height of the housing bubble, greed and stupidity were abundant on an individual and institutional level. There are people who used their houses as the proverbial ATMs, buyers who committed mortgage fraud, folks who foolishly got in over their heads in the flipping game. There are also a whole lot of ordinary people, just like you and me, who wanted a home, who believed in the promise of putting down roots. They saw yards for playing tag, door frames to measure their children's growth on, kitchens to make Thanksgiving dinner in.

Which is why I honest to God don't know how anybody who got rich off the dirtiest, most deceptive aspects of this industry can look himself in the mirror. The ones who fobbed impossible mortgages on unsuspecting buyers. The ones who steered people with decent credit to crippling interest rates. The ones who overbuilt shoddy new constructions without a thought to the communities they were decimating. They didn't just annihilate the economy, they stole dreams and destroyed futures, and they crushed souls.

If there's another word for that than "evil," it doesn't exist in my vernacular. Some days, I think the reason I still cling to my faith is so that I can still believe in hell. And then I can imagine some of these dicks in it.

My friend Andrew Leonard, who writes the "How the World Works" for Salon.com, tells me thusly: "I cannot stress how incredibly historic this is. Since the 1980s and Reagan, we've been under a regime that has sold deregulation as the best way to run the economy. Now you've got banks reporting $10 billion quarterly losses, trillions in loans collapsing, and home prices deflating faster and deeper than since the depression. This stunning story is a repudiation of that narrative.

"Those appreciating houses were setting us up. It seems crazy how interconnected everything is. There are these little Norwegian towns going bankrupt because they were fooled into investing in mortgage-backed securities. The dollar hurting means that oil is more expensive. And there are a lot of investment banks being laid off.

"You can't let institutions like Fannie Mae and Freddie Mac collapse because the global economy goes with them." He says, "Now there's going to be a vast taxpayer bailout of the lending industry, and there's no way that's going to happen without tighter restrictions on what people can and can't afford." Noting the absurdity of having to articulate such things, he tells me, "A few weeks ago, the Fed announced new regulations that lending institutions cannot make loans regardless of the individual borrower's ability to pay back."

One of the things I like about Andrew is his adamant talent

to see the upside, even in a crisis. "I think we're going to see a profound rethinking of how government works the financial industry. Without the bubble we wouldn't have this fundamental reappraisal of how government and industry should interact. This is a chance to reassess, and the timing could not be more perfect. We're making a choice here, and the choice could not be more obvious: we either continue or we start a new path."

Yet the beaten path persists. On a recent unnaturally warm afternoon, I went back to my old neighborhood in Brooklyn. There were new condominiums rising on previously empty lots, and brownstones on either side of my landlady's house were being enthusiastically gutted.

I ran into my former downstairs neighbor, Sheila, and updated her on my adventures and setbacks. "You've had some tough times," she said, dragging on a Parliament. Then she added philosophically, "Whaddaya gonna do?"

Whaddaya gonna do? You're going to just keep going.

It's been a long, strange trip. In the time I've been in this little co-op, I've had career opportunities come my way via my neighbors down the hall. I've had parties and play dates, and I've shared confidences. This little spot on the edge of the city has forced me to change and adapt and fall down and fail and learn and reach out. I've watched the kitchen cabinets collapse and the toilet overflow. I've cried and argued and had sex and laughed in that apartment, sometimes all in the same day. I even wrote a book about it. It has cost me dearly to live here. But it's still my home.

A few months after moving in, I got a predawn phone call

from my downstairs neighbor, Dana, and rushed down to her door. While her son slept in the next room, I kissed her good-bye, and watched her and her husband go off to the hospital to bring their new baby daughter into the world. She's pregnant again now, and their apartment is on the market. It's roughly the size of ours, and she's asking $60,000 more than we paid two years ago. This, in Manhattan, is considered a slowdown.

I hope Dana and I will always be friends and that the easy bond our children have now will follow them their whole lives. But no matter what happens, our lives are forever entwined. I'm part of the story of one girl's first day in the world, because I live in this building, right now.

In my uppermost corner of the city, a condo with park views and decks has gone up on Payson Avenue. Real estate listings have begun referring to our northern Manhattan neighborhood as "NoMa." Buyers are still out there, money is still being made. Two bedrooms in Inwood are going for anywhere from a mere $390,000 to $550,000. But even in the fiercest real estate market in the nation, things are slow. The words "Reduced!" and "Motivated seller!" are appearing with increasingly frantic regularity. It might take a while to sell, but the bottom line is that if I were to put my place on the market today it would probably still net a tidy profit.

Last winter, the rodent-infested deli by the park shut down. After being dark for a seemingly interminable era, a café proffering artisanal cheeses and panini opened in its stead. I sit in The Indian Road Café & Market now, sipping coffee and pounding on keys. I'm surrounded by intent looking caffeine addicts doing likewise at their laptops and bright-eyed young moms feeding croissants to their toddlers in strollers. The usual morning crowd. There is a curly-haired older woman chatting with a friend, wearing a shirt that reads, "Life Is Good." I want to believe she's on to something.

Right outside, water laps at the edge of this island, and the Hudson River flows into the Harlem. Its essence is eternal. Its nature is to move. It is just like all of us.

ACKNOWLEDGMENTS

Acknowledgments pages are always so awkward. They're like the acceptance speech to an award nobody won. Hold the polite applause 'til the end, if you please, because I would be remiss if I didn't express my profound appreciation to the people who've been such a huge part of both this book and the story contained within it.

Thank you to all my friends and family who shared their real estate stories for your unfailing candor and generosity. Particular thanks to Abby, Rebecca, Kristin, Keri, and Shannon, for being indispensable advisers, brilliant pals, and reliable playdate providers. You're my role models as mothers, homeowners, and superheroes.

Thank you to Stephanie for letting me use your apartment as a writer's retreat and for plying me with wine every step of the way.

Thank you to the writers who blazed the trail and offered advice, sympathy, and coffee: Lily Burana, Therese Borchard,

Linda Furiya, Dan Kennedy, Helene Stapinski, and Larry Smith.

Thank you to all my coworkers at Salon.com and my invisible friends in Table Talk for so many years of camaraderie and inspiration. Thank you to Jeffrey P. McManus and the Popcult conference on the WELL, and Fawn Fitter and Byline. Thank you to my colleagues at The Takeaway, for being brilliant at ungodly hours. How do you do it?

Thank you to my amazing agent, Claudia Cross, for unflagging persistence, supreme professionalism, immutable faith, and a wicked sense of humor. You are a true gem.

Thank you doesn't even begin to cover it, but thank you to my editor, Denise Roy, at Simon & Schuster. I cannot imagine a writer luckier than I, to have found not just a smart, talented editor, but also such a wise and funny friend. When the going got tough, you took the title of this book as an imperative. That's above and beyond and then some.

Thank you to Sharon for being my best friend and most quotable person in the world. In life there are the families we're born to and the families we choose. I'm so glad you are my family.

Thank you to Barbara and Jerry for everything, from advice to babysitting to prayers.

Thank you to Jeff for being such an indispensable part of this adventure, for your time and editorial eye, and for being so supportive, through thick and thin.

And finally, thanks to Lucy and Beatrice for being the two most fascinating, awe-inspiring people I have ever known. Thank you for putting up with a bedraggled mom holed up in front of a laptop all this time, and thank you mostly for being my daughters. I love you.

SOURCES

HOME-SHOPPING

page

3   *The average American moves:* U.S. Census.

7   *Houses that went for $600,000: New York,* March 10, 2003.

18   *foreclosure rate:* "Foreclosure Rate Climbs to a Record," *Los Angeles Times*, June 29, 2003.

MATING IN CAPTIVITY

page

37   *"Why let past credit problems":* Peak Home Loan.

46   *While the neighborhood is getting safer:* Aaron Donovan, "If You're Thinking of Living in Bedford/Stuyvesant," *New York Times,* September 21, 2003.

A TOMB WITH A VIEW

page

55   *a crime rate that's nearly double New York's:* Infoplease Crime Rates

for Selected Cities 2003, New York: 2917, Philadelphia: 5553.

67 *In the Bay Area:* Richard Paoli, "Bay Area Home Prices Slip in May," *San Francisco Chronicle,* June 26, 2001.

67 *And in New York City:* Debra A. Estock, "Construction Activity in New York Remains Steady Despite Economic Uncertainty," *The Cooperator: The Co-Op and Condo Monthly,* March 2003.

BACK TO SQUARE ONE

page

75 *This being the land:* U.S. Treasury.

76 *By 2005, 43 percent:* Noelle Knox, "43% of First-time Buyers Put No Money Down," *USA Today,* January 18, 2006.

HIGHWAY TO HELL

page

90 *The homeownership rate:* Danter Company, Home Ownership Rates.

THERE GOES THE NEIGHBORHOOD

page

115 *On October 24, 1981*: Joseph Laura, "Hoboken: Fear of Fire Haunts Many," *New York Times,* November 8, 1981.

131 *In the last five years:* New York University's Furman Center for Real Estate and Urban Policy, "The State of New York City's Housing and Neighborhoods 2006."

Sources

THINK OUTSIDE THE BOROUGH

page

134 *middle-income population:* Alan Berube, "The Middle Class Is Missing," Brookings.

149 *It's funny, because: New York Times,* "Settling for the Upper East Side," August 14, 2005.

SHE STOOPS TO CONQUER

page

158 *I am also creeped out:* http://www.totallycatholic.com.

167 *Today the figure looms:* Camilla McLaughlin, "Buyers Say Size Doesn't Matter," *Realtor,* March 27, 2007, and Christopher Solomon, "The Swelling McMansion Backlash," MSN.

170 *The median first-time homeowner:* Noelle Knox, "43% of First-time Home Buyers Put No Money Down," *USA Today,* January 17, 2006.

ARE WE THERE YET?

page

176 *Inwood outdecibels:* David Seifman and Mark Bulliet, "Sound and Fury," *New York Post,* July 3, 2006.

176 *Over 76 percent of the residents:* factfinder/census/gov, zip code tabulation 10034.

177 *Almost half the total population:* Furman Center for Real Estate Urban Policy, State of New York City's Housing and Neighborhoods, 2005.

180 *In 2005 they will tally:* Bonnie Conrad, "Mortgage Sherpa, The Hidden Danger of Interest-Only Loans," *San Francisco Chronicle,* May 20, 2005.

181 *figure will rise to a staggering near 70 percent:* Kelly Zito, "High Interest in Interest-Only Home Loans Popular but Dangerous," *San Francisco Chronicle,* May 20, 2005.

197 *Yet there are more children:* Sam Roberts, "In Surge in Manhattan Toddlers Rich White Families Lead Way," *New York Times,* March 23, 2007.

THE RATE STUFF

page

228 *L.A. got only a dishonorable mention:* 1998 Sierra Club Sprawl Report.

235 *In 2005 the neighborhood boasted:* Ira Boudway, "Because We've Got the Lowest Crime Rate in 40 Years," *New York,* December 18, 2006.

237 *It's that more people at a higher income level:* Sam Roberts, "In a City Known for Its Renters, a Record Now Own Their Homes," *New York Times,* May 27, 2007.

NICKEL-AND-DIMED

page

249 *By the end of 2007:* CNNmoney.com, "Mortgage Rates Shot Up on Inflation Fears," June 1, 2006.

WHERE THE HEART IS

page

281 *Almost 40 million Americans:* U.S. Census, Renters Four Times More Likely to Move Than Homeowners, October 16, 2007.

288 *mortgage-lending study:* HMDA study of the California Reinvestment Coalition, Community Reinvestment Association of North

Carolina, Empire Justice Center, Massachusetts Affordable Housing Allowance, Neighborhood Economic Development Advocacy Project, and Woodstock Institute.

EPILOGUE

page

295 *$600 billion worth:* Brian Louis, "Rising Subprime Mortgage Defaults Add to Unsold Homes Inventory" Bloomberg.com, March 9, 2007.

295 *By 2007, the value of subprime mortgages:* Associated Press, March 13, 2007

296 *One in ten homes:* Vikas Bajaj and Eric Dash, "Banks Alter Loan Terms to Head Off Foreclosures," *New York Times*, October 31, 2008.

303 *More than $2.28 trillion:* Marketwatch, March 23, 2007.

303 *During the second financial quarter of 2008:* RealtyTrac, "Foreclosure Activity up 14% in Second Quarter. http://www.realtytrac.com/ContentManagement/pressrelease.aspx?ChannelID=9&ItemID=4891&accnt=64847]

304 *Countrywide, claimed $893 million in losses:* Associated Press, April 30, 2008.

304 *In 2007, Angelo Mozilo received:* Reuters, April 25, 2008.

304 *Fannie Mae's CEO Daniel Mudd:* John Brinsley, "Paulson 'Very Optimistic' on Freddie, Fannie Rescue," Bloomberg, July 20, 2008.

304 *Commerce Bank founder Vernon Hill:* Joseph N. DiStephano, Philly.com, "Blaming the Mortgage Mess on the Poor," November 2, 2008.

A FEW FINAL WORDS

We can—and do—argue and finger point over how we got into this our current economic mess. But this much is certain—we won't get out of it without kindess, compassion, and generosity.

The English clergyman Thomas Fuller once said, "Charity begins at home, but it should not end there." If you have a roof over your head and a bed in which to sleep tonight, please reach out and support the organizations in your community that are working to staunch the ever rising tide of homelessness.

When I sold this book to Simon & Schuster, I made a pledge to give 2 percent of the money I earn from it to National Alliance to End Homelessness. The Alliance is a nonpartisan organization dedicated to working with the public, private, and nonprofit sector to combat homelessness in America. You can get more info and find out what you can do locally and nationally by going to http://www.naeh.org.

Carmen would like her friends and neighbors in Maryland to know about Housing for All Calvert and Affordable Development for All Calvert. The organization is a coalition of faith communities, county agencies, and neighbors to assure affordable housing for all citizens of the county. You can find out more at http://www.housingforallcalvert.org/index.html or by emailing info@housingforallcalvert.org.

Kate would like to take a moment to mention an organization she works with in Vermont, Rebuilding Together. It's a national nonprofit volunteer organization that helps low-income homeowners, particularly those who are elderly, disabled, or part of a family with children, with home renovation and repair. Go to http://www.rebuildingtogether.org/ to get involved in your area.

My in-laws have a long-standing involvement with a terrific organization called SHORE—Sheltering the Homeless is Our Responsibility. Since 1985 SHORE has been working to create housing for formerly homeless families in New York's Westchester County. Go to http://www.shelteringthehomeless.org/ for more info.

For some of us, a home is a representation of a lifelong dream. For many individuals and families, it's a desperate need. There are plenty of organizations working to help Americans in need obtain housing or hang on to what they have. (Charitynavigator.org is a great starting point.) Get involved. Take action. Be your brother's keeper. And whether you live in an apartment or a double wide or a McMansion, whether you hang your hat in a ranch or a Victorian or a yurt, I thank you for reading. Get home safe.